KU-485-245

A Premium Business

General Accident

A Premium Business

A HISTORY OF GENERAL ACCIDENT

PETER YOUNG

GRANTA EDITIONS

Published by Granta Editions
25–27 High Street, Chesterton, Cambridge CB4 1ND,
United Kingdom.

Granta Editions is a wholly owned imprint of Book Production Consultants plc

First published in 1999.
© CGU plc, 1999
St Helen's, 1 Undershaft, London EC3P 3DQ, United Kingdom.

All rights reserved. No part of this publication may be reproduced, stored in any retrieval system or transmitted in any form or by any means, electronic, mechanical, photocopying, recording or otherwise, without prior written permission of the copyright holder for which application should be addressed in the first instance to the publishers. No liability shall be attached to the author, the copyright holder or the publishers for loss or damage of any nature suffered as a result of reliance on the reproduction of any contents of this publication or any errors or omissions in its contents.

A CIP catalogue record for this book is available from the British Library.

ISBN 1 85757 068 5

Designed by Peter Dolton.
Design, editorial and production in association with
Book Production Consultants plc, 25–27 High Street, Chesterton
Cambridge CB4 1ND, United Kingdom.
Printed in Singapore by Kyodo Printing Co (S'pore) Pte Ltd.

CONTENTS

FOREWORD

THERE has not been a history of General Accident since 1935, when the company celebrated its first 50 years, and that account was written internally. When the board decided in 1996 to have the story brought up to date for the millennium, it wanted an objective book by an independent historian that traced the evolving culture and fortunes of the company. From a modest office in the Scottish city of Perth, General Accident has grown over more than a century into a global organisation with two-thirds of its business overseas. It is a story of enterprising people in the context of their many territories, economic circumstances, political pressures and advances in technology.

As the last chairman of the company before its merger with Commercial Union in 1998, I am sad that the rapid development of the international insurance market made continuing independence for the company commercially untenable. But I am proud our history now shows what a uniquely interesting and successful company General Accident has been and how its skills and reputation will provide the power unit for the modern corporate giant which is CGU plc.

Sir Alick Rankin
Chairman 1997–8
June 1999

ACKNOWLEDGEMENTS

WRITING this history would have been impossible without the help of a research team. GA staff principally involved were Jennifer MacEwan, the librarian, who made all the arrangements and kept track of the administration; Tom Berthon, the company archivist, and a predecessor Margaret Torrance, who had the foresight to see the value of the past and in 1972 began to establish an official archive; Anne Brodie, archive assistant, a meticulous researcher. Sheila Hay, a genealogist, delved thoroughly into many diverse Scottish and other records with the help of Rosemary Bailey, Muriel Craig and Moira Martin. Janis Whitaker flagged items in the minutes. Stephanie Zarach of Book Production Consultants did much of the research on illustrations as well as on US records. Discussions within this group as well as with members of the history committee, former chief general managers David Blaikie and Nelson Robertson and company secretary Richard Whitaker, revealed fresh aspects of the company and sources of information. Thanks are due to Edward Hunter for access to his family collection, particularly the papers of his father and great grandfather. Dawn Tweedy and Barbara Woodward provided personal reminiscences of the Norie-Miller family.

Among those helping abroad were Eleanor St Clair, John McDevitt and Bob Shea (USA), Andrew Bay, Eunice Sim, Neil Stuart, Katie Walmsley and Tara Wiseman (Canada), Vicki Curtis and Sir Robert Southey (Australia), Ramsay Little, Gay Richards (New Zealand).

Interviews captured much of the detail and period feel that was never written down. Not all sources of such information have been credited in the text, partly because some were agreed as unattributable and crediting everybody would have detrimentally altered the character of the text. I am grateful to all GA staff and relatives, past and present, who have contributed.

For hospitality on my visits to Perth I must thank Brian and Pat Smith, whose guest house at 2 Comely Bank adjoins Francis Norie-Miller's first home in the city.

Organisations
A.K. Bell Library, Perth (Steve Connelly, archivist, Perth and Kinross Council)
College of Arms, London
Dumbarton Public Library
Dundee City Archives

Edinburgh Central Library
Family Records Centre, London
Glenalmond College, Perth
Guildhall Library, London
Guildry Incorporation, Perth
Highland and Agricultural Society, Ingliston (Dorothy Amos, librarian)
Historical Society of Pennsylvania
Mitchell Library, Glasgow
National Library, Edinburgh
New Register House, Edinburgh
Perth Museum
Perth Royal Infirmary
Public Record Office, Kew
Rolls Royce Enthusiasts' Club, Northamptonshire (Barbara Westlake, archivist)
Royal Bank of Scotland, The, archive, Edinburgh
Royal Scottish Museum (Dorothy Kidd, Scottish ethnographic department;
Gavin Sprott, head of social history and technology)
Scottish Agricultural Museum, Ingliston (John Shaw, curator)
Scottish Record Office, Edinburgh
Somerset House, London

Books
A Business Epic, General Accident (1935)
A Century of Progress, General Life (1937)
Bold Century, NZI (1959)
Commercial Directories for Aberdeen (1888–9), Dundee (1886–7)
Fiftieth Anniversary, General Accident Canada (1956)
From Then Till Now, Provident Mutual (1940)
Hunter's Illustrated Guide to Perthshire (1886 and 1928)
Post Office Directories for Glasgow, Edinburgh and Leith (1886–7)
Risks and Rewards, South British Insurance Company (1972)
Romance of a Business, General Accident (1924)

Newspapers and Periodicals
North British Agriculturalist
Perthshire Advertiser
Post Magazine
The Scotsman
Transactions of the Highland and Agricultural Society of Scotland

The two most dangerous
of nearly 200 occupations
were agricultural labourer
and threshing machine owner.

STEAM-DRIVEN | 1

THOMAS Hardy captured in a harvest incident the menace of mechanisation in late nineteenth century agriculture:

The dust, the din, the sustained exertion demanded to keep up with the steam tyrant, are distasteful to all women but the coarsest. I am not sure whether, at the present time, women are employed to feed the machine, but some years ago a woman had frequently to stand just above the whizzing wire drum, and feed from morning to night – a performance for which she was quite unfitted, and many were the manoeuvres to escape that responsible position. A thin saucer-eyed woman of fifty-five, who had been feeding the machine all day, declared on one occasion that in crossing a field on her way home in the fog after dusk, she was so dizzy from the work as to be unable to find the opposite gate, and there she walked round and round the field, bewildered and terrified, till three o'clock in the morning before she could get out. The farmer said that the ale had got into her head, but she maintained that it was the spinning of the machine.

This was not fiction. It was an item in Hardy's article on *The Dorsetshire Labourer* in *Longman's Magazine* of July 1883. By then the reign of the steam tyrant, the steam threshing machine, like the steam plough driven by a traction engine, had spread throughout Britain. Mechanisation was a nationwide response to the drift of labourers to the towns and the need to become more efficient in an agricultural depression. Change from the simple manual methods labourers were used to brought new kinds of accidents, often severe. The revolving spiked drum of a thresher could take in and mangle fingers, hands, even arms.

Perthshire has always been an agricultural county, with both arable and livestock farming. The county seat, Perth, is a market centre, still famed for its October bull sales.

Perth from Kinnoull H

Drive belts could break or slip off, whipping into workers and causing injuries serious to the point of decapitation. An 1878 Act for the Prevention of Accidents by Threshing Machines required the drum and feeding mouth to be securely fenced, but the Act did not extend to Ireland and Scotland.

Scottish farmers hired steam threshing machines, but what their exact impact was cannot be determined because incidents may well have gone unreported and official statistics do not exist. An examination of accident registers for Perth Royal Infirmary, serving an agricultural, industrial and railway area, gives some indicators for 1880–5. Totals of accidents were rising, as were the numbers of amputations and fractures, some of which resulted in death. 'The Registers also record an unusually large number of Accident cases,' noted the annual report for 1882. 'The greater number of those cases were of a most severe and complicated character.' A large increase was dealt with in 1883. Six farmers as in-patients in 1884 suggest there was a common cause.

Classified by occupation, the figures for 1880–5 show that the largest group (934) were labourers, an undifferentiated category that may well have included agricultural casual workers at harvest time. Other categories were domestic servants (336), mill workers (309), agricultural workers (farm servants, ploughmen, farmers and cattlemen, totalling 269) and railway employees (124). What the classification does not reveal is the severity of the cases. Later evidence, based on 20 years' experience of assessing risks, comes in an analysis by the Perth-based insurance company General Accident ready for the implementation of the Workmen's Compensation Act 1906. The analysis shows that the two most dangerous of nearly 200 occupations were agricultural labourer and threshing machine owner (working).

In the late nineteenth century, when mechanised methods were replacing labourers drifting away from the land, steam engines were used for ploughing and threshing.

Severe accidents had been occurring at a time of continuing agricultural depression. Railways and steamships brought lower freight rates, especially from North America, where large land areas were ideal for mechanisation, exposing small farmers to world prices. Over the 25 years from 1860 the price of wheat halved. Imports rose, farm incomes shrank, rents fell, land was allowed to fall fallow. In Perthshire 73,126 acres needed tenants. In its review of 1885 the *Perth Constitutional* summed up the state of local agriculture:

For at least a quarter of a century, the year just drawing to a close will prove decidedly the worst for farmers…The price of wheat and barley is without precedent on a well run 19 years' lease, and the market is in a glutted state…Oats have been

Right
The future directors of General Accident, some of whom subscribed to Perth Royal Infirmary, would have been familiar with the rising number of accidents dealt with there in the early 1880s.

As a child of nine in the West of Scotland Barbara Gibson lost both arms in her father's barn threshing mill, but survived to become a teacher. Long sleeves hid her disfigurement.

lower, but as these are principally required for purposes within the holding, any revenue from this crop is limited…The potato crop was a poor one, and as yet prices no more than cover rent and expenses…The price of beef and mutton is quite 3d to 4d per lb cheaper than it was twelve months ago…The fat market has also been going slowly but steadily backward…The prospect at present is the reverse of cheering, and many anxious and frugal tenants are forced to take a desponding view of the position. One thing appears inevitable, namely, that on all farms where there has been no readjustment of rent as fixed by leases entered into several years ago, the business, though unpleasant to landowners, must at once be proceeded with.

'Abatements of rent' was a harsh cry to the 1,700 owners of 90 per cent of Scottish land.

All this was happening when the employer/employee balance of power was changing. Under the Employers' Liability Act 1880 a workman could bring an action against an employer for personal injury caused by fault or the negligence of another employee. Damages recoverable under the Act were up to three years' wages. Agricultural workers also gained political power, getting the vote under the Reform Act 1884. Moreover, the vote was secret; with a cross on a ballot paper man could cock a snook at master. Apprehensive about the strengthening mood of the lower orders, some saw the enfranchisement as a significant blow to the aristocratic power structure. Through the early 1880s a new radicalism had stirred popular feeling. Henry George's *Progress and Poverty*, proposing a single tax on land value, was claimed to have sold some 100,000 copies in three years. Joseph Chamberlain stumped the country in 1885 by advocating a radical programme including land reform that would give 'three acres and a cow' to agricultural workers. In the Highlands there was crofter agitation.

For farmers the crucial time was harvest, the prime season for accidents, especially when families came out to help. Harvest was soon to be followed by disappointing prices for produce. Farm incomes were less and less able to meet damages incurred under employers' liability. Individualists, farmers would no more have considered co-operative farming like their Danish counterparts than they would have participation in a mutual insurance company to cushion the impact of claims against them. Their financial exposure presented a business opportunity, recognised by a small group who in the autumn of 1885 met in the Perth office of the Royal Bank of Scotland, the agent of which already represented two accident companies. Amid economic, financial and political uncertainty, another accident company could offer farmers and those not covered by existing companies, which were mainly focused on the hazards of rail travel, a modicum of security.

In the general election of 24 November 1885 agricultural workers voted for the first time, electing among the Members of Parliament Joseph Arch, a former farm labourer who in 1872 had aroused the wrath of the gentry when he

Citizens of Perth, like these General Accident staff on an outing to Sma' Glen, could easily get into the countryside.

formed a trade union for his fellow labourers. Just over three weeks later, in a mood of deepening apprehension, a new insurance company was formed. Four members of the Highland and Agricultural Society of Scotland, with the necessary professional support, incorporated on 16 December 1885 a company with a paid-up capital of £5,000 'to insure against all kinds of accidents'. Appropriately it was called General Accident & Employers' Liability Assurance Association.

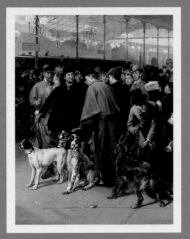

Business did benefit from the railways. They strengthened the rôle of Perth as a regional centre.

QUEEN Victoria on her first journey to Scotland noted in her journal for 6 September 1842:

We very soon came upon Perth, the situation of which is quite lovely; it is on the Tay, with wooded hills skirting it entirely on one side, and hills are seen again in the distance, the river winding wonderfully. Albert was charmed, and said it put him in mind of the situation of Basle.

The situation but not the importance. Straddling the Rhine on one of the major route centres of Europe, Basle was developing as a great banking and commercial city. Since Queen Victoria made her first road journey to Perth it had grown from 1847 as a rail junction, with seven lines converging. In recognition of its status, following a special Act of Parliament in 1884, Perth General Station was remodelled over the next two and a half years. Steam trains brought some soot and grime but Perth remained a relatively clean city in which to live and work. Not being near a ready source of coal and iron, it had none of the dark satanic mills of the industrial revolution. It had all the tone of a county town, with quality shops, two recreation grounds, the North Inch and the South Inch, and from 1887 swimming baths.

Business did benefit though from the railways. They strengthened the rôle of Perth as a regional centre for farmers, transporting cattle and sheep to market and distributing agricultural machinery. On a broader scale they extended the scope in products and services for consumers. Railway lines provided access to national markets for three local industries, all based upon soft Highland water. Whisky was the best known, particularly the Bell's and Dewar's brands. Pullar's was the largest employer, taking in dyeing and cleaning from agents throughout the UK, receiving and returning items by rail. Contradicting Dr Johnson's dictionary definition of oats as 'a grain which in England is generally given to horses but in Scotland supports the people', the

The first office of General Accident in Perth, in part of the building to the left of the church spire, overlooked the tidal River Tay. The larger building on the corner to the right of the spire is the head office, built in 1901. Locals fished for salmon in the river. Occasionally it froze over.

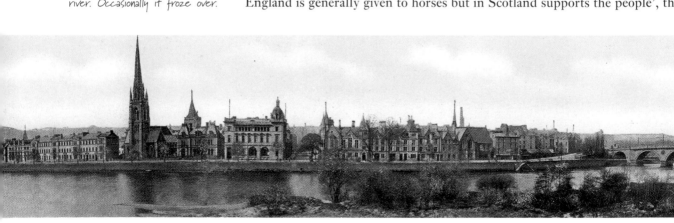

Lower City Mills used water power to grind oats for the staple food in British prisons, porridge.

Railways and the telegraph brought another benefit to Perth: British Standard Time, in practice from the mid-nineteenth century, when most public clocks were set to Greenwich Mean Time, officially from 2 August 1880. No longer nearly a quarter of an hour behind London, the 29,000 inhabitants of Perth were now in time with the capital and General Accident would often claim the company was so in a business sense. The company had been formed in response to specific local needs but from Perth it could do business across the nation. It was no more at a geographical disadvantage than the Glasgow-based Scottish Boiler Insurance and Engine Inspection Company, founded like the Edinburgh-based Scottish Life Assurance Company in 1881 and destined to survive, or the Scottish Temperance Life Assurance Company started in Glasgow in 1883. Like them it had to make its way in a crowded market. In Perth among over 50 agencies, fire and life companies were well represented as were four accident companies: London Guarantee and Accident (by a solicitor), Ocean Railway and General Accident, Scottish Accident (both by William Forbes of the Royal Bank of Scotland, who altogether had ten agencies), Railway Passengers (by the Caledonian Railway at Perth Station).

Apart from William Forbes of the Royal Bank, the general practitioner and local councillor Robert de Bruce Trotter, and solicitor Donald Mackay, the original nine directors of General Accident mainly had country backgrounds. Mackay's brother-in-law, George Kyd, the first chairman, was an auctioneer and land surveyor; William Crawford and Patrick Hunter were substantial tenant farmers suffering from the agricultural depression; William Macdonald a landed proprietor, who also ran the Royal Refreshment Rooms at Perth Station (Patronised By The Queen, The Prince Of Wales, And Other Members Of The Royal Family – Ample Time by all Trains for Breakfasts, Luncheons, Dinners Etc). The two directors in trade were William McKendrick, butcher, and William Muir of 70-year old brewers Muir & Martin. In the tight community of Perth there were many business and social links between the directors, for example through the Dundee, Perth and London Shipping Company and Perth Royal Infirmary, to which Crawford, Macdonald, McKendrick and Muir each subscribed a guinea

George Kyd.

Donald Mackay.

a year, entitling them to recommend for treatment one indoor and two outdoor patients. The founder directors of General Accident each subscribed for 50 £1 shares and were substantial enough men to obtain the bulk of the original £5,000 capital from other sources. For example, £1,000 was procured from Glasgow.

Ground floor offices for the new company, two rooms at Victoria Buildings, 44 Tay Street, overlooking the river, were rented for £29 per annum. Victoria Buildings was the address of agents for seven other insurance companies. From here the business was developed, the first policy being issued on 1 February 1886 covering for 15 shillings the employer's liability of John Burns, a Perth cabinet-maker. The first claim, of which no record exists, was paid in May.

Setting rates in accident insurance is very much a matter of experience and hope. Accidents, where and when they will occur, are less predictable than the longevity of men and women for life assurance. Mortality tables and individ-

ual medical examinations are a more reliable guide to underwriting a risk than frequencies of past accidents. There is no guarantee of a maintained pattern. True, through trial and error, occupational risks can be classified and special factors taken into account but nobody can foresee a spate of accidents or a particular disaster.

Accident insurance was a comparatively recent introduction, having been started in response to a run in the late 1840s of railway accidents, which according to *The Times* 'are almost of daily occurrence, generally ending in loss of limb, often of life'. Registered in March 1849, the pioneering Railway Passengers Assurance Company originally insured against fatal and non-fatal railways accidents, defined as occurring when a train was in motion. Having raised capital beyond its needs, in 1852 the company obtained parliamentary sanction to insure against accidents of all kinds. The company secretary, William

As a railway junction, Perth had a bustling railway station, the atmosphere of which is conveyed in George Earl's 1895 painting **Perth Station, Coming South**. Queen Victoria used to stop here on the way to her Highland castle, Balmoral.

Vian, used his own judgment to draw up premium tables for this class of insurance. These became the basis for other companies' premium structures, the fourfold classification of risk by occupation coming into use from 1857, moral hazards being uninsurable. With technology changing, experience of occupational hazards took time to accumulate and initial rates were not always an accurate reflection of risks. To try and ensure that claims did not exceed premiums, the prudent approach was to calculate a risk factor for a given situation and for safety increase it by a margin consistent with being profitably competitive.

Further, the underwritten risk had to be spread so that it was not concentrated, whether geographically or within a particular category. Hence an early move of General Accident was to establish local boards of directors in London and Glasgow, men of influence in their communities who could bring in business through their connections. In Glasgow the company went on to share colliery business with the Mercantile Accident and Guarantee. Later, the two organisations co-operated in insuring the Birmingham & Midlands Tramway Company. An office was opened in Edinburgh and one in Manchester was considered a priority, but its opening was delayed. Elsewhere agents were appointed as business-getters.

As an insurance company is basically writing a series of IOUs under certain conditions, it needs the security of adequate capital and an investment income. Part of its risk can also be laid off through reinsurance, which General Accident effected for the fatal part of its personal accident policies. Its early reinsurance treaties were continental, with AGF in France and Munich Re from 1892. In other respects the company was determined to make its own way. At their first meeting the directors discussed an amalgamation approach from the Mercantile Accident and Guarantee Company and 'resolved that such a step was not advisable'. Within two months of its formation authorised capital was increased to £100,000 with share issues to be made when deemed desirable. An advertisement in *The Scotsman* of 4 February 1886 stated that the prospectus had been issued for the further development of the business, that the first issue was £20,000 in £1 shares, and that it was intended to apply for an official quotation on the Stock Exchange. As well as contributing to the opening of more offices increased capital provided 'ample security to the assured'. One of the company's developments, probably inspired by the popularity of Perthshire as a tourist destination, was personal accident policies for tourists, issued for one, three and six months. Accidents could always occur on the railways, pleasure steamers or boating on the Tay, while walking or shooting. Early investments were in mortgage companies, especially in Australia. A year later, by mid-1887, railway stocks were favoured, investments being of £2,000 to £2,500 in debenture bonds and other first-class securities.

Before the company was a year old differences of opinion arose between Perth and London. The London secretary, who had failed to bring in sufficient business under his agreement, and a local director had to make the more than 400-mile journey to Perth to try to resolve differences. These fundamentally came down to a question of authority. It was agreed that the power of London to appoint agents was restricted to its own area and the Home Counties. Everywhere else came under Perth.

No sooner was that settled than the Glasgow board suggested that 'to make business workable and profitable' the head office should be jointly in Perth and Glasgow, with the overall board consisting of six directors from each. The proposals amounted to a reconstitution of the company. To add to the problems in Glasgow the resident secretary, 25-year old James Marwick, just qualified as a member of the Institute of Accountants and Actuaries, stated that to continue acting for General Accident he would need £200 per annum. The main board decided against an increase and expressed the hope that he would continue on his existing terms. He did not, choosing to set out on his own, opening an accounting partnership in Glasgow as Walker & Marwick. He was destined to return to the aid of General Accident before the century was out. Meanwhile the company secretary, Walter Ireland Jr, defecting to a rival company as a director and secretary, resigned with two other officials. The share prospectus of the rival company included Dr Trotter, deputy chairman, as a director, but he refused to resign from General Accident immediately.

At the end of its first financial year, 31 January 1887, over 1,000 policies had been issued with a premium income of £2,833, against which claims amounted to £335. After deduction of expenses the surplus amounted to £784, out of which a four per cent tax-free dividend was paid, leaving a balance of £585. On the face of it the company with its staff of three clerks and four outside officials

Patrick Hunter, one of the original directors of General Accident, was a substantial tenant farmer living outside Perth, where he cultivated three farms. The land held more interest for him than the law, which he studied but did not practise.

On the formation of the company he became its first deputy chairman and then chairman for 10 years, from 1891 to 1901. Altogether, he was a director for 20 years, resigning in 1905.

One of the largest shareholders, he held 1,805 shares, valued at £5,302 3s 9d, the largest item in his personal estate. In the year of his death, 1906, his son William succeeded him as a director.

had made a creditable beginning, but it was falling apart. It could not stay as it was. If it was not to go under it had to put itself on a firmer footing on its own or through amalgamation. The latter option had been rejected once. Local insurance companies were still being formed, more so in the provinces than in London, to meet specific needs. Names such as London Provincial Horse and Carriage, Dewsbury and District (for plate glass), the Engine and Boiler Insurance Company convey their character. For the most part such companies, undercapitalised and serving restricted markets, were too small to survive. Their failure rate was high. At the same time, with the consolidation of local banks and the fall in the number of provincial stock exchanges, financial power was moving to London, since the collapse of the Paris money market in the Franco-Prussian War (1870-1) the undisputed capital market of the world. Whither General Accident? It had asserted the authority of Perth over its London office and had refused to share power with Glasgow. Nestling in a small suite of offices in The Gateway to The Highlands, how could it survive over the ensuing months and in the long run achieve anything like a national standing? It needed a strong saviour.

He was the first of three outsiders who were to change the fortunes of General Accident decisively.

SALVATION was at hand, 60 miles away in the Glasgow-based company Mercantile Accident and Guarantee, a contemporary with which General Accident had co-operated but refused to merge. Its assistant manager for little over a year was Francis Norie Miller. At the age of 27 he had behind him a career in London with three other insurance companies: London & Lancashire Fire; Ocean, Railway & General Accident (1880–1), on which he commented 'I was considered to have degraded myself almost outside the pale of civilisation when I went from a fire company to a casualty company'; chief clerkship of the accident and guarantee departments of Employers' Liability Assurance (1882–5), where a fellow employee described him as 'an alert and rather restless young man; a good colleague, joining in all sports and entertainments'. Tennis and, later, golf and horseracing were his favourite sports. Of the four companies for which Norie Miller worked until 1885 all but the London & Lancashire became part of Commercial Union, with which General Accident was to merge in 1998.

Norie Miller was the only official in Employers' Liability with any experience of accident business and saw the possibilities of development at a time when there were only nine companies transacting that kind of insurance. Of these the leading company, Railway Passengers, had a premium income of less than £200,000 and the other eight a total of £119,000. Six of the eight, catering principally for personal accident and fidelity guarantee, were formed between 1869 and 1877 and some had regional names, e.g. London Guarantee and Accident, The Lancashire and Yorkshire, Scottish Accident.

Employers' Liability Assurance, started as its name states following the 1880 Act, foresaw wider opportunities including the USA. Setting up there involved American representatives visiting the UK, correspondence, and transacting accident insurance for railway servants, for which Norie Miller was responsible and made profitable. He listened eagerly to a senior colleague, Stanley Brown, giving an account of his first visit to the US and 'his description of the buildings there'. The temples to business now included fully steel-frame buildings, the first of

In this 1882 photograph of the Employers' Liability Assurance staff the 23-year old Francis Norie Miller is in the back row, fifth from the right.

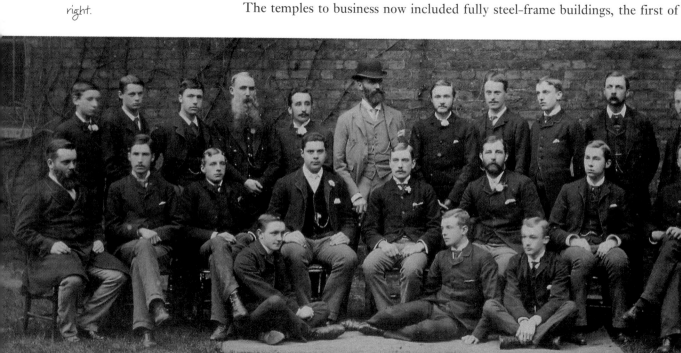

which was erected for Home Insurance in Chicago in 1883. What would soon become known as skyscrapers set a young man's imagination soaring.

Having been born at Stoke Newington in 1859, gone to school at Holt House, Cheshunt, Hertfordshire, and worked in London, Norie Miller brought experience of accident insurance and a perspective not limited to Perth. He was the first of three outsiders who were to change the fortunes of General Accident decisively. The younger of twins who at school was not good at spelling, he had inherited a head for figures from his father, Henry, who became chief of the statistical department in Her Majesty's Customs. His Scottish mother Ann gave him her maiden name Norie, by which his father used to address him and Francis was later to hyphenate, Norie-Miller sounding better than plain Miller. Originally it looked as though he was destined for a career in law but his inclination was towards business as the fitting outlet for his energy and, some said, charm. He was a businessman, a strong character who loved work, his only physical handicap being chronic bronchial asthma, for which his chest was poulticed. Congratulating him on his appointment in Glasgow, his father wrote: 'If you do not move <u>on</u> some one will step before you and your opportunity is lost for ever. You will find living in Scotland is much colder and you will have to be very careful and wear plenty of flannel.'

On 18 February 1887 he met the directors of General Accident, who were 'very favourably impressed…and considering the high character of his recommendations agreed to offer him an engagement' as secretary. He asked for a day or two to discuss it with friends and on 21 February he accepted a two-year contract 'subject to the Board's sanctioning certain alterations of the proposed terms'. His terms, including a salary of £300 p.a. and 2½ per cent on the profits in excess of £50, were accepted by telegram forenoon. In future he would claim that he had actually taken a drop in salary to secure the opportunity. He soon moved to Perth with his wife Grace, son Claud and daughter Elwena, their removal expenses costing the company £15. The family rented for £34 a year a substantial semi-detached villa at 4 Comely Bank that he later referred to as 'a £30 a year cottage'.

From his appointment the tone of the minutes changed. An item would often begin 'On the recommendation of the secretary…' There was a clearer statement of the terms of insurance, the limits of territories and the commission rates on various classes of business. Within two months he had submitted proposals for covering risks on tobogganing and marine passengers' effects, got board meetings changed from weekly to monthly, been authorised to settle claims up to £10 without reference to the directors, and set about removing bad and doubtful risks. As part of his dynamic commitment to his new employers Norie-Miller arranged for proceedings to be taken against his former company and penalties recovered for a palpable imitation of General Accident's name on

Francis Norie-Miller's first home in Perth was at 4 Comely Bank, just off a main road running down into the city.

the Mercantile's Birmingham office. In April 59 agents were appointed, including one in Cardiff for the whole of Wales, Monmouth and Hereford; in July he was given permission to visit the company's representatives in Liverpool, Manchester, Birmingham and London, where the local board of directors had been dispensed with; in August a further 74 agents were appointed.

In all this activity unsatisfactory levels of business and irregularities in accounts were not allowed to pass unnoticed. As well as paying attention to detail Norie-Miller advised on major matters. Not until he returned from England did the directors proceed with the recommended £1,000 investments in various railway stocks. By September, when a resident secretary was appointed in Dublin for Ireland, so much was happening that board meetings were again held weekly. In October the solicitor agreed that the company could transact fidelity guarantee business. For promotional purposes 10,000 pocket diaries were produced for 1888, when a share issue was authorised to raise further capital. Application forms for the issue of 30,000 £1 shares, of which 10 per cent would be paid up, stated that 'Immediately on the completion of the present issue, it is intended to make application for an official quotation on the Stock Exchange for the shares of the Association'. Nothing came of it.

Looking back at the time of the company's jubilee, Norie-Miller gave this early period of the business a grim romanticism:

Below and facing page
Calendars were used for promotion.

I recall (to give an example of many similar experiences) journeying by night to Nottingham in the corner of a Third-class Compartment; arriving there for breakfast, making various calls in the town, completing some business arrangements, then going to Leicester and working there till about 8 o'clock and catching the night train back to Perth, so as to carry on the necessary work that fell to the Chief Official at the Head Office of the Company. This required untiring energy and one was undoubtedly helped by the fact that the looking forward to bigger things smoothed the rough edges of personal inconvenience and disappointments that always come to those who are doing things.

At other times he maintained he could sleep better on a train than in his own bed.

An innovation in 1888 was his arrangement with *Malcolm's Diary and Timetable* to insure for £100 passengers killed in railway accidents, provided they were carrying the diary. This penny premium for every 25 diaries sold, half of which was spent on advertising in the diary, marked the start of a profitable line in coupon insurance. The idea was soon taken up by the *Railway Herald*, *Bright Thoughts* and *Gossip* and spread to football accidents with *Football News*. *Fishing Gazette* covered both railway accidents and death by drowning while fishing. Under personal accident policies an annual £1 premium assured £300 on death or permanent total disablement, £150 for permanent partial disablement and £1 10 shillings per week during temporary total disablement. George Bernard Shaw, who wrote parts of his plays 'in Great Northern express trains', took out a coupon insurance about 1905.

Such was Norie Miller's reputation that in 1888 his old company continued to use his name in a prospectus, the further issue of which was stopped. Business was growing, especially with several tramway companies throughout the country. Pay-outs were small. For example, an employers' liability claim for a child killed by Glasgow Trams was settled for two guineas (£2 2s). Although the *Insurance and Financial Gazette* revealed some of the practices in reducing commissions and questioned whether the company was 'in a position to pay either dividends or directors' fees' when it was 'struggling to get on its feet', growth gave General Accident confidence in itself. In 1889, when Norie-Miller had been promoted to manager and presented with a gold watch because the directors were anxious to keep his services, the managers of all accident companies in Scotland were invited to an Edinburgh meeting to examine the formation of a tariff association, which would agree basic rates. General Accident declined to join because it was of 'not much advantage'.

Most of its claims were under employers' liability. It went into burglary insurance in 1890, incurring its first claim in Birmingham, for £250. Norie-Miller remembered an American named Smith calling on him in Perth:

This man Smith had an idea that burglary losses could be insured against, and had laid the particulars of his plan before the Mercantile of Glasgow. I ridiculed his suggestions because they seemed to me absurd. But he was persistent, and convinced me finally that it was possible to make the business a serious insurance undertaking. My mind made up, I remember how I hurried to get my inspectors out first so as to be the first company to transact burglary insurance.

Mercantile of Glasgow beat General Accident by several weeks but later, when Mercantile ceased business, General Accident was able to claim it was the oldest burglary-writing company in the world. It was also later able to take the idea back to the US.

By 1891 the organisation had been reconstituted as The General Accident Assurance Corporation with over 100 shareholders and was known as the new company. Norie-Miller, who had had an assistant secretary for two years and had been approached by a rival company 'of better standing', had his salary increased to £450 and a bonus scheme. A tangible indication of the volume of business was the purchase in 1892 of a desk and a Yost typewriter for £26 5s, half a year's salary for a clerk. Another typewriter was bought for £17 in 1894 and a telephone installed, the idea having been rejected two years previously. Expenses compared favourably with those of other companies.

From 1895 the company had an agreement with the Scottish General Fire Company, which gave it a percentage of that company's premium income. (This company was not the Scottish General of 1939, which had been founded in 1919 as Scottish Automobile & General and was acquired by General Accident in 1933.) In 1900 Scottish General Fire and General Accident merged and General Accident was admitted to the Fire Offices Committee. In November 1896, the month of the Locomotives on Highways Act repealing an earlier law requiring motor vehicles to be preceded by someone holding a red flag, Norie-Miller told the board that he was about to issue a special prospectus to insure motor cars at a premium of £2 per cent. Features included a variable rate of £1 10s to £2 10s, foreign use excess of £10, premium reductions for owner-only driver or membership of a recognised organisation such as the Motor Union or Automobile Club, policies transferable to the next owner. All of these may have previously occurred under individually written policies preceding formal printed proposals. No office has yet been credited for certain with issuing the first motor policies. What can justly be stated is that under Norie-Miller's initiative the company readily adopted innovations. One of the maxims he never tired of repeating was 'The man with little risk has much rest' and he was quick to identify risks and rate them.

For handling business arising under Joseph Chamberlain's Workmen's Compensation Act 1897, which applied to all accidents suffered by certain categories of employees, General Accident policy in competition with companies quoting 'ruinous rates' was 'to take only the best class of risks and at a fair premium'. It had to take into account deferred liabilities and the likelihood that successful claims would be more numerous than expected. By 1896 cycle insurance was being written and a marine department insured the lives and property of passengers and mariners against loss at sea. In 1899 the Scottish Live Stock Insurance Company was registered at Norie-Miller's instigation, he joining the board, to protect General Accident's agencies from other livestock companies that were getting into the accident business. Because of its diversification into new markets the company had to increase its capital. In 1897 the authorised share capital of £100,000 was fully sub-scribed so the amount was doubled. The company was anxious to dispel any doubts about its independence and integrity. In 1899, after making changes to the articles of association, it was listed on the London Stock Exchange, which added to its credibility.

Coming down to the office from his home at 4 Comely Bank and crossing the river by the Perth Bridge, Norie–Miller saw the Post Office on the corner of the High Street and Tay Street as the site for the future head office of 'The General'. In 1895 he proposed making an early offer for the building and £2,500 was accepted. The building was demolished and the foundation stone of General Buildings laid on 25 July 1899. Two years later the £20,000 building was occupied and promoted as the image of a well-founded company, its marbled ground floor giving the visitor an immediate impression of cool solidity.

For prestige, titled and double-barrelled names were recruited to the board. Men such as the Earl of Dunmore, Lieutenant Colonel H.S. Home-Drummond, Unionist MP and future prime minister Bonar Law, and Sir C.B. Wollaston-Knocker did not necessarily know much about insurance or provide useful business connections but they brought a respectability to the corporation and inspired confidence in the premium-paying public. Lieutenant Colonel Home-Drummond of Blair Drummond was named in advertisements as chairman of the company, with the additional information that he was Vice Lieutenant, Justice of the Peace and Convener of Perth County. In the same advertisement Norie-Miller's name and title appeared in larger type. Company standing in motor insurance was increased by the appointment in 1903 of an advisory board including Lieutenant Colonel Arthur F. Mulliner, a founder of what became the Royal Automobile Club and head of a firm of motor carriage manu-facturers, and The Hon C.S. Rolls, third son of Lord Llangattock and winner of the Automobile Club's Thousand Mile Trial in 1900, the promoter who in 1906 would enter a partnership with the engineer Sir Frederick Henry Royce to produce in 1907 the first of a line of classic cars, the Silver Ghost. Rolls was also instrumental in interesting the future King Edward VII and his Queen in the pleasures of motoring. In 1903 too the company took a stall at the first Official Show of the Society

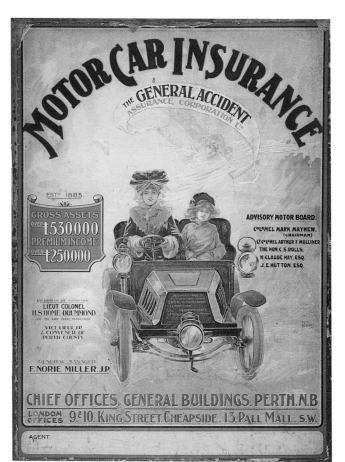

One of the first motor insurers, the company established its reputation through the appointment of an advisory motor board from the fledgling industry, advertisements and stands at exhibitions. This advertisement was used in 1903, the year of the first official Motor Show, at which General Accident had a kiosk.

Coming from his home across the Perth Bridge, Norie-Miller saw the Post Office building (inset) on the corner of the High Street. He regarded it as a prestigious site for the next headquarters of his company, outgrowing its first offices 150 yards along Tay Street.

In 1899 Lady Georgina Home-Drummond laid the foundation stone of General Buildings, which was to be the company head office for over 80 years.

of Motor Manufacturers and Traders, a body formed the previous year. There had been displays in London before but this one, a gathering of 185 international exhibitors at the Crystal Palace, where steam, electric and petrol cars also ran in the grounds, was the first Motor Show. Vehicle prices ranged from £165 for a two-seater 6 h.p. Continental to £1,500 for a 30 h.p. four-cylinder Fiat, imports then accounting for over 80 per cent of the UK market.

Back in Perth, head office rules and regulations, signed by Norie-Miller, were strict, as the following extracts from 1904 show:

Each clerk is required to sign the Attendance Book in his or her Department immediately upon arrival in the morning. At 9.00 a.m. a red line will be drawn by the Chief Clerk in each Department, and any clerk arriving after that hour must sign below the line, giving the time of arrival, together with an explanation as to the cause of being late.

The Lady Superintendent of the Typists' Department has full control of all the lady typists or lady clerks in the Building, and is responsible for seeing that proper order and decorum is maintained, not only in the Office generally, but in or about the passages and cloakroom. Any unnecessary noise, conversation or laughter, waste of time or inattention to duty, must be immediately checked and all cases of insubordination at once reported to the Secretary, whom failing, the Assistant Manager.

In order to provide against accidents, no clerk under 17 will be allowed to make use of the Lift except when he or she is accompanied by another of at least that age. Infringement of this or the preceding rule will be severely dealt with.

At the close of business each evening, all desks must be absolutely cleared of all books and documents, which must be returned to their proper places.

Smoking is strictly prohibited in the Offices and the younger members of the staff must refrain from playing or loitering in the passages and corridors, or indulging in boisterous behaviour, but at all times must maintain a quiet and business-like demeanour while in the building.

Certainly it was so when Francis was around. He himself would check the attendance register and, ever conscious of his own health, pay particular attention to the sick list. A married couple were not allowed to work in the same department; nor, sometimes, in the same office if it was a small one. One of them, usually the woman, had to apply for a transfer to another office, or leave. So women on the staff had to choose carefully, weighing up the pros and cons before getting married. They could, however, get a dowry from the company, which compensated for the loss of their accrued pension rights.

Male clerks were typically paid a pound a week. L.S. Lowry, on the claims staff of the Manchester office from 1907 until being made redundant in 1910, saw his annual salary rise from £46 16s to £52. Typical advertised prices at the time were:

a blue serge suit 25s; a tweed coat from 27s 6d to 34s 6d; a pair of boots 14s 9d; Lotus shoes for ladies 12s 9d; an embroidered white flannel skirt 7s 6d; ready made costumes from two guineas; tweed and cloth costumes from four guineas; a child's cashmere frock 4s 6d; 'real Scotch blankets' from 10s 6d to 22s. One could enjoy a three-course meal in a restaurant for a shilling. Tea was 1s 8d a pound and claret 16s a dozen bottles. At sale time clothing and furniture cost less.

At those prices Norie-Miller and his family lived well. His salary rose from £3,000 to £4,000 p.a. in 1908. That year, when the government introduced old age pensions for the over 70s, the company arranged its own scheme, under which employees retired with up to two-thirds of their salary averaged over the last seven years, which was a generous provision. The company also established a provident society, which provided for the treatment of employees in Perth Royal Infirmary.

Working for General Accident was respectable. It was looked upon as a profession, a minor one maybe but not a trade, when trade was still looked down upon. Pay in insurance might not be that different but status was, certainly in the minds of the staff. Outside staff (inspectors) dealing directly with agents were performing a service. They were providing something intangible, beyond price, peace of mind, freedom from worry if the worst happened. Inside staff, also presentably dressed, could pride themselves on doing a clean, quiet job to the same end. They were more than a cut above those working amid dirt and noise on some railway jobs or in factories. Whisky might appear a pleasant, old-established industry to be in but as a job it usually came down to bottling, labelling, wrapping and packing. Moreover, it could be casual, with a lull in the summer 'silent season'. Social differences like that counted in a small community like Perth and an ambition for one's children on leaving school could be to join 'The General'.

Business expanded to fill the new premises. In 1904 the Law Fidelity & General Insurance Company was acquired and in 1906, when fire business was increased with the purchase of the Regent Company and life assurance was embarked upon, the overall name changed to General Accident Fire and Life Assurance Corporation (GAFLAC). About 1903 the General Life Assurance Company had successfully opposed a name change to the General Assurance Corporation on the grounds that there could be confusion harmful to its business. GAFLAC, later the name of Norie-Miller's racehorse, was now the acronym of a composite office that could appeal to the heads of middle class families, who insured their lives and property.

At the lower end of the social scale the company was probably the first to receive a claim under the Workmen's Compensation Act 1906. On the day it came into force 'a servant girl in the employ of one of our policyholders jumped down from a table and a rusty nail entered her foot'. In the first year of the Act claims were to amount to nearly £50,000. Rates were reckoned to be 30

25

FRANCIS NORIE-MILLER

While employed as a clerk in the Manchester branch L.S. Lowry was studying drawing and painting at the Municipal College of Art in the evenings. This drawing, A Portrait of a Man, was made in his third year as a part-time student.

per cent too low and there were too many hazardous risks, all sufficient reasons for not entering that business in Australia. At home, risks were classified in four categories by occupation, nearly 200 professions and trades being listed.

At the company's coming of age in 1906 the first issue of the staff magazine, *The General's Review*, reported:

> *a yearly income of close upon £500,000, a Subscribed capital of £400,000, and Reserves of £200,000. The Staff at the Head Office numbers 125. There are 27 home and foreign branches, 12,000 agents, and business is transacted in nearly every quarter of the globe.*

There was no doubt who was the general in charge of the troops. Norie-Miller reinforced the association by issuing a series of bookmarks featuring contemporary generals: Lords Kitchener and Roberts, Generals French and Ian Hamilton, Lieutenant General W.H. Mackinnon. Confident in General Accident setting its own rates, Norie-Miller 'absolutely declined' to join the Accident Tariff Association in 1907 for the terse reason 'We think it is supreme folly for Companies to fix exorbitant rates.' In 1908 the company resigned from the Fire Offices Committee for various reasons:

> *First, I consider the conduct of many of the older Offices in the Committee towards this Corporation and other of the younger Offices quite unworthy.*
>
> *Second, I am convinced that as a result of their conduct it is quite impossible for a progressive Office to obtain sufficient facilities for reinsurance unless they are outside the Committee.*

As well as being a workplace the company was a social and sports centre. Francis Norie-Miller used to invite groups for recreation to his home at Cleeve on the outskirts of Perth.

Third, I am of the opinion that many of the ratings for Home business are distinctly unjust to the Assured, and that British manufacturers and merchants are being forced to pay for the heavy losses incurred by those Companies doing business in the United States.

In 1908 it became the first insurer to introduce a no-claim bonus into house-hold insurance, a free sixth year. That year it first issued policies for royal cars, covering HRH The Prince of Wales. Plate glass for shop fronts, which from the mid-nineteenth century had led to the formation of many local semi-mutual insurance companies, followed in 1909 when the Northern Plate Glass and the Scottish Live Stock insurance companies were both acquired. Around this time an innovation was a combined fire, burglary and domestic servants policy.

Prestige in Perth, where the head office was about to be extended, was matched in London with the move in 1911 from off Cheapside to the new General Buildings at 99 Aldwych. Once again the question of Perth or London as the place for head office came up, Norie-Miller being firmly in favour of Perth:

1. There is no doubt that the rapid strides we have made in our business in foreign countries is to a large extent due to our being a Scotch [sic] Company.

2. Our building in Perth is so constructed that even if it were possible to let it there are no business concerns in the city that could afford to pay a rent adequate to the accommodation and size and appearance of the rooms in the building.

3. In Perth we have a staff averaging about 200. It is a fact that the cost of living in London is a third more than in Perth. Moreover, in Perth we are able to get the best students in the County, the remainder going to London and other large centres, and there is no question that in the country clerks work much harder and have a greater interest in their work than is the case in London. As against this, by amalgamating the London and Perth staffs a saving might be affected [sic] in numbers, but we would require to take from Perth at least 150 of the staff. The cost of removal of 20 married members, taken at £60, would be £1,200. The other 130 would require to be put down at £5 each, so that the removal of the staff would come to about £2,000. Then if one-third were added to the salaries of members of the staff this would mean another £5,000 or £6,000 a year.

4. Whereas it would be impossible to get adequate rents for the Head Office, the surplus offices in London could be easily let at a rental which would return a high rate of interest on our Investment.

5. It may be argued that in the case of our foreign officials coming to Perth an extra ten hours are added to the journey each way, but that on a journey of from 3 to 50 days is not considerable and while it is much harder on the General Manager, I think the Representatives of the Company appreciate the opportunity it gives them of visiting Scotland.

A.E. Cooksey sits in front of filing boxes which were still used to keep papers in order in the 1980s.

6. There would doubtless be a considerable saving in the travelling expenses of the Executive, but these have latterly been greatly reduced.

Although for business convenience he had acquired in 1910 a four-storey house in London, 5 Orme Court, Bayswater, Norie-Miller's home was in Perth, a small estate he bought in 1900 and renamed Cleeve, after the village in Somerset where his father came from. Francis often said: 'So long as the Tay flowed to the sea so the General Accident would remain in Perth.'

Letting offices in the new building in London was not easy and the company looked far and wide for tenants. Early in 1910 the Hon R.G.D. Fitzgerald, a director on its New South Wales Board, spoke to Sir George Reid, who was about to take up his appointment as the first High Commissioner in London, offering him space until Australia House was built (1912–18). Subsequently Fitzgerald wrote to the Australian Prime Minister, Alfred Deakin, confirming the offer. It was not taken up.

London did score a triumph for the company over which J.E. Pollard, manager of the West End branch, could not contain his enthusiasm in a four-page letter of 26 April 1911 to Norie-Miller:

I am extremely pleased to be able to apprise you of the fact that His Majesty the King has approved of the Royal Warrant being granted, subject to my personally applying to the Crown Equerry and signing for same…

The bestowal of this Warrant will mark an epoch in Insurance History – a few minutes' thought will convince you of the gigantic importance of the 'General' being the first and only Company thus privileged. We at once soar above the heads of our competitors, be they tariff or non-tariff Companies, and hold a unique position, bearing the prestige of being The Office exclusively selected by Royalty…

Then, again, what a powerful business-yielding weapon is at once placed in the hands of every official or agent throughout the world, silencing, as it must do, the voice of adverse criticism…

Leaving the Imperial for the personal point of view, I may mention that it is only by my personal influence and owing to the fact that I held a Captaincy under the late Master of the Horse (the Duke of Portland), who was my Colonel, the late King Edward being my Honorary Colonel, that I have been able to secure such an unprecedented honour for the Insurance profession.

I have been working on this secretly for several years, and naturally feel a certain amount of pride at the success of my efforts, and consider that the remuneration you should offer me should be a cash bonus of One Hundred Guineas, (which, I may mention, would not cover the expenses incurred), my salary being, at the very least, doubled. Apart from my having obtained the Royal Warrant this would not be excessive after sixteen years' service in control of one of your best and most lucrative

Facing page
The Aldwych office was furnished in a grand style befitting the chief office for London.

BY APPOINTMENT

Branch offices, and having regard to the fact that I have had no increase for several years…

It is imperative, if I am to take advantage of the opportunity, that I should have a larger salary to enable me to push for business in the Royal Circles, and you are aware that I have always been in the habit of spending a good deal of my remuneration in the interests of the Corporation…

In response Norie-Miller interviewed him on 8 May and conveyed the essence of the meeting to one of the directors, Sir William Taylor, the surgeon-general:

The fact of Mr Pollard's name appearing on the Royal Warrant seems to have caused him to lose his head altogether…I told him that his attitude was impertinent…I declined to admit that he was out-of-pocket to any extent whatever, but in view of the special circumstances of the case I actually offered him a bonus of £50 and an increase in his salary of £50 per annum, making it £450. This in my opinion was generous in the extreme, and to my great surprise he scoffed at the proposal. I have therefore given him a month's notice to leave the service of the Corporation.

Yet not six months earlier Norie-Miller had been full of praise for a member of head office accounts department who was leaving to join another firm in the USA, congratulating him on his appointment and presenting him with two trunks, a suitcase and a hard case: 'We feel certain that, in his new sphere, he will do credit to himself and to his training at Head Office.' In 1914 the London manager, Ralph Sketch, was treated with his successor to a lunch at the Waldorf Hotel, where amid the London board, staff, agents and friends, Norie-Miller congratulated him on his new appointment as manager of the casualty department of Norwich Union. Other farewells, reported in *The General's Review*, confirm the view that those managers leaving the corporation, even to join rival companies, went with presents such as a barometer, brushes, entrée dishes, pipes, a soup tureen, and the best wishes of Norie-Miller, who regarded them as graduates of his academy. What it did not pay to do was to cross him.

He was not to receive another challenge to his autocracy until after the 1914–18 war, and then from an unexpected quarter.

Following the sinking of the **Titanic** on her maiden voyage in 1912, General Accident paid £1,500 on the life of the purser, Herbert McElroy and £1,000 on the chief engineer, Joseph Bell.

Philadelphia was a port,
and in area the largest
city of the US, offering
opportunities in insurance.

SINCE Scotland provided a better education than opportunities for using it many of her countrymen emigrated, developing abroad their talents as architects, builders, engineers, financiers, lawyers, managers and traders. It was the Scots who provided the bulk of the capital for the development of the United States between 1873 and 1914, investing in railroads, mines, timber, agriculture and industry. Money came from the financial capital Edinburgh, from commercial centres such as Glasgow and Dundee, and from Aberdeen with its legendary reputation for thrift. Investment trusts of families such as Airlie and Low, names occurring among the directors of General Accident, were participants.

With their money and skills the Scots brought traditions such as Burns Night and their native game, golf. The sport began to have a vogue in England towards the end of the nineteenth century and from 1888 was taken up in the USA. For example, in 1890 the Philadelphia Country Club was founded and golf links laid out on its rolling land at Bala.

In neighbouring Welsh-named suburbs lived two partners in an insurance agency, William S. Muir at Haverford and J. Paul Haughton in Bryn Mawr. On reading in the insurance press that General Accident was the first company to start burglary insurance in the UK, Haughton, an agent for the New England Accident Company, which was involved in this line of business, saw another opportunity for the Scots. He wrote to Perth suggesting that the company should open a burglary office in the US. When the company declined, Haughton persisted, winning the support of Norie-Miller.

Commuting into Philadelphia on the Main Line of the Pennsylvania Railroad, Haughton had a perspective on a divided city. His short journey took him from the sedate suburb of Bryn Mawr, a site suitable for the young ladies' college founded in 1880, to the dark alleys and courtyards of 'trinity' houses occupied by immigrants. On three floors – 'Father, Son and Holy Ghost' – lived whole families, who sometimes kept animals on the ground floor. Like many northern cities that imported labour for industrial development after the Civil War, Philadelphia had grown. Between 1880 and 1900 its population increased from almost 850,000 to nearly 1.3 million. Immigrants came from Italy, Russia and Eastern Europe, many of them Jews fleeing pogroms, to join the older British and German settlers. But of all the immigrant groups the most significant was the black population, the largest of any northern city, being exceeded only by Baltimore, Washington and New Orleans and amounting in 1900 to 5 per cent of the city's total.

Growth of the city had created a new commercial, industrial and professional middle class. Prospering from the textile, iron and steel industries, the shipyards, oil and sugar refineries, and many small businesses, they wanted to protect their property.

Philadelphia was a port, and in area the largest city of the US, offering opportunities in insurance. Since the eighteenth century it had been involved in marine, fire and life insurance, in the nineteenth adding livestock, accident, travel, boiler, glass and fidelity risks. Its insurance centre had over a hundred companies. Further, like Perth, Philadelphia was a railway centre, with routes to New York and the North East, Washington and the South, Chicago and the West. Pennsylvania was the Keystone State; travel to other states, opening up business and keeping in contact with agents would be straightforward.

Prospects were not as grand as they had been for another Scot, Andrew Carnegie, who had amassed a multi-million dollar fortune in another Pennsylvania city, Pittsburgh, but there was a business opportunity in the new class of insurance against burglary as well as in accident and health (no state-assisted scheme against injury existed) and there was money to be made. Since the economy had emerged in 1897 from four years of depression the time was ripe.

On 17 October 1898 the General Accident board unanimously agreed to go into Canada and America. Following transatlantic correspondence, early in 1899 a cable was sent to Haughton inviting him to come to Britain and meet the directors, which he did on 26 January, when it was decided to appoint him, aged 27, and Muir, 34, as general managers for the US on 'terms and conditions to be agreed by the board on the understanding that their whole time would be given to the business of the Corporation'. For the corporation it meant the substantial deposit of bonds with the insurance commissioner of New York State. The agreement with the Muir & Haughton partnership was completed by mid-February.

So important was the venture that it delayed opening in France and Scandinavia though an agent was appointed in Belgium. Keeping an eye on his performance was easier than monitoring the handling of a much larger volume of business by four employees at a greater distance. Transatlantic differences soon became apparent. Muir toadied in a handwritten 16 August letter to Norie-Miller: 'The refrain in all your letters "keep down expenses" is (notwithstanding that we hear it so often) pleasant to our ears.' In his reply of 5 September Norie-Miller was firm:

I deeply regret that you have been in any way put out by my constant reference to the keeping down of expenses and I feel sure you will appreciate the delicate position in which I am situated in many ways.

First, as you are aware, it was almost entirely due to my solicitation that my Board agreed to enter into business in America and when agreed at our various interviews with Mr Haughton when here it was on the distinct understanding that $200,000 was to be the gross amount you would require to deposit in the Country. They now find that it is nearly $400,000 and that we still require to remit more so

The Philadelphia head office
of the US branch was situated
in the insurance quarter of
the city and the historic area
associated with American
Independence.

that this, combined with the fact that the expenses appear to them so heavy, causes them to constantly urge me to write to you on the matter.

By 5 October Muir had become disturbed:

> *Our first impressions of the auditors you have appointed were the reverse of agree-able as we all found Mr Marwick [the former resident secretary for General Accident in Glasgow] very uncouth & illbred & very presumptuous as to his position.*
>
> *He dropped into the office yesterday afternoon unannounced, spent the balance of the afternoon & was here a few hours this morning & before acquainting himself in any way with our system & our necessities, started in & spent almost all his time telling us how to keep our books.*
>
> *We shall be pleased to receive at any time suggestions from your auditors but cannot & will not submit to instructions from them although we will cheerfully open our books for their inspection & auditing.*

There was a suggestion that the General Accident account was unprofitable to James Marwick in comparison with, say, large US railroad accounts and that his attitude was a ploy to get rid of the account.

Norie-Miller made the position clear:

> *I want you to understand that Auditors in Britain act for the Shareholders as opposed to the management, and you will always find them very inquisitive but we do not mind it as they often discover points which we would like discovered...I am quite sure when you come to know Mr Marwick that you will be good friends as when the usual Scottish roughness works off you will find him, I hope, very kindhearted.*

Muir's experience was otherwise, causing him to write to Messrs Marwick & Mitchell in New York on 22 November:

> *As your Mr Marwick contemplates visiting us next week for the purposes of con-tinuing his audit, it is our desire to inform you that as heretofore every facility will be afforded him to perform his work, and all the records of our office, which are prop-erly subject to his examination, will be fully and freely at his disposal, provided his duties are performed with civility and without such offensive language and manner as has heretofore characterized his conduct.*
>
> *Our reasons for this position are that Mr Marwick's conduct has heretofore been so offensive and of such character as to disturb our own peace of mind, demoralize our office force, and excite unfavorable comment from those who have occasion to visit our office, and is likely to seriously embarrass and damage our position as*

J. Paul Haughton and William S. Muir were
the first two managers of the US branch.

Managers in the opinion of those who have overheard his remarks and witnessed his ungentlemanly and insulting conduct.

He has reached the extreme limit of our patience and forbearance, and a repetition of his previous actions and conduct will not, for one moment, be tolerated.

Muir in a parallel letter to Norie-Miller looked for 'your strong co-operation for a correction of this evil...to curb these men'. He went on about:

our submission to such indignities as we have suffered this week. The mental and nervous strain of the business is enough under ordinary conditions and the experience of the last two days with the man Marwick has brought me nearer to a nervous collapse than any amount of hard work under ordinary business conditions could have occasioned.

Norie-Miller remained firm and Marwick, Mitchell & Co continued as auditors.

There were other problems. For instance, a UK board – there was no US board as it was a branch office – minute of 8 January 1900 noted that Muir & Haughton had issued a burglary policy for 'Messrs Chubbs' business, extending the risk agreed to be covered by the Company and being an entirely different form to that approved of by the Head Office'. Unilateral action continued. A minute of 23 March records:

A letter from Messrs Muir & Haughton dated 10th March and received this day stating that they had made arrangements for the purchase of the business of the Provident Accident Company of Philadelphia was read and, while the Directors generally approved of the purchase on the lines explained by Messrs Muir & Haughton, they thought it better that the Manager should further correspond and report to them more fully on the whole case.

Further, on 16 July:

After full consideration the Board unanimously decided to transact Employers' Liability business in America. The Manager was instructed to inform the American Managers that they must not enter into any arrangements whatever for taking over of any Company's Employer Liability business without first receiving the full consent in writing of the Directors. The Manager was also instructed to intimate to the American Managers that they were expected to so regulate the business that no further remittances of any kind would require to be sent to America by the Corporation.

In person a US manager was overtly compliant. On 31 August:

James Marwick, who founded what later became Peat Marwick. His name survives as the M in KPMG, one of the world's largest accountancy firms, which remained as the auditor to General Accident for the whole of its history.

The Board afterwards met Mr William S. Muir, the Company's Manager in America and fully discussed past and future business. The question of transacting Employers' Liability business, which had previously been decided upon, was very carefully considered, and it was unanimously decided only to transact this business as members of the Tariff Association, Mr Muir heartily concurring in this decision.

Business grew in burglary, teams (horse-drawn delivery services) and, with the acquisition of the New England Mutual Accident Association of Boston and the services of Franklin J. Moore, in commercial accident. General Accident had originally reinsured the New England Association and went on to reinsure the Provident Mutual Accident Association of Philadelphia in 1900 and the National Indemnity & Insurance Company of Baltimore in 1901. From 1902 the liability business was given a boost by Walter E. Hoag, who had been with the London Guarantee and Accident Co of Chicago. By 1903 General Accident was operating in 19 states and had accumulated $500,000 in assets, a sum that enabled it to purchase a building diagonally across the street from its previous headquarters. This had been above a cigar shop once the rooming house of buxom Dolley who had married one of her diminutive boarders, James Madison, the Virginian who played a major rôle in the Continental Convention and became fourth US president in 1809. The new office at 400 Walnut Street was a two-storey building originally built in 1871 for the Enterprise Insurance Company, right in the heart of the insurance district. Early in 1904 C.H. Boyer, who had experience in industrial accident and health insurance, approached the company with the offer of moving into that line, which soon showed a good premium income. In mid-1905 Muir and Haughton were doing well enough to join the prestigious Philadelphia club the Union League.

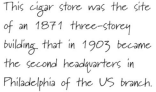

This cigar store was the site of an 1871 three-storey building that in 1903 became the second headquarters in Philadelphia of the US branch.

Unfortunately they were only the first of a sorry succession of managers no better than their moral climate. The commercial community had a lenient attitude to certain crimes. In the late nineteenth century plundering of the Philadelphia treasury, 'boodling', was a common practice, described at length in Theodore Dreiser's moral tale *The Financier*, set in the 1860s/early 1870s but published in 1912. City contracts were awarded by politicians in return for favours. The state government was owned by big business, Standard Oil under Rockefeller being reputed capable of doing anything with the state legislature except refining it.

Facing page
This new six-storey office building was erected on the south-west corner of Fourth and Walnut Streets.

When all around seemed to be making a fast buck, why be left out? Muir and Haughton took that view as revealed by *United States Review* on 26 April 1906:

> *The revocation of the contract of Messrs Muir & Haughton…as United States managers of the General Accident Assurance Corporation, Ltd., of Perth, Scotland… has proved the sensation of the week in insurance circles…About two weeks ago Mr F. Norie-Miller, general manager of the company, at the head office, and Col. Home-Drummond, the chairman of the Board of Directors, arrived in this country and found the situation in their offices so unsatisfactory that the above summary action was deemed necessary and with the characteristic deliberateness and firmness of the English [sic] offices, was promptly decided on, notwithstanding repeated overtures for a readjustment.*

In an interview Norie-Miller explained the background:

> *There is no reason why Messrs Muir and Haughton could not in the course of a year or two have each made at least $25,000 per annum under their agreement with us…It not only gave them a guaranteed income at the time, of $7,000 per annum each, which was very much in excess of anything they were previously making, but it also gave them the prospects of making the splendid income…They, however, do not appear to have been satisfied with this, and we have just now found to our great surprise that for some years they have been giving a great deal of their time and attention to other lines of business, notably the General Trust Company, various fire companies and also carrying on a large fire business in the office of our company…It is a significant fact that when Messrs Muir and Haughton came to remove their papers from our vault, which is a good sized room, and it was crowded before, it was left practically empty, showing that they had carried on extensive operations…without any payment being made to us for rent, clerical assistance, etc.*

He went on to reassure the insurance world about the sterling strength of the corporation and the qualifications of its new US manager, Franklin J. Moore, who was soon appointed a director of the newly formed Canadian company. Muir and Haughton countered with their own version of events in the local press, contending that the business of the fire and other companies in which they were alleged to have been involved was conducted by relatives, and filed a $750,000 claim for the breaking of their contract. Norie-Miller attended the 11-day trial, at which the plaintiffs had in his view at least three personal friends on the jury:

> *Our witnesses numbered 43 and the evidence they gave was practically uncontradicted. It showed that Messrs Muir & Haughton have devoted during the last 18*

months at least a considerable portion of their time to other businesses, Trust and Investment Companies, Fire Companies, etc. We also proved beyond any question of doubt that they had purchased furniture and typewriters, employed stenographers and extra clerks to do the work of their Companies and paid for everything they required out of our funds. We also proved that they themselves incurred travelling and other expenses in connection with these companies which they charged to our company. We also proved that they had floated the Delaware Insurance Company with power to do a Casualty business in opposition to ourselves, and had asked Mr Boyer that either he or his wife should take charge of the Industrial Department of this Company, and there is not the slightest doubt from letters which were produced that they had written to Agents and others, that it was their intention to immediately switch off all the officials and business of our Corporation to their own Company. Notwithstanding all this the jury, in consequence of their being appealed to by Counsel on the other side to give justice to young American citizens as opposed to a wicked foreign Corporation actually were eleven to one in favour of giving the plaintiffs a verdict of one million dollars, and there would have been no verdict at all had the others not come down to the final verdict of $75,000 at the request of the minority of one.

In a subsequent compromise this figure was finally settled at $50,000 (£10,000) payable to Muir and Haughton over three years with General Accident paying its own costs. The company was satisfied with the settlement, having estimated it had been wrongfully charged £4,000 p.a. for expenses incurred for other companies and that it would save at least £6,000 a year under the agreement.

As in the UK, the US branch colourfully promoted auto insurance.

Business looked up. In 1907 the first automobile policy was written. Based on an original from Perth and necessitating an amendment to New York law, which made no provision for collision insurance, it combined in one contract legal liability for the running of a car, indemnity for damage to car, damage to property of others, loss by burglary and theft, accident insurance for owner and paid driver. The following year, 1908, a new six-storey office building was erected on the south-west corner of Fourth and Walnut. Reinsurance was undertaken for the burglary, theft and personal accident business of the People's Surety Company of New York, the accident and health business of the United American Life Insurance Co of Delaware and the burglary and theft business of the Metropolitan Surety Company of New York. In 1911 the corporation extended its operations into fire insurance by buying the 80-year old Potomac Insurance Company of the District of Columbia, the only private insurance company ever chartered by an Act of Congress and signed into law by President Andrew Jackson.

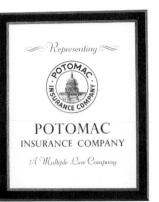

That same year, the superintendent of insurance for New York severely criticised many of the industrial claims settlements as being less than was fairly due and securing compromise settlements by unfair and improper methods. So Norie-Miller, accompanied by the chairman, the Earl of Dunmore, and another director, James Simpson the general counsel, once again dispensed with the US managers, this time Franklin J. Moore, and C.H. Boyer, the manager of the industrial health and accident department who, with relatives, was responsible for the bad practices. These included profit-sharing by agents and officials on sums saved on settlements and 'evading payments to beneficiaries resident in foreign lands of laborers killed here'. Looking back to 1906, Norie-Miller later wrote:

We appointed as United States Manager Franklin J. Moore and appointed with him a board of directors who we thought were very good men in Philadelphia. They certainly were men of good standing there. They, however, backed him up in what we considered was reckless underwriting. His one object seemed to be to build up a large income and not to take good care of the underwriting, which, following our usual con-

This glass sign depicts a 1910 Columbia touring car selling at $2,750, with cape top $2,900.

servative policy at home and other parts of the world, we thought desirable. He was also very reckless in his use of our funds and as a result we had to dismiss him and at the same time put an end to the local board.

In his place two managers were appointed, John A. Kelly, 'a general insurance agent of New York who did a very large business for numerous

Claud Norie-Miller, the elder son of Francis, gained experience in the Canadian company immediately before moving to the US branch.

companies', and Claud Norie-Miller, Francis's elder son, who for the last five years had been the company's manager in Toronto. Having a member of the family on the spot was a solution that did not work. Early in 1912 the headquarters of the US branch was moved from Philadelphia to New York without telling Perth. Further, in Francis Norie-Miller's words:

Kelly continued the policy of building up a huge income which we did not desire and at the same time appointed his own firm general agents for the whole of the State of New York and Northern New Jersey, placing about one million dollars of our business through that agency without asking our consent or letting us know the change which he had made. It was only upon further information received from our Joint manager there that the Board became aware of this during my absence in Africa. Immediately upon my return I came over to New York in February [1912] and, after making large reductions in the expenditure, reported to my Board that Mr Kelly must, in my opinion, leave, as he could not hold the position of Senior Manager and at the same time be an agent of the Company. My opinion was confirmed by the dictum of the Insurance Commissioner who insisted that such an arrangement must end and accordingly it has been stopped. At the same time we have taken steps by cancelling a large amount of business and generally limiting our underwriting to decrease our income in New York by a very large amount of what we considered too hazardous business...I am confident that the United States, which has never given us any profit, will in future years give us the same profit that we have been obtaining from other parts of the world.

Norie-Miller later talked of 'Kelly's wickedness' but his trust in his elder son was misplaced. He too had been corrupted and abused his position by taking short cuts to wealth. Bad business continued to be written in 1912 and 1913. Given power of attorney on 2 February 1914, Claud disillusioned his father, who was grooming him as his dynastic heir in the growing corporation. Soon he was being referred to by title not name. In January 1915 Norie-Miller senior was given, with Frederick Richardson, then assistant London manager, power of attorney for the US 'to do and perform all necessary acts and things as they may deem necessary or advisable'. Claud had put his father in an invidious position, as revealed at a board meeting of 8 February:

The General Manager submitted various letters from the United States and the Board having considered the replies made by the United States Manager to the charges made against him note that he denies the charge of failing to give his full time and attention to the business of the Corporation, but that he does not deny, and must therefore be taken to admit, the charges against his moral conduct. In the opinion of the Board that conduct, associated as it is with a former employee of the Company known to the American staff, and persisted in in spite of warnings and remonstrances is inconsistent with the responsible position of manager of the Corporation's business in America, and with the respect and confidence with which it is necessary he should be regarded by the staff. They accordingly instruct the General Manager to intimate to him that his contract of service with them is cancelled, and that in the meantime and until further enquiries and arrangements can be made he must regard himself as holding office entirely at the pleasure of the Board. The Board further instruct the General Manager to offer the United States manager any position in Perth or London.

Liability underwriting in Philadelphia shows how the American office readily adopted typewriters and telephones.

The US financial position was affecting the corporation as a whole:

The United States Manager's letter of the 29th January re remittances was read. The General Manager explained he thought he could get $10,000 from Canada and $10,000 from Shanghai to enable such remittances to be made and he desired to send from this side $30,000 and this it was agreed to remit at once. This $30,000, with the remittances sent prior to the close of the year, would only leave $35,000 to be remitted to the States to fulfill the General Manager's promise to the New York State Department in the early part of last year.

By the end of April $125,000 had been sent to the US, which had to make do with as little as possible because, with the needs of the general business, the corporation could be forced to take its overdraft with The Royal Bank of Scotland up to its limit. The situation had deteriorated to the point where Claud could no longer remain in the corporation. In July it was decided that the US headquarters were to be moved from New York back to Philadelphia and he was asked to leave by the end of 1915 or earlier as determined by the general manager on receiving six months' salary in lieu of notice. His father's ultimate loyalty was to the corporation and his immediate responsibility was to shore up the finances and get a responsible manager who could turn the US operations into profit. By September Richardson was put in control of the US, assuming his position as manager on 1 January 1916. On 22 December a statement of remittances and securities sent to the US amounted to $500,000, made up from Shanghai ($10,000), Canada ($30,000), Paris ($50,000), Perth ($170,000) and $240,000 in shares of The Potomac. For the Perth portion Norie-Miller considered a private placing of £30,000 of preference shares with a syndicate headed by Clarence Hatry, a financier later to be exposed as a fraudster. The corporation had had to rally to the aid of the beleaguered US office and the rescue of the general manager from his son, who resigned officially to go into the brokerage business.

In 1916 conscription intervened. The errant 32-year old Claud was rehabilitated by dying a hero's death when his troopship *Transylvania* was torpedoed in the Mediterranean on 4 May 1917. A lieutenant, he assisted nurses into lifeboats but was himself reported missing, presumed drowned. Privately, his son's departure had brightened the father's prospects within General Accident. Not until 1924 was he able to have a memorial rood screen installed in the remodelled St Ninian's Cathedral, Perth; it could have been for the American cross he had had to bear.

The early years of the
century were a period
of overseas expansion for
General Accident, in Europe but mainly in
the British Empire.

HAVING crossed the Atlantic, it was easy for an official to make a comparatively short journey north to the first dominion, Canada. General Accident had been looking at the possibility of starting there. Scottish influence had been strong since the eighteenth century and, unlike the French presence, was spread with a work ethic across the nation. Almost every member of the original syndicate for the Canadian Pacific Railway (completed 1886) was a self-made Scot and at the turn of the century Scots were just under 15 per cent of the population.

In the spring of 1903 J.W. Mackenzie of Halifax, Nova Scotia, wrote to Perth about opening up business there but the directors decided against it. Much of the overseas expansion was occasioned by established insurance agents wanting to increase their range of representation. They got to learn about General Accident either by word of mouth or from reading the insurance press. For instance, *The Index*, an international review of insurance trade and finance published in London and New York, ran a front page adulatory profile of Norie-Miller in 1890. When he met fellow travellers aboard ship they may well have already known much about him and were keen to associate themselves with his successful company.

In 1904, when his directors had changed their minds, Norie-Miller was authorised on a visit to Canada to negotiate on the takeover of the Accident & Guarantee Company there. Shortly afterwards a loss of about £8,000 in the Toronto conflagration was reported, which deferred a proposed arrangement to enter the fire business with the Anglo-American Insurance Company. Lack of cash postponed a takeover of the Accident & Guarantee Company and after protracted negotiations the deal with Anglo-American came to nothing, ostensibly because General Accident stipulated that before acceptance Marwick, Mitchell should audit the accounts but in reality it was because The General was getting too good a bargain.

Going it alone under a special act of Parliament, the company formed in July 1906 the General Accident Assurance Company of Canada with headquarters in Toronto and paid-up capital of £10,000, chiefly invested in municipal debentures. W.G. Falconer, an Edinburgh solicitor who had done legal work for Perth, and Norie-Miller's son Claud, who had worked for the company in Paris, Amsterdam and Antwerp and more recently in Philadelphia, Boston and Buffalo were appointed as joint secretaries. Directors were mainly prominent Canadian businessmen.

Within a year, during which it had been writing accident and health and liability policies practically the same as Philadelphia, the new company had established agencies in all the important towns of Canada, where there were the most reliable agents and the more profitable business with a lower expense

Overseas visits were social as well as business occasions. Here Francis Norie-Miller takes a leisurely stroll on board ship for a visit to France in June 1912.

ratio. Most of the business came from Ontario and Montreal, then the commercial capital though, according to Claud Norie-Miller, in Quebec towns it was not fully developed, 'the population being almost entirely French, a class who do not insure to any extent'. Business from the Maritime Provinces, Winnipeg and the West involved greater expense in handling claims. Losses were incurred for the first two years. In 1908 the Canadian Casualty & Boiler Insurance Co was acquired and the company followed Perth into fire insurance, T.H. Hall being appointed to run that branch. Like Francis Norie-Miller, he had worked for the London & Lancashire and the two men were of similar energetic stamp. On appointment, after making the necessary

Francis Norie-Miller believed strongly that buildings reflected the character of The General. The branch offices in the Belgian capital, Brussels (facing page), Copenhagen (right) and Amsterdam (above) are all examples. The last named occupied a prominent corner site.

deposit in Ottawa and assuring himself that the Toronto agents were thoroughly capable, Hall spent over three months selling in every sizeable place in Western Canada. Within six months fire premium income came to more than $100,000.

The early years of the century were a period of overseas expansion for General Accident, partly in Europe but mainly in the British Empire, the largest empire ever known, covering one quarter of the world land surface and population. In Western Europe the company had had a Belgian branch since 1899 and a French agent, Michel & Cie, since 1896, which was helpful when a branch was opened in 1902, A. Michel becoming a local director. Michel & Cie were to be associated with General Accident for nearly a century as reinsurance brokers. With the French connection, the company also did business in the Argentine, Mexico and Russia. The Netherlands and Norway branches opened in 1902; in 1903 Gibraltar and Spain. Of doubtful value, the Spanish business was transferred in 1911 to Compagnie d'Assurances Generales. Denmark and Switzerland opened in 1904. Belgian business, which since 1905 had included workmen's compensation, was enlarged with the purchase of the Royal Exchange portfolio for £10,000 in 1909, by which time business was also under way in Constantinople.

Australia was the first of the dominions in which the corporation set up, in 1903 appointing W. Medhurst Taylor, a broker of Melbourne, who approached the company to become its agent. He initially worked purely on a commission basis for fire business in Victoria but the intention was to give him Australasia as his territory. Melbourne, where Taylor had gathered a number of insurance agencies, had also been recognised as the interim capital of the federal government until a site independent of the six states could be established. From Melbourne the business, all under the tariff agreement, expanded through the purchase in 1904 of the Australian interests of the Magdeburg Insurance Company and the appointment of Taylor as the manager for the whole of Australia. His territory covered Australia including Tasmania, New Zealand and the Pacific, a large area progressively covered through agents and branches. Since the Commonwealth of Australia came into being in 1901 the economy had recovered from its depression, riding on the back of the sheep. The wool clip formed a half of rising exports, which comfortably exceeded imports, providing local capital to expand commercial and industrial activities. Export of wool and sheepskins by William Haughton & Company provided sizeable fire insurance business and in 1904 the company was appointed chief agent for South Australia. The company's similar exports from New Zealand provided business from that territory.

A branch office in Sydney opened in 1908; an agency was established in

Townsville, Queensland (1907), and a branch in 1910, when the 'goodwill and connection' of the agents was bought for £400. A similar pattern followed in Tasmania in 1911. Fiji was handled from 1908 by an agent. In 1907 the range of cover was extended with the addition of automobile, burglary, employers' liability, fidelity guarantee, personal accident and sickness, plate glass, public liability, and workmen's compensation. The portfolio of the Bombay Company was acquired in 1909. Although the product and territorial coverage had widened, things did not go smoothly so Ralph Sketch, the then foreign manager, went out to Australia to reorganise representation. On the expiry of his five-year agreement Taylor agreed to split his office in Melbourne between his own and General Accident business in Victoria, with Sydney becoming the head office in new premises under an interim manager until W.G. Falconer transferred from Canada. Taylor stayed as manager for Victoria for 18 months and Falconer for two years full-time, in 1912 appointing Taylor's successor, G.R. Anderson, to take over Australasia. It all seemed more trouble than it was worth for meanwhile the UK board decided to dispose of the Australian business. Immediate action was postponed.

It was also decided at the same time not to open in New Zealand because of the high costs of starting a new business and 'especially in view of the fact that the Government is at present engaged in a fight with the Insurance Offices for the business'. In 1905 the government had founded the State Insurance Company to compete with the tariff companies, which held monthly meetings of four regional associations to monitor compliance.

A Malayan outpost of the company.

In New Zealand gold miners supplemented their low wages by 'accidents' entitling them to workmen's compensation. A little finger rated at about $50; a thumb up to $500. If a genuine accident did not occur in the Waihi goldmine, for a small fee Lionel the Lopper was on hand to help. Compensation was paid by New Zealand Insurance, a company acquired by General Accident in the late 1980s.

Norie-Miller wrote to Muir in Philadelphia in 1899:

It is very pleasing for me to note from your P.S. that the best element in America sympathise with us in connection with our War [Boer War 1899–1902]. *It is a dreadful thing to lose so many Officers and men even although we are victorious, but I fear it was absolutely necessary for us to punish these Boers who are practically only half civilised. It will open up a magnificent Continent for us in the future and immediately the War is over I intend having a Branch Office in South Africa and working that whole District with energy.*

Not until 1908 was a branch established when Norie-Miller visited the territory, acquired the Industrial Life and Accident Assurance Company and opened a chief office in Cape Town, with sub-offices in Johannesburg, Port Elizabeth and Durban. As elsewhere, prominent local citizens were appointed to the board, among them Dr (later Sir Thomas) Smartt, who had been besieged with Cecil Rhodes in Kimberley during the Boer War, and Jacobus Graaff, co-founder of the Imperial Cold Storage and Supply Company. Within a year, motor business was being written on rates more competitive than those of the tariff companies, which seems to have inspired a counter-campaign in the insurance and financial press. The industrial life business was sold to African Homes Trust. In 1909 the first local board was appointed in the Transvaal, with Sir William St John Carr, a mayor of Johannesburg after the Boer War, in the chair. To take advantage of expansion in the ostrich industry, an office was opened in 1913 in Oudtshoorn but reduced to agency status after a few months when ostrich feathers went out of fashion, cutting the income of the 'feather barons'. Earlier in Egypt, then under the administration of Lord Cromer, the company was represented from 1903 in Cairo and from 1905 by F.W. Cuming in Alexandria. In India the company was represented from 1902 by C.H. Forbes & Co with headquarters in Bombay.

In 1903, Britain being the leading foreign power in China, a Far East branch was opened in Shanghai, a treaty port of the declining Manchu dynasty. Japan, Mauritius and Trinidad were also opened in 1903 and in the following year

Burma and Ceylon. Hong Kong had to wait until 1906 and the Bahamas 1908. Although general business in the Philippines was reported in 1911 as being unsatisfactory, prospects were explored in other former Spanish territories: Cuba, Panama, South and Central America. Motor insurance was undertaken in Chile in 1914. In 1912 an agent was appointed in Khartoum. The geographical spread, by now covering the most significant markets in the world, raised the question of whether the company should engage in marine insurance, but for the time being it did not venture.

These investments abroad were made at a time of increased emigration from the UK to the Empire and in spite of setbacks in the USA, the main source of overseas business. They represented in total a modest outlay for the return because the business was brought in by agents paid on commission. Judging by Australian commission rates, this was generous. For example,

The Cairo office.

When ostrich tail feathers
went out of fashion South
African breeders of the bird
could no longer afford so much
insurance. Accordingly, the
General Accident branch at
Oudtshoorn, on the Little Karoo
in Cape Province, lost its status
and became an agency.

Right: The Cape Town office.

appointed as chief agent for South Australia, initially on fire business under the tariff, William Haughton & Company received a commission of 35 per cent; the agent for Queensland 30 per cent and £100 p.a. office allowance. In Fiji, where the prospects must have been limited, the rate was 25 per cent. Such levels were strong incentives to securing business, as Norie-Miller well knew.

In spite of the difficulties
and sorrows of war and
the problems of dealing
with overseas interests that were not
performing well General Accident emerged
from the war materially strengthened and
with greater self-confidence.

THE German invasion of Belgium in August 1914 halted 15 years of company expansion overseas. Reinsurance was also affected. General Accident immediately ceased ceding business to two German companies with which it had treaties and, under those with French and Belgian companies, for the time being it had to pay claims without obtaining recoveries. Belgium, which represented the company's largest European investment, was the hammer-swing route the German army took to Paris. By 20 August the capital, Brussels, had fallen and the enemy was on its way to Antwerp. While the French office was prepared, if necessary, to move from Paris to Lyons, the company's staff in Antwerp fled to London before their city fell on 9 October, in the fighting their office sustaining only broken glass on the ground floor.

In London they were looked after by the War Refugees Committee, which was given gratis all the unlet offices at 99 Aldwych, which also became the home of the Belgian consulate. On 22 September Her Majesty Queen Mary visited the offices to inspect the work of the Committee, with the reception and placement of refugees not only from Belgium but also France and, later, Greece and Serbia. Soon afterwards bomb insurance of £40,000 at 2s 6d per cent was taken out on the premises, £25,000 of it being reinsured. Financial help was given to refugees in the form of a £1,000 donation to the Prince of Wales' National Relief Fund, to which the staff decided to make a monthly contribution from their salaries.

In what they expected to be a short adventurous break from the clerical routine, staff were also volunteering for the colours. A month after the outbreak of war 260 staff, largely made up of 60 per cent of head office personnel, were reported to be fighting. *The General's Review*, which they would receive while on active service, published a Roll of Patriots. So that they would not be worse off, each one was to have his service pay made up, those receiving under £1 10s a week to get full pay and those who had £1 10s per week or more would receive full pay less the actual cash payment made by the War Office or the governments of the respective countries. The directors put on record:

their high appreciation of the splendid patriotic example shown by the staff of the General Accident in Great Britain, Belgium, France, South Africa, Canada and other Colonies, in so readily enlisting in the armies of their respective countries, and also their appreciation of those members of the staff who, not being privileged to fight for their country, so readily agreed to perform equally loyal and patriotic service by undertaking the work of their brothers who are away, and subscribing so handsomely to the various Relief Funds, as well as assisting in Red Cross and other work at home.

Within a few days of the outbreak of war women were busy knitting socks and other comforts for the troops.

In September one inspector and two clerks from the Antwerp office were killed at the front and in October the chief statistician in the Paris office lost his life in action. The effects of the war were summed up in the annual report:

> *The Board with regret have come to the conclusion that it is prudent to pass the Ordinary Dividend for the past year. The dislocation of business in consequence of the War is emphasised in our case by reason of the fact that while no business is transacted by us in either Austria or Germany, we do a large Continental business, principally in Belgium and France. No complete Statements of Accounts for these two countries later than 31st March and 30th June 1914 respectively have been available, and only three months' profits in Belgium and six months' profits in France are included in the Revenue Accounts.*

Financial losses in the US had not helped. Continuing in 1915 and more than absorbing the profits from the working of the business elsewhere, they were

Soon after the outbreak of the war the chief office of the company in London, 99 Aldwych, became an unprecedented hive of activity. Belgian refugees awaiting registration for accommodation crowded the pavement outside. Troops on leave had to be registered here. Later, refugees from other nations joined the throng.

So important was the work of the War Refugees Committee that Queen Mary inspected its operations on 22 September 1914.

given as the reason for again passing the ordinary dividend. A loss in Canada had not helped either. Dividend payment was resumed for 1916.

Conflict in Europe also directly affected some business in the neutral US. For instance, John H. Buddemeyer, the Buffalo agent of General Accident, asked German policyholders to leave the Scottish company as a matter of patriotism and transfer their business to the Casualty Company of America. The procedure was called 'twisting'. By the spring of 1915 it was claimed that some 200 of General Accident's 1,500 patrons had changed companies since the outbreak of war in Europe. Through the Supreme Court in Buffalo the company secured an order restraining its former agent and his employees from interfering in any way with its business. In British territories the company was able to profit immediately. For instance, in Australia, where the Aachen & Munich Insurance Company ceased operations, General Accident's Adelaide agents were quick in securing the transfer of the business to their books.

At home the company offered aircraft insurance against 'loss or damage to property or contents occasioned by bomb dropping or other aircraft risks', which were not covered under an ordinary fire policy. In 1916 its proposal form was more strident: 'The Menace of the Air! Zeppelins!! Insure against Mutilation and Death.' The campaign worked, producing a profit of some £60,000.

E.T. Thorpe, an inspector at Birmingham branch, had been in the Territorial Army before the war. Following war service in Egypt as a signaller, he returned to the UK and visited Birmingham office during an air raid in mid-1916. After being commissioned in the Royal Warwickshire Regiment he transferred to the Royal Flying Corps. He is seen here as an aviator with 30th Squadron in 1918. In WW2 he was manager of Southampton branch.

What had been expected to be a six months' campaign turned out to be a war of attrition, for which few were prepared. By mid-1916 90 per cent of General Accident male staff were with the colours and the balance of 36 had been given exemption, conditional upon their remaining with the company. Since the start of the war the company had paid at the rate of £14,536 per annum to its staff with the colours, but they had all received notices that from 1 May instead of receiving full salary less army pay and allowances they would receive half-salary with army pay and allowances. Where army pay exceeded the half-salary they would receive full salary less army pay, the reductions amounting to a substantial saving for the company. Two months after it came into effect five staff, three of them officers, were killed in the first major British offensive of the war, the Battle of the Somme. Near the end of the year cash advances to Belgian refugees in London 'of position and repute' from whom the Belgian manager 'had been getting or hoped to get business' amounted to £6,913 9s 2d. Henceforth advances were to be restricted and interest added, payable either half-yearly or added to the loan.

At home staff were still supporting the war effort. From early in 1917 they could subscribe to the government's War Loan by salary deductions. With so many men away, their work had to be done by women, who had to be trained. They were no novelty in the company. The first woman, Mary Shelton, had been employed in 1894 at an annual salary of £20. Three more were recruited in 1897, more since. What was different in the Great War was their significant number, which could not but help change, if only temporarily and superficially, the masculine culture of the company. For instance, Miss Helen Shand, who in late 1916 took over as chief clerk in Inverness from William Fraser when he was called up for war service, was probably the first woman to reach a senior position in a branch. It was 'a lady clerk' who on the Tuesday morning after the Easter Rising 1916 showed initiative. She went into the office at 104 Grafton Street, Dublin, which had been slightly damaged by rifle fire, to take all the letters out of the box, carry them up and lock them in the safe with other papers that were of value.

Lads were also recruited at low salaries. James Mitchell, later to become staff superintendent in head office, was offered at the beginning of 1917 a starting 'salary of £18 per annum, this to be increased by £6 per annum so soon as you are proficient in shorthand and typewriting'. The offer was made on headed notepaper to which had been added in bold print:

WAR NOTICE – In consequence of the War the cost of Reinstatement of Property has increased at least 50%. Property Owners should take out Bonus Fire Policies and effect a saving of 20% in premium. Merchandise and Stocks of every description have also advanced in price. All Fire Insurances should be increased accordingly.

Staff assembled on the roof of the Aldwych office in 1916 show the large number of women employees during the war.

The German declaration in February 1915 that the western approaches to the British Isles were a war zone, where mines were laid and submarines operated, did not deter Norie-Miller from transatlantic crossings. So pressing were problems in the US branch in 1915 that he had to go to Philadelphia, as later in the year did Richardson to take control. Altogether Norie-Miller crossed the Atlantic eight times during the war.

Keen to keep and develop profitably the US business, into which it had poured so much money and management time, the board was nevertheless ready to dispose of other overseas businesses. On 14 April 1915, examining the results for Australia, Mexico, Argentina and South Africa, the board was unanimous that the business of these branches should be discontinued or disposed of. The board expected the Australian manager to arrange disposal. Shortly afterwards the local directors incurred the displeasure of head office for defiantly making a compulsory deposit of £6,000 under the Workers' Compensation Act, an action that nearly resulted in the manager being dismissed. Mexican business had already ceased though the manager was still there. The Argentine, which needed the consent of the partners for withdrawal, had a low claims but a high expense ratio. South Africa had to be put on a proper footing before it would be possible to dispose of it without heavy loss; in 1914 over half of its losses were through the costs of two lost actions, and workmen's compensation and motor insurance were also in the red. Two years later it was discovered that the accountant had embezzled £1,000. In 1916 Australia, where local industries such as the manufacture of wool textiles were developing to make up for reduced imports from the UK, provided some consolation by moving into profit for the first time, which encouraged the board to enter marine insurance in the territory. This was not to include hulls or cargo in sailing vessels, i.e. the risks were almost gilt-edged, being practically confined to cargoes of coasting steamers.

The year 1917 was one of mixed fortunes. In Canada the loss ratio for the first six months was high but was compensated for by the prescience of the fire manager, Hall, who wrote to Norie-Miller on 11 December:

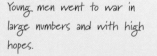

Young men went to war in large numbers and with high hopes.

Referring to your cable of the 8th inst in which you enquire whether we are affected by the Halifax Explosion it is with considerable satisfaction that I have to report we will not lose one dollar in Halifax because of my decision to withdraw from that City five years ago. [In 1912 he had written to Norie-Miller, 'Nova Scotia has had anything but a satisfactory record…I was always afraid of Halifax City, which is almost entirely of Timber construction.']

Over 3,000 dwellings were destroyed by fire in the recent conflagration as well as a large part of the waterfront, also large public buildings, so that the loss to the Fire Companies is bound to be pretty heavy.

A collision of a Norwegian steamer and a munitions ship had caused the explosion. The second half of the year was also marked by a conflagration in Salonika, which alone caused a net loss of £50,000. In spite of that and the US net loss of £55,000, the foreign profit was £42,000 against the home figure of £92,000.

The guns fell silent on the eleventh hour of the eleventh day of the eleventh month 1918. By mid-December the Belgian manager planned to return to his office and resume business, claims having been lodged against Germany both for the actual loss incurred and the loss arising from the destruction of the portfolio of business. The total debit amounted to almost £267,502, the claim being in excess of this, and the directors were confident that a substantial sum would be recovered. In London the company would have to wait until May 1919 to reoccupy its Aldwych offices lent to the War Refugees Committee, which had dealt with half a million displaced people. The effort was recognised in 1921 when Norie-Miller, who had been addressed by exiled Belgians as 'Monsieur Le Général', was awarded La Medaille du Roi Albert by the Belgian king. Nathaniel Forte, the London manager, was also decorated, as was Francis's wife, Grace. The Norie-Millers had given over their London house to Belgian refugees,

After the war a memorial to those in the company who had fallen was unveiled beside the entrance of General Buildings in Perth.

among them the manager from Antwerp. In Perth, as a memorial to sons of the county who had given their lives, the *Perthshire Advertiser* opened a penny fund for the restoration of St John's Kirk. General Accident headed the subscription list with 25,336 pennies.

At home business throughout the war had on the whole proceeded satisfactorily, the conflict making people conscious of covering risks on properties and contents. Because of the repeated air raids there had been an increase in war business; General Accident, for example, had increased the cover on its London office from £40,000 (£37,000 building and £3,000 furnishings) to £60,000. Since the government had assumed responsibility for war risks on shipping the company did take a small line with an underwriter at Lloyd's.

In spite of all the difficulties and sorrows of war – 38 staff were killed – and the problems of dealing with overseas interests that were not performing well, notably the US, General Accident emerged from the war materially strengthened and with greater self-confidence. When the industry trade body, the British Insurance Association, was formed in 1917 General Accident was an early member but resigned seven months later, preferring to go it alone. On 20 March 1918, after 31 years' service, Norie-Miller, who the previous year had been made the first president of his local Rotary Club, was at last made a director of the company he had done so much to build. It was a sure sign that he had shed the American albatross. In July 1918 Norwich Union offered to buy General Accident. The offer was rejected.

Motor insurance was the
main line of growth.
Recruiting so many agents
reinforced the company's status as the country's
leading motor insurer.

HAVING lost his elder son, Norie-Miller, rising 60, as a personal priority brought into the company his 30-year old second son, Stanley, who had been wounded but had survived the war in France. Serving in the Black Watch Royal Highland Regiment, which Perth regards as its own, he was mentioned in despatches and awarded the Military Cross. Like his father, Stanley had studied originally to follow a legal career, but whereas the father had chosen insurance his second son, who felt more for his mother than for his father, had his future mapped for him. Not surprisingly, his rise was rapid. In the summer of 1919 father and son went to the USA to inspect the major overseas branch; in the autumn of 1920 Stanley was appointed joint foreign manager, in 1923 deputy general manager, and in 1926 a director. There was no doubt that General Accident was a family fief, but Stanley's authority was more apparent than real. For instance, in 1923 a routine letter went out to the foreign branches asking for information to be used in compiling a 40-year history of the company. The letter, beginning 'Dear Sir' and ending 'Yours faithfully, F. Norie-Miller, Director and General Manager', was initialled by Stanley per his father.

Early in 1920 a proposed fusion of interests with Royal Exchange was rejected so General Accident went ahead with extending its own head office and, partly stimulated by the acquisitive activities of competitors, buying other companies. It strengthened its interests in life assurance by acquiring two established companies: in 1923 The English Insurance Company (slogan: 'Honesty – the best policy'), founded in 1869 and retained with its own identity; and in 1925 The General Life Assurance Company, which began in 1837 as The Protestant Dissenters' and General Life and Fire Assurance Company. Its branch offices were closed and staff integrated into General Accident. North of Scotland Plate Glass Insurance, acquired in 1924, added to that line of business, the next similar acquisition, Windsor & Eton Mutual Plate Glass, occurring in 1933.

Transport was a growth business. In 1919 the company undertook aviation insurance through the Automobile Insurance Company, which General Accident had already registered, the name being changed to The Automobile and Aviation Insurance Company. Development of aircraft and, to a lesser extent, aerodromes had been stimulated by war. For example, the Royal Flying Corps had trained at Turnhouse aerodrome near Edinburgh from 1915. Civil aviation was set to grow and, as with motor insurance at the end of the nineteenth century, the company wanted to be involved early.

Marine business, in which a modest beginning had been made in 1917 through Lloyd's brokers Hartley Cooper & Co, was strengthened in 1922 with the appointment of an offshoot of William Haughton, agents in Australia, as joint managing agents in London. Motor insurance though was the main line of

Francis Norie-Miller, racehorse owner, was sufficiently well known to become the subject of a **Mayfair** cartoon by Spy.

growth, Britain's first real mass-market car, the Austin Seven, being produced in 1921. Two years later General Accident took over from bus operator Thomas Tilling its insurance subsidiary The Road Transport & General, which kept its name and some 650 offices, competing with its new parent. Motor Credit Services, formed by Tilling in 1922 and in which General Accident acquired a 50

per cent interest in 1923, became wholly owned in 1925. It provided hire-purchase for cars and another source of new policyholders.

Many more came through mass production and the presence of Lord Morris on the General Accident board. From 1924 every Morris car coming off the production line was sold with a free General Accident comprehensive car policy, the reduced premium of about £7 being paid by the manufacturer. Whereas the company was selective in accepting life assurance proposals and workmen's compensation, avoiding for example unremunerative colliery business, it now covered a large group of drivers irrespective of their record. The scheme lasted for two years, during which some 90,000 vehicles were covered but claims were so great from bad and novice drivers that it was not renewed. In the short term General Accident lost money not only through the higher volume of claims but also the increased expenses of more claims and engineering staff. As a strategic move the scheme was of long-term benefit both in its publicity value and in providing the company with a nationwide network of garages selling Morris cars. Recruiting so many agents reinforced the company's status as the country's leading motor insurer, a fact emphasised in its advertising. 'A feature of special interest to Motorists is the Progressive Non-Claimant's Bonus Scale – up to 20%.' In 1925 the company joined the Motor Tariff Association.

Earlier the company had come into public notice for a less welcome reason, a strike widely reported in the national press for at least nine months from November 1920, although the dispute about union recognition had started in the previous July. It arose at a time of increasing trade union membership and strikes, affronts to authority so soon after the Russian Revolution of 1917, when the spread of Bolshevism was feared. For Norie-Miller it was the first challenge from some of his labour force who wanted to organise. The Guild of Insurance Officials, founded in 1919, knew that younger lowly paid members of General Accident staff wanted to be represented collectively, especially in the isolation

In 1931 the company was granted a Coat of Arms. The lamb in the centre is the holy lamb of the City of Perth. Flanking it are eagles, which also appear in the Perth Arms and indicate the corporation's interests in the USA. The lion in the crest is part of the Arms of the Earl of Airlie, a director in 1931, and the cross it supports is an allusion to Norie-Miller. Above the motto, 'I warn and I protect', are Scottish thistles.

of Perth where the company could pay less than the going rates. Replying in July 1920 to the union secretary's letter, the company chairman, William Low, took the line that:

> *Our Corporation was very generous to the employees when on service, and I quite understand the General Manager resenting the dictation of a newly organised body that is not familiar with all the facts. Your Guild may serve a very useful purpose for educative, recreative and benevolent purposes, but I cannot conceive a body of semi-professional men and women being bound down to a dead level of remuneration. These may apply in Trade Unions where the labour is equalized, but are totally inequitable, in my opinion, for appointments where varied capacity and training prevail.*

Most of the staff appeared to have agreed with the board, which by the end of September had received:

> *letters signed by over 80% of branch staffs expressing their loyalty to the Directors, Executive and the Corporation; and also their entire disagreement with the statements that had been made by a Representative of the Guild of Insurance Officials that they were not loyal to the Company. It was decided to inform each Branch Manager that the Board had received these statements with gratification.*

The Guild claimed these expressions of 'loyalty and gratitude' were not spontaneous but engineered from Perth, where in 1914 the watchword had been 'Go fight for **our** liberty!' but now it was 'No fighting for **your own** liberty!' Young men and women 'in the land of Bruce and Wallace' had been dismissed solely because they were union members. A parliamentary question was asked, the Ministry of Labour became involved and a mediation committee was formed, but the company rejected any intervention. Following a ballot, out of the home staff of 631, of whom just over a half were believed to be union members, a total of 133 (63 of them women) withdrew their labour. Some Guild members were induced by increased salaries to resign membership, regarded as a moral victory for the union. A few got better jobs elsewhere. At the end of 1920 two rallies by 'organised brain workers' at Central Hall, Westminster, protested against General Accident management's unconstitutional action, reckoned to be unique in the insurance industry. *The*

Facing page

The company had a well-staffed stand at the 1925 Motor Show in London.

The market for vehicles and hence new policyholders was enlarged by the provision of hire purchase facilities.

Economist called it 'an indefensible act of tyranny'; *The Policy-Holder* stated that Norie-Miller 'was about half a century behind the times…quite out of touch with modern ideas and methods…the sooner he retires the better.'

Adamant, he blamed the episode on 'two principal agitators…women of about 40, who were old enough to have given sounder advice to the young people' but 'had little to do'. To a certain extent he blamed himself in that 'when the Armistice came' he 'endeavoured to retain…all the girls who had taken the place of men, as well as giving the men back their own positions, hoping to gradually fit the women into some position'. In a message to staff he dismissed the affair as 'a storm in a teacup' and 'Gilbertian', claiming that it had brought 'a largely increased volume of new business' and support for the company. Publicly he stated that no strikers would be taken back nor would their relatives be employed either; in the personnel department he had a black book kept recording their names.

Norie-Miller also adopted a similar persistent attitude to the Church of Scotland, the trustees of which in 1928 were about to place all its insurance on kirks and manses with one lead company. The trustees had selected North British & Mercantile and English tariff companies to share the risks. As this meant General Accident would lose its existing business with the Church, Norie-Miller played the Scottish card:

As the largest motor insurer, the company took prominent advertisements.

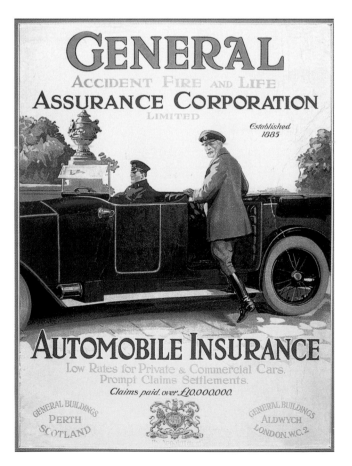

> *We are a Scottish Company, with our Head Office in the City of Perth and Branch Offices in all the large towns in Scotland; we employ six hundred officials in Scotland, the majority of whom belong to the Church of Scotland; many of our directors are very large Heritors and supporters of the Church, and we already have Insurances to the extent of nearly half a million pounds on Church of Scotland property.*

He also stressed that his company's offer, in no way inferior to that of a tariff company, represented an annual saving of £3,500 to the Church. In increasing polite acrimony, Norie-Miller sustained the correspondence for over three months, accused the chairman of the trustees of having a dictatorial attitude, and published the correspondence.

Most employees, glad to have a job when unemployment was rising, were content to accept the patriarchal culture. For those who could not

A feature of life in General Accident was the number of families who worked for the company generation after generation. This was particularly so in the relatively small community of Perth.

William C. Hunter (above), the son of Patrick Hunter, one of the original directors of the company, became a director in 1906, the year of his father's death. Like his father, he studied law but unlike him did practise, as a solicitor in Edinburgh for over 50 years, having been admitted to the Society of Writers to the Signet in 1888.

He followed his father as a member of the Highland and Agricultural Society, showing a particular interest in the Shorthorn breed. When William died in 1941 he too was the senior director.

In 1919 his son Patrick came into General Accident on the foreign side of the business.

Right, Richard Munro, chauffeur to Francis Norie-Miller from 1921, was not an employee of the company but three subsequent generations of his family went into it.

From 1927 Richard drove Norie-Miller's first Rolls-Royce, a third-hand 1920 Silver Ghost. New maroon models were bought in 1932 and 1937. Although the steering had been changed for driving on the left in Britain, Richard drove the Cadillac, a present from the US branch, less happily because it was like a tank.

After the death of Sir Francis in 1947, Richard Munro and his wife continued as chauffeur and housekeeper to his widow, his second wife, Florence, who moved from Perth to Bournemouth.

Richard Munro's son James was the first of the family to work for the company, in the post room at head office from 1930 to 1933. After his untimely death at 18 in a swimming accident, his brother David (top right, in the RAF in WW2) joined the postal department in 1933 at an annual salary of £39. On his first day his father drove him to the office sitting in the front seat of the chairman's new Rolls-Royce. The chairman (below right)

was in the back seat. David never travelled in the car again.

When a department wanted a junior the head post boy was promoted. David moved into the fire department, spending his time before World War Two in Perth and post-war in Glasgow branch. David Munro completed 46 years' service with the company, retiring at 63 in 1979.

afford further education it was Hobson's choice. They might mutter that the wages of sin were death and the wages of General Accident were a damned sight worse but they had security. The company provided an income and often a focus for their lives. In 1924 it paid the weekend or excursion fares of staff interested in visiting the British Empire Exhibition at Wembley, where it had a kiosk. From 1923 there was an athletic and social club in the London area, which in 1928 got a sports ground at Sunbury-on-Thames. In 1926 a music and dramatic society was formed in Perth, where ready for the fiftieth anniversary a sports and social centre would be established in 1934.

After the Wall Street crash of 1929 employees were even more grateful. Deep in the consequent depression, in September 1931, taking their cue from the Chancellor of the Exchequer in the National government, whose emergency budget cut government employees' salaries and the dole for the unemployed by ten per cent, most of the directors urged that the company follow suit. After all the King had patriotically accepted the same reduction in his income. Norie-Miller opposed such a cut. He argued that staff should be informed, no increases would be awarded at the end of the year and those who left should not be replaced, their work being shared among existing staff. Rigid economy was to be exercised on all expenses and staff should try to secure business from their friends. His course was adopted by the board. Letters from all home branches, without exception, expressed thanks.

During the 1920s the branch network had grown and local boards of directors, 'gentlemen of great local influence', formed at new centres. In mid-1931 *The General's Review* reckoned: 'It will soon be almost as difficult to live 10 miles away from an office of the "General" as to live 10 miles away from a railway station.'

Branch colour schemes were chosen by the general manager, who also sanctioned decoration expenses. Otherwise branch managers were kings in their little kingdoms, watching every penny. Every outgoing letter was logged and the junior clerk had to balance the post book at the end of the day before he was allowed to go home. Staff were cheap and there was little investment in office equipment: typewriters and carbon paper, dictating machines the wax cylinders of which were shaved for reuse, a telephone, little used for outgoing calls. Cost control was strict, as 18-year old Bill Hartley found when he joined the Liverpool office in 1931 at an annual salary of £30:

The visitors' room was a dingy ante-room off a main corridor. Visitors came into three-quarters darkness. When somebody in the office became aware of their presence he went to a cubby hole, slid back an enquiry hatch and switched on the light. When attending the counter you had to be very very quiet. As soon as the footsteps of the

The company kiosk at the
British Empire Exhibition,
Wembley, 1924.

departing visitor rang out you had to switch off the light because the branch manager was listening for the click of the switch. If you didn't switch off the light you were taken to task. I protested that it was unfair to expect the public to walk into a dark-ened room. In vain.

Bill nearly resigned because he thought the company was being mean on claims too:

In the office I saw a man with his arm in a sling accompanied by his wife and small child, obviously a workmen's compensation claimant. One of the claims staff had given him a wad of notes, a sum of money he had probably never seen. I was sure the value of his claim had been reduced by as much as 50 per cent, but there was the appeal of ready money. He had been bought off.

Times were hard and Bill stayed, though at one time he thought he had lost his job for refusing a half-a-crown tip for carrying Norie-Miller's case. Eventually he rose to be a general manager and a director of the company. One of his predecessors, J. Mayhew Allen, who became General Accident actuary and secretary in 1906 and later actuary and manager of General Life, also felt that times were hard and was responsible for serious defalcations along with two colleagues. Believing they were underpaid, they charged expenses improperly or unnecessarily incurred, sometimes fictitious, including golf club subscriptions, the upkeep of their private cars and telephones. The trio were dismissed in 1932 and, as the corporation wanted to avoid the publicity associated with a criminal case, civil proceedings were taken for the recovery of money. In 1934 one of the defendants, represented by Norman Birkett KC, brought actions for libel and wrongful dismissal against Norie-Miller, defended by Sir Patrick Hastings KC. After a five-day hearing the jury found for Norie-Miller, who was awarded costs.

In 1933 two clerks, found guilty of fraud with an outside confederate over coupon insurance in the *Daily Express*, were sentenced to nine months' hard labour. There may well have been elements of fraud, getting something on the insurance, in the higher ratio of fire losses paid during depressed years, reaching over 50 per cent in 1921–2, 1930 and 1932. Within the company women who could not afford to resign on getting married were not above

Facing page
Traffic passing the London chief office in 1929 shows how taxis had increased metropolitan motor traffic.

Administration in UK branches, as here in Glasgow, was largely done with pen and paper.

On 10 August 1935 Francis Norie-Miller as Member of Parliament for Perth was introduced to the Duke and Duchess of York, visiting to open the Art Gallery and to receive from the Lord Provost, Thomas Hunter, the Freedom of the City. The company insured the cars of the royal household.

removing wedding rings and passing as single, a practice easier away from the small community of Perth, where one could more readily be accused of being married.

As the depression eased some areas, notably the Midlands and South of England, showed signs of prosperity. Most obvious were so many houses being built for owner-occupiers and the increasing numbers of motor vehicles on the roads. Both developments helped General Accident's business; a Scottish company, it had most of its UK business south of the Border. Private house-building, peaking at 350,000 new properties a year in the middle and late 1930s, was for the suburban middle class and better-off working class, who needed the protection of insurance for their greatest asset and its contents. They were in good company. From 1930 to 1936 General Accident held the household insurances, including 'jewellery as per schedule', on 145 Piccadilly, the home of HRH The Duke and Duchess of York. Norie-Miller was introduced to them in Perth before the Duke succeeded as George VI in 1936, when policies were issued for The King's House, Burhill, Surrey, and The Royal Lodge. The general trend of more households for smaller families with greater disposable income would continue to boost General Accident's business.

During the decade the number of motor vehicles doubled to three million in 1939, two million of them being private cars, affordable by white-collar workers and in families where the wife too was working. More cars meant more accidents, which had led to the standard knock-for-knock agreement between some insurers, reached in 1929. Injuries occurred every three minutes and 17 people were killed every day, figures which the Road Traffic Act 1930 set out to improve. One of its provisions favouring insurance companies was compulsory cover for third party risks, which in turn during the Depression gave the staff many hours of overtime dealing with the rush of previously uninsured motorists. General Accident increased its stake in motor business by acquiring in 1933 a controlling interest in Scottish Automobile & General, which had been founded in 1919. Although cars were becoming more necessary for getting business General Accident staff were not provided with them. Nevertheless, when they were used branch managers insisted on their being kept shining clean to reflect the company. Charles Heath joined the Leeds branch of Road Transport & General in 1937 for an annual salary of £150, rising to £175 in 1938:

When I became an inspector the company wanted me to have a car, for which it would lend money. I bought a secondhand Morris 8 for £60, less than half the cost of a new model, and was paid three ha'pence a mile, receiving a penny as an expense and the halfpenny being kept in reserve for a new car or items like new tyres.

He was fortunate. Elsewhere in Yorkshire one General Accident inspector covered all the Wolds and part of the Dales by bus, cycle and on foot. The annual allowance for wear and tear on bicycles was 30 shillings. Looking back, Heath saw it as a deflationary era of cheap labour:

In head office there was a huge motor department of low-paid, elderly clerks who ticked proposals against a standard yes/no pattern. If there was a difference, they referred it to a supervisor.

In spite of safety measures such as the introduction of the Highway Code (1931), Belisha beacons (1934), and driving tests, at first voluntary and then compulsory (1935), the average cost of claims continued to rise. An excess of £2 10s was applied to accidentally damaged items such as mudguards or a puncture in the canvas of an open-topped car. If a horse had tried to make a meal of a roof there was a case for negotiation. 'Rural' areas, including cities such as Chester and Exeter, had inadequate roads, producing a high incidence of claims because they were crossroads for commerce and holiday traffic. Standards of driving were not high and not encouraged by the practice of driving out for a drink at a prominent new roadhouse, where 'One for the road' was a common invitation. Ability to walk a straight line afterwards was a rudimentary test of sobriety.

General Accident offered £5,000 for the exclusive right to advertise in the 1935 edition of the Highway Code, 15 million of which were to be produced, but the Ministry of Transport decided against any advertising. In 1938, the year after the company issued its millionth motor policy, Norie-Miller commented:

It only remains now for young drivers, who will be interested to know that they are responsible for the large percentage of accidents, to show some respect for the law and regulations...and restrain that insane longing for excessive speed.

He also criticised the 'unnecessarily high damages awarded in certain courts'.

A particularly unprofitable place for car and workmen's compensation insurance was Eire, the new name for the Irish Free State and one that had to appear on policies following the new constitution at the end of 1937. Although Eire was an independent nation and had in 1936 passed an insurance act intended to bolster local companies against foreign competition, General Accident in common with other insurance companies nevertheless continued to treat the country as part of its UK branch network. Workmen's compensation claims there were high because the fixed compensation rate was only marginally below the average wage and there was little encouragement for people to get back to work if they could avoid it. Anyway, there were few jobs to be had. The Irish economy, predominantly agricultural, had been badly hit by the depression. Motor premiums were inadequate, especially with the size of third party claims growing after the Road Traffic Act 1933. Irish juries could be lavish with other people's money. Against this background of adverse claims experience the company decided not to write new business in those two lines in Ireland from early 1938.

A court case that attracted public and insurance notice in 1937 was *Digby v. General Accident* because it involved the film star Merle Oberon and a point of principle. As a lawyer Stanley Norie-Miller took a personal interest on the General Accident side. Injured in her own car being chauffeured by Digby, Merle Oberon accepted damages of £5,000 against him. He in turn sought indemnity from General Accident under her policy. General Accident, while conceding that Digby was covered against liability to third parties, maintained that, as the policyholder, Miss Oberon could not be a third party to her driver's negligence. This interpretation of the policy was upheld in court. Digby went to the Appeal Court, which ruled that he was entitled to indemnity by General Accident. Still convinced by the original verdict, the company took the case to the highest court, the House of Lords, which in 1943 found for Digby. The judgment of their lordships was that the policy indemnified the policyholder for any claims by any person, not any person other than the policyholder, for injury. Furthermore, the policy indemnified any person driving with her permission as though that driver was the policyholder. For the purposes of the claim made by her against him, Digby was the policyholder, General Accident were the insurers and Miss Oberon was the third party. Henceforward, insured drivers could claim the same indemnity as though the policyholder were driving. Merle Oberon's accident and unavailability were also the pretext for her future husband, the film producer Alexander Korda, to stop the shooting after five weeks of the epic *I Claudius*, which was behind schedule and over budget.

Greater mechanisation in industry also led to more accidents involving death and injuries, leading to more workmen's compensation claims, exacerbated when premiums fell along with wages. Norie-Miller continued to trumpet the strength of the company in meeting claims. In 1934 he issued a letter reiterating the tariff/non-tariff situation:

Merle Oberon on the set of the film I Claudius. The emperor was played by Charles Laughton (right).

We wish to point out that the only true test of the strength of an Insurance Company is its financial position as disclosed in its balance sheet. Whether Tariff or Non-Tariff, every company stands entirely by itself, and its funds alone are responsible for meeting liabilities under the policies issued…We endeavour to work at a lower percentage of management cost than most Tariff Offices, and we feel that, but for the existence of ourselves and other Non-Tariff Companies, an extra burden might be placed upon manufacturers and others by higher rates being charged.

He signed it Chairman and Managing Director, having been made chairman in 1933 on the resignation through ill-health of William Low and his own son Stanley taking over as general manager. The whole tone of the letter was one of rugged independence, the company standing resolutely alone and remaining outside the British Insurance Association apart from a brief membership from 1936 to 1938. General Accident, which in 1931 had opened a trustee and executory department in London, felt and looked stolid. In 1935 the company's fiftieth anniversary coincided with the silver jubilee of King George V, the two events being marked by a bonus of one week's pay, limited to £20, for staff, and a bonus and increased dividend, each one shilling, for shareholders. Ready for the anniversary, the company had built a pavilion by the Tay and equipped it as a sports and social centre in what became known as the Norie-Miller Park. A laudatory history, *A Business Epic*, was published in which Norie-Miller was

In this aerial view of Perth the company's sports and social club is seen at the top centre.

recognised as a man of influence beyond the industry, having just been elected National Liberal MP for Perth. Early the following year he received a baronetcy. His golden jubilee with the company, the peak of his achievement, occurred in 1937, when he was given various gifts and worldwide congratulations.

In January 1938, concerned over damage to property that might be inflicted by enemy aircraft, he took a unilateral decision to underwrite war risks on private houses and small shops in the UK, a move he reckoned would protect the company's fire business. His decision was both contrary to the policy of the British Insurance Association, of which he claimed to be unaware although the company was once again a member, and was taken without consulting his own board of directors. As managing director, Francis Norie-Miller had drafted a minute to the effect that the board had unanimously adopted his proposals for war risks. At the February board meeting the inaccurate minute was altered but, notwithstanding that, in a letter from Nice where he was getting some winter sunshine Francis instructed his son Stanley as general manager to prepare and despatch 4,000,000 prospectuses. When Stanley pointed out the estimated cost would be £40,000, Francis modified his instructions to reduce it to some £7,500. Stanley had also been deprived of his right to revise board minutes drafted by his father. In a private and confidential memo to Fred Richardson in the USA, who had been a board member since 1928, the senior director, William Hunter, a relative of one of the original directors, Patrick Hunter, was forthright:

> *It is not suggested that the Corporation has so far suffered serious losses by reason of any recent action of the Managing Director, or that he has recently brought it under any dangerous commitments, but it is felt that the time has come when his health no longer permits of his exercising satisfactorily the wide powers of Managing Director and that his attitude to the General Manager and to certain members of the staff has become such that the successful conduct of the business cannot be maintained. It is thus not unlikely that the Board may soon be called upon to take some action, more or less drastic.*

Another director felt 'the future of this Corporation is very much at stake'. At 78 Francis, who made accusations of 'hole and corner work' behind his back, was losing his grip.

Richardson suggested to certain directors a reorganisation, which was put to the board. Near the end of 1938 Norie-Miller resigned as managing director, and became governor with a salary of £10,000 p.a. free of tax. Although edged upstairs, he remained a presence.

When car sales slumped,
shrinking other industries
and raising unemployment...
the Depression made little impact on General
Accident's business.

In 1920 the expense ratio was as low as 33.2 per cent and in 1921 the US branch remitted $182,703.82 to Perth, with nothing having to be sent in the other direction.

Insurance companies needed their wits about them to combat the crime wave:

The year just ended [1920] is admitted to have shown the most colossal Burglary Losses in the history of the business...The crime wave has swept the entire country, and it is practically impossible to pick out any particular locality that is worse than the rest...We have been called upon to settle claims for articles ranging from a five-gallon oilcan to a half horsepower electric motor, which only goes to show that the 'crooks' are not fastidious in making their selections, and, to accomplish their ends, have even resorted to posing as clowns, and finally as insurance inspectors, in order to get details of the places they intended to rob, their methods indicating that they are part of a well-organized gang, the head of which it was found was operating a high-class automobile business on the surface, in which he was being given unlimited credit, and who, outside of this business, was taking orders from large commission houses all over the country for any and all kinds of goods, and after locating just where the articles were, sending his men to rob the places. It has been found necessary, in face of these conditions, to be more conservative in the underwriting of burglary lines.

Richardson's approach was methodical. In 1916 he asked a meeting of casualty and surety underwriters:

Why do we need to concentrate on the study of statistics? To me the answer seems to be that we must lay a solid foundation of knowledge in order to be able to provide the wide open contracts which will be in demand to meet the needs of the great period immediately ahead of us.

To him the lessons of great and permanent value, worth repeating in the boom of the 1920s, were:

1 That the selection of risks is the first principle of insurance. By that is meant selection by the company and not selection by the assured.
2 That economy of administration is imperative.
3 That fairness and promptitude in the adjustment of claims is the debt we owe to the policyholder.
4 That allocation of a large part of the profits to reserve is necessary in order to provide security.
The security of our policyholders must depend upon the degree of skill and

integrity that we put into discriminating between one piece of business and another. It is not fair to honest assured to put their premiums in the same pot with the premiums of the dishonest and irresponsible.

This applied in particular to the question of compulsory automobile cover, being discussed by a number of states in the mid-1920s: 'Solution is being sought of a problem that arises out of the cheapness of automobiles, whereby many cars are owned and operated by people who are judgment-proof.'

In his three-yearly report ending 31 December 1922 the New York insurance superintendent commented: 'The outstanding feature of the report is the low cost of the company's business and its economical management expenses.' By 1924, 25 years after starting in the USA, the company was able to open an 11-storey head office at 414 Walnut Street, Philadelphia. It was an occasion for a three-day celebration attended by top management from Perth. In keeping with Prohibition, the only Scottish spirit at the public events was in the form of 'a handsome young piper who struck the appropriate note for the occasion and his stirring piping gathered the assembly together'. In the world's largest insurance market the real hero was Richardson, who had turned the branch's fortunes round, over the three years from 1920 showing an underwriting profit.

The 1920s, especially the latter half, were the decade of the auto. By 1929, when 4,455,100 cars were produced, the automobile industry was the largest in the US. It acted as an economic motor, demanding production of its materials and components, stimulating the construction of suburbs, highways and small wayside businesses. All enlarged the market for insurance, April/May being the prime months for auto cover. With the growth of trucking traffic, in WW1 the company had entered inland marine insurance, protecting goods in transit. In 1926 total General Accident premium income topped $10 million for the first time, never to fall below it, and there was an underwriting profit every year until 1951. Richardson's achievement was recognised in 1928, when he was made a director in Perth. Commitment to underwriting, he emphasised, was crucial to the company's fortunes. At a convention of agents in October 1929, the month of the Wall Street Crash, he predicted that a time was coming when companies that depended on profits from investment returns would be unable to survive.

Frederick Richardson, who turned round the US branch, could be mistaken for an American, but was an Englishman.

GAFLAC Society — General Accident Assurance Corp, June 1934, appears to be celebrating the achievement of a champion swimmer.

ACCIDENT ASSURANCE CORP. JUNE 9, 1934.

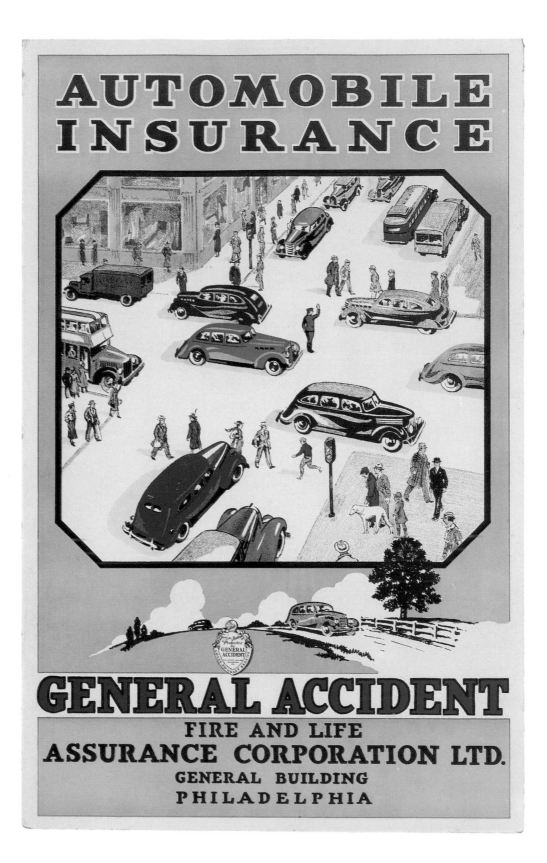

His policy of selecting risks and going for quality assurance paid off. When car sales slumped, shrinking other industries and raising unemployment, forcing one family in Philadelphia to live on dandelions, the Depression made little impact on General Accident's business. Reductions in premium income were marginal, the upward trend being resumed in 1934. The much smaller Potomac was less fortunate, recording underwriting losses every year from 1920 to 1932 with the exception of 1923. Defalcations were optimistically estimated at $150,000 in 1931, when the loss on building loans was reckoned to be slightly over $100,000.

Recovery during the latter half of the 1930s was steady, with new branches being opened in Chicago, Columbus, Dallas, Indianapolis, Los Angeles, Springfield and Washington DC. General Accident performance over the decade was better than the US economy as a whole, Gross National Product in 1933 being nearly a third less than in 1929 and, in a deflationary spiral, the dollar value of production remaining below 1929 until 1941, when under the Lend-Lease Act the country geared up for war production. The Depression affected the nation in varying degrees for ten years but the company for only four.

Richardson, born in Newcastle-upon-Tyne, was the last Englishman to run General Accident in the US. Physically he could be mistaken for an American and in true American fashion had seen and pursued business opportunities. When he took over in 1916, in the words of the *United States Review*, 'the General Accident operations had proved an unfortunate and costly experiment…the United States branch had been a veritable sink hole'. Under his leadership assets had grown more than 10-fold and policyholders' surplus more than 16-fold. Over the 10 years from 1928 operations had been conducted at a total expense ratio of 32 per cent, compared to an average of 38 per cent for the 10 largest casualty companies, which had a loss ratio only 0.1 per cent lower. Asked how he did it, Richardson replied: 'I make all my profit on the business I do not write.' Behind his quip lay an occupational underwriting policy that listed accountants, farm agents, ministers and nuns as good auto risks and bartenders, doctors and waitresses as bad. In an age when racial stereotyping and consequent prejudice were common, his conservative approach could include for instance the refusal of individual proposals from Japanese-Americans.

Facing page
US advertisements were colourful.

T.H. Hall in his Toronto office in 1929.

Thomas Hall, in charge in Canada, was a man of different stamp. Regarded as a capable administrator who in 15 years had never failed to deliver a profit in the fire department, he had the limitation of not really grasping the casualty side of the business. Having edged out his rival and taken his title of general manager of General Accident Assurance Company of Canada, he left casualty temporarily the poor relation. The deficiency was made good by appointing more agents and, in order to hold the necessary agencies in various districts, registering in 1920 a third entity, Scottish Canadian Assurance Corporation.

Hail was a business entered in 1919, severe hailstorms in the western states being a particular risk in property damage. Plate glass followed in 1922. As in the USA, business prospered enough to justify a new head office, a move into prestige premises in Bay Street, Toronto in 1923. In 1924 Hall was moved up from general manager to managing director of the local company even though from Perth he was consistently regarded as a man who did not easily delegate, who occupied too much of his time with detail work and worried too much over matters of minor importance. He was unable to buck as successfully as Richardson in the US the downturn in premium income following the Depression and, although income recovered after 1935, by 1940 it had still not reached its 1930 level. In 1935 a loss of over $100,000 was recorded. It was clear that the business had grown beyond his capacity to keep an eye on everything and in 1936 at 64 he appointed as joint managers the secretary, Geoffrey Malcolm, and his own son, Douglas, who had managed the Winnipeg branch.

In Australia progress was uncertain. The Queensland branch was closed in 1919 and the business sold to an agency. Head office authorised the opening of an agency for fire business in Samoa in 1920. In the same year the Australian board recommended the purchase of freehold property in Sydney 'as it is destined to be the greatest city in Australia', but no such property was bought for 13 years. A Melbourne freehold was bought in 1925, becoming the first of the General Buildings in the territory. During the 1920s state government insurance departments, notably in New South Wales, Tasmania and Western Australia, secured much of the business, particularly in workmen's compensation. Further sub-branches were not established until a decade later: conversions from the Haughton agencies in South Australia and Western Australia (1930); Queensland again (1932).

These followed a major change of policy in mid-1930, when the company resigned from all Australian tariff associations except marine and started operating as an independent office. One of the questions, for instance, was whether the company could offer special terms to the Royal Automobile Club of Queensland when rates were fixed by the state government. General Accident was able to do so and it opened a branch in Brisbane. Being independent deprived

Public liability was one of the company's lines. In Australia the company was asked to quote on the risk of leading an elephant through the streets of Sydney as part of a promotional campaign for tea. H.G. Daley, an inspector, weighs up the risk.

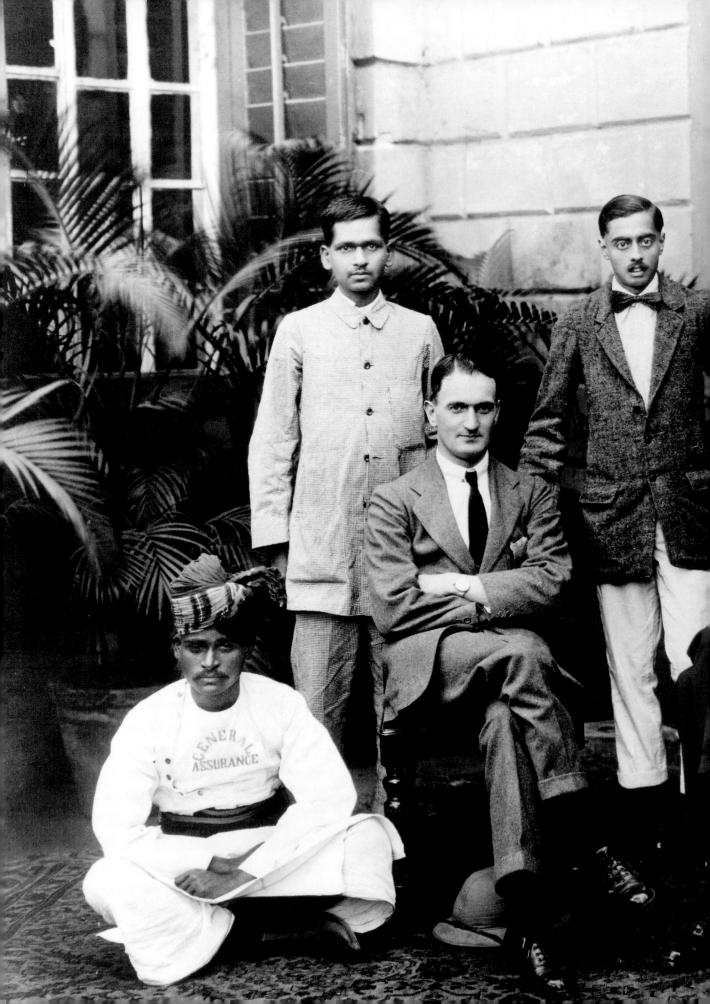

In the early 1920s local staff were in the majority in the Calcutta office. The manager was A.G.F. Smith (centre left); G.M. Rose, his deputy, is seated next to him.

it of a place on schedules of major business such as fire but it could be more competitive. From the mid-1930s, when wool prices improved, there was more business to compete for at sharper rates. This was pursued by a Scot, Alexander [Sandy] Doig, previously manager in Aberdeen, much more cautiously than by his predecessor, George Anderson, who had been dismissed in 1929 for arranging two reinsurance treaties that progressively increased losses and also being dilatory in cancelling them. Doig's work in declining all reinsurance and improving office routines was described by one employee as 'a cleaning up of the Augean stable and the best action ever taken in our Australian history'. Life could be leisurely though. When Doig took home leave in 1932 he was away for six months.

Occasionally Scottish ways worked in the company's favour, for instance in securing business among the Presbyterian community of Adelaide. Frugality was evident, the purchase of an £18 10s 10d bicycle for the Geelong inspector in 1921 meriting a board minute. By the late 1930s Western Australia had bought two cars but, to keep their costs down, staff had to maintain them. Perth there out-Perthed head office in deference, the staff standing to attention to welcome the manager with a concerted 'Good morning'. As in other parts of the world, there were instances of fraud during the Depression, the most notable being a claims clerk colluding with a motor repairer to manufacture claims. An architect's insistence that he had never had an accident and was entitled to a no claim bonus sent the pair to prison.

The last major Empire territory without a local representative was New Zealand, the small business of which had been handled from Australia in accor-

Cape Town office had its own print room for producing South African material in English and Afrikaans.

dance with the tariff. In 1925, a year before the economy turned down in the latter half of 1926, Neville Newcomb Ltd, auctioneers and estate agents based in Auckland, the most populous area of the country, were appointed agents for ten years. During the decade they managed to develop the business in spite of the adverse economic situation, but not profitably. On the expiry of the agreement, when there was a mild improvement in the economy with rising export prices for wool and meat, General Accident formed its own company, sending out as manager Colin Little, fire superintendent from the Liverpool branch, who had hoped to become manager of the Shrewsbury office. In an amicable arrangement some of the Newcomb staff transferred to General Accident, with Newcomb retaining a national agency for fire and accident insurance on a commission rate up to 25 per cent and special provisions for the Auckland area. Head office of General Accident was in Wellington, the seat of government and central for travel to both North and South Island. Staff were stationed in main branches: Auckland and the two main centres of the lighter populated South Island, Christchurch and Dunedin. To be more competitive, the company withdrew from the tariff associations except the marine. In 1937 it ceased transacting compulsory third party motor insurance because of the unsatisfactory way in which risks had to be accepted.

South Africa, where transit and marine insurance departments were established in 1918 and 1921, became the base for expansion into Southern Rhodesia (from 1980, Zimbabwe), Moçambique and Nyasaland (from 1964, Malawi). In keeping with its status General Accident had a new office built in Johannesburg, opened in 1925. After the Depression offices were opened in Pretoria, Bloemfontein, Salisbury (from 1982, as the capital of Zimbabwe, Harare) and Bulawayo. Agents were appointed in Kenya, Uganda and Tanganyika (from 1964, Tanzania). The Indian Guarantee & General Insurance Company, founded in 1872, was acquired in 1922 and continued as a subsidiary with its own board in Bombay.

By this time, although General Accident was most strongly represented in the English-speaking world, its policies were printed in 11 different languages. Over 50,000 people, either on salary or commission, were reckoned to be selling policies, but this may be a round figure chosen by Norie-Miller. Inter-war overseas expansion mainly filled in gaps of representation in other parts of Africa, the Caribbean and Latin America: British Honduras and Santo Dominica (1920); Costa Rica and Ecuador (1921); Bermuda, El Salvador, Guadeloupe, Jamaica, St Kitts & Nevis (1922); Antigua, Guatemala, Kuala Lumpur, Virgin Islands (1924); Colombia, Cuba, Greece, Sudan (1925); Malta (1926); Haiti, Nigeria, Puerto Rico (1927); Curacao, Barbados (1928); San Domingo (1929); Belgian Congo, Iraq (1930). The Depression postponed further openings until

In 1927 the Far Eastern manager, T.E. Mitchell, and staff presented Francis Norie-Miller with a Chinese umbrella to mark his 40 years' service. Embroidered in gold, silver and other colours on deep orange silk, the umbrella has three main figures: the God of Health, the God of Officials and the God of Longevity. The bird on top symbolises long life and fruitfulness.

1936, when Martinique was the first, with West Africa, both British and French, following in 1937.

This breadth of representation enabled the corporation to accumulate a fund of knowledge about good and bad risks, not just in weather patterns and other hazards that could be studied in textbooks. For example, Perth was able to reply to a City broker's enquiry:

We do not insure sheep going across the Equator, they die like flies sometimes. There are some technicalities about it; for instance shearing on board before they reach the hot zone in certain seasons and so on. Shearling rams are fed on highly nitrogenous food for getting abnormal Show bloom, and this makes a greater hazard.

The Shanghai office, in Hong Kong Road, had a large local staff.

The livestock manager must have had access to a wide knowledge of animal husbandry since he finished his reply by stating 'For anything special you can wire and we will reply within five minutes.'

A disturbing event was the Sino-Japanese War, which broke out in mid-1937. Within five months Japanese forces had captured Shanghai, where General Accident had its Far Eastern branch. At first the office was moved from Hong Kong Road to 'more convenient and centrally-positioned premises in the building of the Chartered Bank at No 18 The Bund'. That was a temporary solution and in the spring of 1938 the Far Eastern office was transferred to Singapore. Business in China continued through the agents W.R. Loxley & Company, which celebrated its diamond jubilee in that year.

Worldwide representation was now almost complete, mainly through branch offices and agents, with some agents being given power of attorney to act on behalf of the corporation. Ultimate authority though remained with Perth, which exercised it not primarily through travel and telecommunications but rather through the influence of Norie-Miller. In 1928 the corporation had the grand telegraphic address of Bullion, Perth but only three outside telephone lines. Senior management did sail to major outposts, it was sometimes thought more for recreation than action, but the farthest outpost necessitated weeks if not months away from the office. In 1923, for instance, there was a prospect of coming to an arrangement with the government of Jamaica on insuring banana crops against damage from hurricanes. Occupied with the takeover of The English Insurance Company, Francis Norie-Miller was unable to go. He proposed sending his son Stanley with the London manager, Nathaniel Forte, who had more insurance experience. Faced with a year or so's absence, Forte, who when a young man had spent time in Barbados, stated that he could not stand the summer heat in the Caribbean. It 'would for me prove suicidal'. He also had to consider 'the precarious health of my wife, and my old mother'. In reply to his suggestion for a maximum stay of six months ending in June, Francis was:

extremely disappointed…it will be quite useless for any official to go out to Jamaica to commence writing an entirely new form of insurance, and to take in hand the building up of the necessary organisation for so doing, unless such official can remain there for a reasonable period. A stay of only the first two or three months until June, as you suggest, would

Jamaica had its winter attractions, but in 1923 before air conditioning it was a less desirable destination in summer.

WINTER in the
WEST INDIES

R.M.S. "ORCOMA." 11,571 tons gross register.

JAMAICA
"THE ISLAND OF SUNSHINE"

Pacific Line

be merely a waste of the Corporation's money. I do feel that the highly paid officials of the Corporation should be available, at any time, to take up important matters of this kind, and that is why I am so disappointed to find that you do not seem at all anxious to try to make a success of this undertaking.

Mr G. Scott-Pearse went instead.

As air travel was in its infancy, something of a hazardous novelty, an overseas visit tended to turn into a cruise, a grand tour of a few countries. Communications were little faster than in Victorian times, delays in receiving answers to letters being accepted as normal, sometimes even being taken advantage of. Cablegrams and international phone calls were kept to a minimum. What really held the scattered offices together was Norie-Miller's personal authority, his personality percolating to the lowest echelons of the organisation through the media of the staff magazine and press articles, copies of which were sent overseas. Official accounts were supplemented by gossip that spread quickly on the company grapevine and amplified his authority. When overseas offices did not adhere to his principles they could incur losses, as India did in the 1930s. He left no doubt anywhere that it was one company and he was at the head.

Amidst the turmoil of war the spirit of community within the company strengthened.

MOST local UK memorials list more killed in WW1 than WW2, reflecting the greater mechanisation of warfare over an interval of 20 years. For General Accident it was different. Against 38 dead in WW1 the company roll of honour 1939–45 listed 151 names, 13 of them from overseas: Australia, Belgium, Canada, Netherlands, New Zealand and the United States. It was a sad reflection of the growth of the company between the wars.

Before war broke out, the board had decided on 31 May 1939 that in the event of war staff on active service would have service pay and allowances made up to the salary received at the time of mobilisation. By 24 January 1940, less than five months after the outbreak of war, 664 staff were on active service, a difference of £20,529 p.a. between office salaries and Army remuneration being made up by the company. Once again women had to be recruited and trained to take on the work. A year before the war Norie-Miller had written to the London manager, G.M. Rose, saying 'I have decided that I will give a medal to everyone of those who takes the place of a man and does work which the Branch Manager approves.' He could hardly have envisaged the scale of the replacement. Norwich branch, for example, was without 95 per cent of its male staff. There was no shortage of applicants to fill the vacancies. In Perth there was a waiting list, as Lily Turpie discovered when in 1941 she joined straight from school at the age of 14:

It was easier to get in if you had a relative already in General Accident, provided the relative had not been on strike in the 1920s. My uncle and aunt were strikers and didn't get their jobs back after the strike. I got into the livestock department at a salary of £39 a year because, although I was the niece of strikers, I had a different name. After typing renewal notices for cattle and horses, many of which had names, I went into personnel, what was called the field department, where the black list of strikers was kept under lock and key.

Lily went on to serve the company for over 45 years, becoming private secretary to three successive chief general managers from 1972 until her retirement in 1986.

The first member of staff to lose his life was A.G. Dick from Manchester on 23 November 1939 when the lightly armed merchant ship *Rawalpindi* was sunk in the Indian Ocean. Two years after war was declared, on 3 September 1941, the board decided to set up a widows' pension and benevolent fund, the idea being extended in the following February to include subsistence for widows and children.

After the fall of France in June 1940 and the consequent possibility of a German invasion of the UK the board, now meeting every two months, was

concerned that the head office in Perth could be cut off from effectively exercising its functions. Accordingly, emergency arrangements were made for a
committee of the board, under the deputy chairman Fred Richardson, to take
over direction of the company if need be. Power of attorney was granted to
overseas branch managers 'in the event of communications being interrupted
between Great Britain and the countries in which these Branches are situated'.
Further, plans were made for the evacuation of head office to Canada. Basic
records such as reinsurance treaties, agreements and statistics of foreign
branches and agents were packed up and sent in batches to Toronto, where
T.H. Hall was empowered in certain circumstances to assume the title of world
manager. In the state of emergency Perth put aside its earlier criticisms of his
management style involving too much attention to detail that ought to have
been delegated. He would have been in good company because Canada was the
territory to which the royal family and the government would have evacuated.

Damage on the home front was greater than in WW1, greater than the company anticipated in October 1939 when it issued proposal forms for an air raid
personal accident policy paying a sum assured up to £1,000 on any one life not
involved in civil defence work. The company's City, Plymouth and Portsmouth
offices were destroyed in 1941 air raids, causing disruption to business and
extra work because an extra copy of records had to be created manually. A
1,000lb bomb dropped outside the Bristol office on 3 December 1940 rendered
the building unfit for occupation and the staff had to move to the nearby
Clifton sub-office and sports pavilion. Coventry had to be evacuated in
November 1940 because of danger from an unexploded bomb and five months
later a blast bulged in the back wall, but the structure was sound enough for
work to carry on. When the first floor ceiling was brought down and all the win-
dows of Hull office smashed in a heavy daylight raid in May 1941 staff continued business on the ground floor. A year later Exeter office received a direct hit
and was gutted by fire, most of the important papers surviving in an underground strongroom. The head office of General Life with its records had been
evacuated from London to Perth.

General Accident's chief office in London suffered twice. Following the
blitz of high explosive and incendiary bombs, by early December 1941 air raid
damage to the Aldwych office, based on 1939 values, amounted to £70,928. A
bomb came through the roof, exploding on the third floor and stopping the
clocks at 3.06 a.m. On many mornings London streets were a sea of broken
glass, impossible to walk on, and services such as water and electricity were
cut off. Nevertheless staff were glad to have survived and be at work to tell
their tale. As well as providing shelter during night raids the office opened
its canteen to people in uniform. A narrow escape from a direct hit occurred on

Aldwych was hit in the
1941 blitz, causing disruption
outside and inside the office.
Staff sheltered in the
basement.

30 June 1944 when a V1 rocket, a 'doodlebug', landed just up Aldwych. Casualties were brought in off the street.

Overseas offices were affected too, as they had not been in WW1. In the US a War Damage Corporation was established by Congress to issue insurance cover against war damage. All the insurance companies, including UK companies operating in the US, agreed to participate. General Accident did so via its subsidiary Potomac, with a limit of $40,000 possibly rising to $48,000 on either profit or loss. In Australia an underground shelter for 100 people was built below the company's offices at 105 Pitt Street, Sydney. It was a sensible precaution. Japanese submarines were patrolling off Sydney harbour. On 19 February 1942 Japanese aircraft bombed Darwin, killing at least 243 people, damaging most buildings and destroying the majority of Allied ships in the harbour.

That event sent shock waves of fear as far away as New Zealand, where there was talk that a torpedo had been fired across the bows of an inter-island ferry. Colin Little, the General Accident manager, enrolled in the fire police section of the Home Guard, which did weapons drill with broom handles. Petrol was rationed so, to carry on business, his car was converted to a gas-assisted system, which involved fitting a firebox and furnace into one front mudguard and a filter plant and storage cylinder into the other. On longer journeys he had to stop every 100 miles or so to rake out the ashes in the firebox and stoke up again with coke from the boot. Other vehicles had canvas balloon bags of gas on roof racks.

Branch typists practised working in gas masks.

When the Japanese were advancing in Burma the agent in the capital, Rangoon, walked some 800 miles to Calcutta in India, where he handed over the books and cash to the local agent.

Net assets of the company in Western European countries occupied by the Germans in the summer of 1940 could only be recorded: Belgium £42,068 6s 3d, Denmark £29,633 0s 1d, France £74,876 8s 2d, Netherlands £10,486 11s, Norway £8,907. In Belgium the company was taken over and run by a German insurer, Victoria, and handed back after the war. On the liberation of Paris in August 1944 a General Accident employee was pleased to note that the company's office was intact.

Under German occupation business could be almost as usual as Robert Le Sueur in Jersey, the largest of the Channel Islands, recalled in a post-war talk:

Many people left the island before the invasion of 1 July 1940. On that day a clamour of people called at the office to check that their life assurance policies were in force. Anybody who was anybody at the office happened to be on holiday in England. The total staff consisted of me, the office junior aged 19, who suddenly became acting resident secretary, and a very pregnant typist who should already have left but stayed on to help out. As the weeks went by she had to sit farther and farther away from her typewriter.

After the invasion, when communication with our district office in Southampton was cut off, a dozen or so offices represented on Jersey got together and formed the Associated Offices Central Fund. Regular meetings took place between the managers, many of them quite ancient compared with me. The premiums received by all offices were pooled and used to deal with claims, a small amount initially being deducted to pay office expenses. At first claims were only dealt with in part but as funds grew they were dealt with in full, if possible. Cover provided was mainly fire only on houses and third party and fire on cars, vans and lorries. Some comprehensive policies were in force but as there were no replacement parts very few accidental damage claims were settled. Only one life claim was received. No policies were issued during the occupation, only a form of cover note. Quite surprisingly, a lot of new business was arranged.

The insurance company managers agreed to restrict their income to £3 a week, a figure that made me quite happy as my income at the time of the invasion was less than £1 a week. All transactions were in German currency but as the General Accident bank account was in sterling so the bank had to transfer the currencies. People hoarded sterling. After the German setbacks in North Africa and Russia at the end of 1942 German soldiers were paying the exchange equivalent of five pounds for a one pound note. That's when we knew that somehow we were bound to win the war.

Petrol was rationed so the staff collected the premiums on bicycles. When the pregnant lady had to leave there were over 100 applications for her job. I also

In January 1940 members of Exeter branch took blood tests in preparation for donations to the transfusion service.

arranged help in the office by a commercial traveller in his 50s who, unaware of the local situation, had come across to Jersey on the last boat. He was later deported to a labour camp in Germany, as were all non-natives.

Conditions in the office were very poor: no heating or lighting. Staff wore gloves with the fingers cut out and wrapped themselves in blankets to keep warm. If a customer came into the office the staff had to extricate themselves from a cocoon of blankets. We were not allowed any milk for tea or coal or gas for heating. Staff got very run down as the available food was of poor quality.

The only inter-General Accident correspondence was between the Jersey and Guernsey offices. One topic was the war risk exclusion clause. Did this apply when an accident occurred involving a vehicle belonging to the military authority? Or involving a civilian driving his vehicle being used for military purposes? R.H. Le Prevost, the resident secretary in Guernsey, felt that on moral grounds we shouldn't insure civilian vehicles being used for these purposes.

Three days after the liberation of the Channel Islands, on 10 May 1945 Le Prevost wrote to Mr Thorpe, the district manager in Southampton, explaining that Mr Le Sueur and he:

had worked quite independently of each other and in two entirely different ways, although we have been in constant communication with each other and have visited each other on three occasions and have endeavoured to help each other *whenever we felt that we needed moral support. I think the Jersey method of working, that is in conjunction with the other companies, will have proved the more satisfactory of the two.*

He went on to compare the current and pre-war figures. Very little of the non-motor business had disappeared but motor income had dropped to almost as many pence as it should be pounds. At the end of the occupation the only motor vehicles on the road were those of a few bakers, the doctors and some members of the administrative body. The Germans had bought the office car, which they exported, and separately his own car for £85, which he had spent on the struggle for existence. His bicycle tyres were completely worn out. Kitchen chairs had been smashed for cooking the few vegetables they had been able to obtain. Clothing had been a problem but he was able to benefit from a deceased acquaintance of the same size. His secretary 'had had the misfortune to lose her mother and, callous though the remark may sound, she is now reasonably clothed.'

In June 1945 the Southampton district manager was expecting details of five years' transactions to be sent to him within the next fortnight. When the situation had been explained to him the staff started working seven days a week to clear the paperwork. No sooner had that started than Perth insisted on a campaign of rewriting all home policies issued before the German occupation.

The impact on UK staff was much greater than in WW1. At the outbreak of war staff had numbered 4,251; by mid-1942 they were down to 2,951, with 1,540 at war. Casualties then amounted to 91: 40 killed, 12 missing, 39 prisoners of war. In October 1942 the Ministry of Labour recommended that office hours be increased. General Accident complied by raising the working week by five and a half hours from 37¼ to 42¾ a week, increasing salaries by 10 per cent, with a maximum increase of £50. Typists, for example, worked two nights a week from 6 p.m., being paid 1s 6d an hour. If a mistake was made in typing a renewal notice, the document had to be started again but there was also a concerted effort to save paper. For example, the reverse side of a 1928 letter was used by the motor claims department in head office for the carbon copy of a letter sent to the Legal & General in 1941. Inevitably there were postal delays affecting the confirmation of cover and the settlement of accounts, adding to the frustrations of wartime shortages and the difficulties of managing private and business lives while coping with extra demands. Periodically, gas mask drills lasted for an hour, head office staff being inspected by Stanley Norie-Miller himself. As well as working longer hours staff undertook duties such as firewatching, service in the Home Guard and as air raid wardens, which in major cities exposed them to risk of injury. Voluntary effort also went into fund-raising events such as War Weapons Week. Other work included adding pieces of camouflage to netting, and sewing or knitting garments for servicemen and prisoners of war, organised by Our Boys Committee. Prisoners of war received parcels from head office, branches, and from Philadelphia through the American Red Cross. Through the Red Cross, prisoners also kept up their studies and were able to sit examinations of the Chartered Insurance Institute.

Amidst the turmoil of war the spirit of community within the company strengthened. Alfred Pearson, from 1944 assistant general manager, wrote personally to everybody who had been called up. Each letter, individually typed and signed, concluded with a reminder not to forget the old folks at home, remember to write to them. Barbara Easton, secretary to the assistant Aldwych manager, appreciated the personal understanding by those less exposed to the conflict:

> One kind gesture from Perth to London was for General Accident people to open their homes to London staff for a holiday away from the bombing. Living in North London, I took advantage of this offer and stayed with a Mr Perkins and his family. The fare to Perth was £5 and the train was six hours late arriving back in London because of enemy activity, the sort of hold-up that seemed the norm at the time. We always felt head office never realised the true feeling of working through the many problems in London.

The assistant manager, Edmund Norie Snell, a nephew of Francis Norie-Miller, understood and invited her to his home in St Albans, Hertfordshire, where she had the security of sleeping in a bed under which he stored the Home Guard sten guns. The US branch, from which over 230 employees had joined the US armed services, rallied to the cause by sending food parcels, a welcome supplement to plain rations. American staff collected enough money to provide a mobile canteen van that in 13 months served more than 250,000 meals to people affected by the blitz, victims and the armed and auxiliary services.

Throughout the war the slogan as far as possible was 'Business as usual'. For the first year at least coming into the office every day, Francis Norie-Miller was not going to be deflected from continuing the growth of his company. One danger he foresaw was that, with Labour as part of the coalition government and the collectivist mood in the country, a Minister of Insurance could be appointed with powers 'to legislate for insurance companies and practically manage their business'. Insurance companies in general were concerned about their future rôle, particularly after the publication in 1942 of the Beveridge proposals on social insurance and the civil service 18-month study of their implementation, which led to the formation of a Ministry of National Insurance in November 1944.

In 1940 what Norie-Miller feared was that, with government intervention, companies might be made liable for the insolvency of one of their number. This was one of the reasons why he stood out alone against a collective £60,000–70,000 rescue of the Universal Insurance Company in 1940, believing:

> *To support a company which was started with inadequate capital and which seems to have been mismanaged, seeing that they are now unable to meet their liabilities (a feature which the Board of Trade ought to have enquired into two years ago) is not in the best interests of those Insurers who are offering real protection. Companies with little or no capital above the mere deposit should not be encouraged to take business at inadequate rates and rely upon other Insurers to meet their liabilities when they themselves are unable to do so. The publicity which the failure of the company will receive is the best thing that could happen for other Insurance Companies.*

Norie-Miller resisted approaches from Sir Brian Mountain, managing director of the other major non-tariff company, Eagle Star, and Montagu Norman, governor of the Bank of England, who was concerned that allowing any scandal

In 1941 the US branch supplied to the Church Army in the UK a mobile canteen. It served over 250,000 refreshments to blitz victims, rescue parties, workers in Air Raid Precautions, soldiers, firemen and demolition squads in its first 13 months. Insulated compartments kept stew, soup, coffee and tea hot for hours. General Accident branch staff helped run the canteen part-time.

Liberation! On 9 May 1945 a crowd gathered outside the General Accident office in Guernsey for the liberating commander to appear from the Royal Court House opposite. Unconditional surrender was effective from 8 May, VE Day. On the left in the office window is Reg Le Prevost.

about an insurance company would enable 'Lord Haw-Haw', the British traitor who broadcast subversive propaganda from Germany, to 'make a great song about English insurance companies starting to fail and it might do untold harm to the financial structure generally of the City'. An appeal to the national interest from one governor to another failed to impress Norie-Miller, who preferred to conduct his own business on a sound basis. 'The Public deserve to lose when they have been so foolish as to expect that they could buy ten shillings worth of Insurance for five shillings.' He was also right on two other counts: although a rescue package was put together, the Universal Insurance Company failed and William Joyce, 'Lord Haw-Haw', was treated as a joke by the public, receiving his just deserts when he was captured, found guilty of treason and in 1946 hanged.

Business through the war was satisfactory. One area that suffered was motor insurance, so many cars being laid up for the duration of the war and only at risk from fire and theft. The situation was exacerbated in 1942 when the basic petrol ration was withdrawn, prompting the company to reduce private car premiums by 20 per cent. This was partly justified by better claims experience offset by an increase in accidents in 'blackout' conditions. A blow to pride was the withdrawal in 1941 of the Royal Warrant, held since 1911, on the grounds that the warrant was no longer granted to companies providing a service rather than a product.

Soon after VE Day, 8 May 1945, a victory bonus to staff was declared, two per cent of existing annual salary for each complete year of civilian service with the corporation during the war with Germany, with a maximum of £50. It included commissionaires, caretakers, messengers and filers, whether permanent or temporary, home and foreign, and the staffs of all subsidiary companies. Pensioners who had retired during the war received a bonus based on salary at the time of retiring, as did those civilians called up for active service or directed to work of national importance. Unfortunately, after the war when the company wanted to get a licence for extra paper to produce a war record it was impossible and the highlights featured in a special issue of *The General's Review*.

Amid the jubilation the company's independent stance was modified. Facing the challenges of adapting to the post-war world and with Norie-Miller in a titular position, the company felt it needed something of the strength of the industry on its side and rejoined the British Insurance Association, which it had left in 1938.

His father, Francis, had been an innovator, a risk-taking entrepreneur with an expansive approach; Stanley was a cautious consolidator, proceeding in judicious increments.

WHEN Bill Hartley rejoined Liverpool branch in 1945 he soon became aware that women had become dominant while he was away on war service in the UK and Middle East. On asking a woman to do something, he was struck by the tone in which she replied 'I'll come in a few minutes'. Harkness, the chief clerk, made it plain to him: 'You can't talk to young ladies like that.' Not that staff were overburdened with work. With staff returning from the war, there were for a while more people than work for them to do. They could take their time.

In essence they found little had changed. General Accident was still the same frugal company. Internally, a new envelope was never used if an old one would do. To save postage, juniors in branches delivered local mail by hand. There were frequent exhortations not to use the telephone, especially not in the morning when calls were dearer. Chief clerks in branches gave underlings permission to use it, whether the call was for business or a personal emergency. In Dublin one of the duties of the most junior clerk, often fresh from secondary education, was to go down to the basement in his white shirt and shovel the heap of coal delivered through the hole in the pavement. His dirty shirt was tolerated for the rest of the day.

In head office the pre-war hierarchical structure remained unchanged, along with the Dickensian high desks and stools to match. People at differing levels within the organisation addressed one another as Mr, Mrs, Miss or simply by surname. For a while staff were told not to wear cloth caps to the office so they stuffed them in their pockets before arriving. Senior managers still entered by the revolving doors at the front entrance and were entitled to ride in the lift while the rest of the staff came in by the back door, where they encountered the timekeeper, himself sometimes under the eye of the staff superintendent. In what was still the pinstripe era in business, jackets stayed on in the office. Officially, staff could not make tea; unofficially, messengers made it and brought a few cups round. The lunch hour and a quarter, during which some people walked or cycled home because they could not afford the bus fares, was also a strictly timed period.

One Saturday morning off in three was something to look forward to. Pay was better than pre-war, but the cost of living was higher. A young woman in her made-to-measure green overall, laundered every fortnight, debated with herself whether she could afford to spend the whole of her brown wage packet on a hair perm that week. If she had a personal problem she could go to the lady superintendent, who as well as organising social events such as the children's Christmas party acted as an agony aunt. To attend to medical matters a Perth doctor came in daily. Taken with the non-contributory pension scheme, the annual outings 'doon the Watter' ('down the Clyde') – senior staff had their end of the excursion train – the sports facilities in London and Perth, the latter having a recreation pavilion destined to remain 'dry' until after Sir Stanley died, the company was a mini welfare state.

Post-war business was satisfactory. At the end of 1945 the net loss in territories occupied by the enemy amounted to only £26,660. There was a strong revival in the demand for all forms of life assurance. Accident and general premium income also rose but so did claims, the beneficial effects of rate increases lagging behind rising costs. The marine department, since 1938 under the sole agency of William Haughton & Co, began underwriting aviation risks in 1945 and was set to grow to the point where in 1954 it would become a full in-house department of General Accident. Overall, in spite of the end of workmen's compensation business in 1948, the general trend of income, profit and reserves was upwards.

The significant event for General Accident was not the end of the war but the passing of Francis Norie-Miller. Obsessed as always with his health, he had his doctor visit him at least once a day throughout his final year. Against the doctor's advice Francis insisted on going to the 1946 Derby at Epsom. Weakened by the hard winter of 1946–7, the coldest for 53 years, he did not leave Cleeve, his Perth home, for the last three months of his life, for the first time missing the company's annual general meeting, held in May. He died peacefully at the age of 88 on 4 July 1947 and company offices were closed for the Monday of his funeral. For just over 60 years his name had been so synonymous with General Accident that many, including those within the company,

The year of the East Coast floods, 1953, produced a mass of claims. Some claims came from the company's home city when the Tay overflowed.

thought he was the founder, a belief he did not always deny. What he had done was save the infant company, which otherwise might well have foundered or been taken over, and with entrepreneurial flair developed it as a genuinely national and then international organisation. Its beginnings were not promising and circumstances were not in its favour. His achievement was to overcome them through a Victorian work ethic. He often talked of 'working the business' and his favourite text was:

Francis Norie-Miller's favourite text.

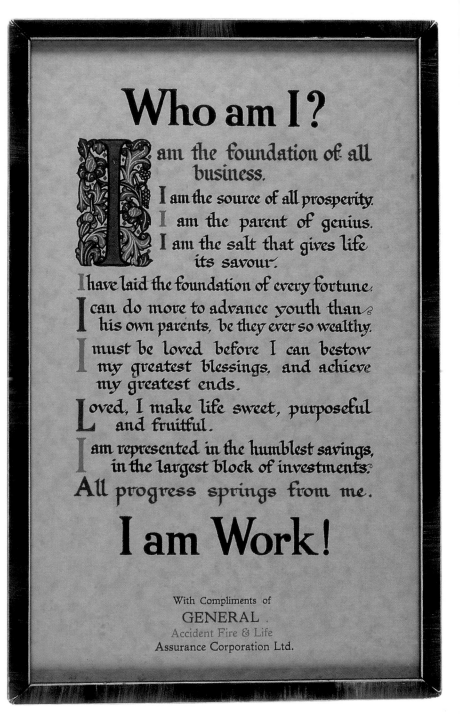

Who am I?

I am the foundation of all business.

I am the source of all prosperity.

I am the parent of genius.

I am the salt that gives life its savour.

I have laid the foundation of every fortune.

I can do more to advance youth than his own parents, be they ever so wealthy.

I must be loved before I can bestow my greatest blessings, and achieve my greatest ends.

Loved, I make life sweet, purposeful and fruitful.

I am represented in the humblest savings, in the largest block of investments.

All progress springs from me.

I am Work!

With Compliments of
GENERAL
Accident Fire & Life
Assurance Corporation Ltd.

The text, sounding like advice in pokerwork, was first used in the General Accident booklet published to mark the first 40 years of the company and issued at the British Empire Exhibition held at Wembley in 1924. Showcards of the text were distributed to agents in 1927 and at the end of the century it is still to be seen in some offices. Alan Bennett, the dramatist, saw it in the Lancaster branch in July 1975 while he was waiting to fill out a claim form and made it the curtain of a play about two gossipy office non-workers, *Doris and Doreen*, transmitted on 16 December 1978 by London Weekend Television.

The rise in General Accident's status was not unique. Other insurance companies, notably Norwich Union and companies in Liverpool where there was a background of marine insurance, had grown from provincial bases and flourished. Norie-Miller's achievement was personal. Starting as a pound-a-week clerk, he had risen at a young age to the top of what he always thought of as a profession rather than a trade and had gathered the support of the titled, gentlemen of high standing and repute in business, the professions, the military and landed gentry, as he was not slow to emphasise. On the way he had achieved a longed-for respectability, becoming a pillar of the Perth community and receiving some national and international recognition. When, on medical advice, he retired from the chairmanship in 1944, his successor, Fred Richardson, paid tribute at the 58th annual general meeting:

He was bent on making the name of the General a household word and to this end no channel was left unexplored. He came to a company that had an annual income of four figures. He bequeaths to the future a company with assets of over £25,000,000.

He had also given it an independent character. Staying in Perth under his direction, the company had gone its own way, keeping an eye on what was happening in the City of London but not automatically following the herd. This was most evident in being stubbornly a non-tariff company in the UK, but joining the tariff abroad where it was most suitable. Similarly, the company had an on– off, mainly off, relationship with the industry body, the British Insurance Association. To his peers in the industry Norie-Miller had been a maverick, but always in the interests of his company.

A mobile crane was badly damaged when it fell into the Clarence Graving Dock, Liverpool. In the accident two petrol tanks burst and some 40 gallons of fuel flooded the area. Fortunately it was prevented from bursting into flame, thus limiting the claim on General Accident.

His single-minded determination, strengthened by kneeling in prayer at his bedside, was also his weakness. He demanded and rewarded conformity, would not tolerate what he saw as rebellion from subordinates. Some who joined after the Second World War, felt that the company had lost out, especially in head office, through employing in the 1930s lowly paid conformists, who remained when younger members went into the armed services. Lining up at New Year, faithful employees were admitted to the boardroom, shook his hand and were grateful for the salary increase granted. If you belonged to Norie-Miller's masonic lodge or Rotary Club or had a relative in the company you were sure to have the security of a job for life, whether you were up to it or not. At least getting a job was not dependent on one's religious affiliations as it was in some Scottish companies, especially in the Glasgow region. In General Accident there were instances of the faithful being promoted beyond their abilities and perceptive newcomers were not slow to see mediocrity around them and the lack of scope for new ideas. Jim Mahon, a solicitor, felt he had joined a company of amateur gentlemen in which service was more important than ability. The situation was not uncommon in British companies at that time. There were also a few who, had they not been deprived of further education by their pre-war economic and social circumstances, could have benefited from going to university. Instead they had learned within the university of insurance life, rising above the routine to become managers with a broader view.

That Stanley, almost 59, was not in the mould of his father, except for being a shrewd businessman and having a weak chest, soon became apparent in family and company terms. His father's will had made many small bequests. Some people felt they were a genuine personal thanks for good deeds in his lifetime, others a piece of mischief-making beyond the grave. Stanley consulted the head of legal affairs within the company on his rights and employed outside solicitors. With his sister Elwena and father's widow, Florence, the secretary whom Francis had married in 1934 after his first wife died in 1931, Stanley contested the will on the grounds that his father had claimed he was a domiciled Englishman often resident in Scotland. His last will had been made in England under English law, but because he lived principally in Cleeve it had to be granted under Scottish law. Lord Mackintosh in the Court of Session heard evidence on how Francis played the dual rôle of a Scottish and English gentleman as occasion demanded. Witnesses went into his family background, character and habits. It was said that sometimes he wore the Robertson tartan and stood up in front of guests to eat his porridge Scots-style. The outcome in 1949 was that Florence was awarded £100,000 and Stanley and his sister £50,000 each, the intended small beneficiaries getting nothing. Stanley also became president of the premier club in Perth, from which his father had been blackballed.

Stanley Norie-Miller.

Within the company Stanley made the significant step of bringing in the first important outsider since his father was recruited 60 years before. On 1 October 1947 Aonghais (a Gaelic name for Angus, pronounced Innis) Macdonald joined the company as investment secretary. Insiders were suspicious of him. Although he was undoubtedly a Scot, by Glasgow training an investment banker, he was not from the insurance industry. Coming from the malted milk drink company Horlicks, which promoted an end to 'night starvation' and the benefits of sound refreshing sleep, what could he possibly know about General Accident's business and ways? Aware of being an intruder arousing jealousies because he was stepping over long-term General Accident people, he devoted himself to investment management and watched the progress of the company under Sir Stanley. As the relationship between the two men developed, Stanley relied more and more on him for advice and gave him greater responsibilities. Twenty years after joining Macdonald was to achieve a significant acquisition that had a long-term impact on the company's fortunes.

In his private and business life Stanley was basically a disappointed man. He was the younger son, through whom his father had realised his dynastic ambitions for the dishonest and deceased elder. Deprived of his chosen career at the bar, Stanley had been a reluctant but conscientious successor, supported in business by his wife, Grace, who had not succeeded in giving him an heir. Their

Murrayshall was the Perth home of Stanley Norie-Miller and his wife Grace.

only son to survive among seven miscarriages died at the age of nine months. Stanley was the end of the line. The couple were married in 1921 and in 1928 Francis had bought and had had renovated at a cost of £26,000 the derelict Murrayshall on the outskirts of Perth, giving it to them as a present and a place to entertain for General Accident. This they did but people in trade were not welcome. Nor had Francis given them anything towards the upkeep of a large property that after their passing would become a hotel.

Stanley was always careful to distinguish between his personal and company affairs. Margaret Torrance, his secretary from 1959 until his retirement, like her predecessor who had served him for 40 years kept a postage book for his personal mail, which was never put through the company. If he amended a letter he would not have it retyped because that meant the waste of a sheet of paper. He did not pay himself a high salary, treating company money as carefully as his own. His principal relaxation was playing bridge at a penny a hundred, the reckoning of 'in' or 'out' being done at the end of the year. On board ship he relaxed even more and played housey-housey [bingo], for which the prize could be a bit bigger. When subordinates presented development proposals his key question was 'What will it cost?' and, on receiving a figure, his standard reply was 'We will think about it'. His father, Francis, had been an innovator, a risk-taking entrepreneur with an expansive approach; Stanley was a cautious consolidator, proceeding in judicious increments, not a succession of inspired leaps. For instance, a figure of £5–6 million was put forward as the cost of redeveloping head office to bring together the scattered departments of the expanded group together for greater efficiency and Stanley was quick to say that was 'Much too much'. Nothing was done.

Seeing a discreet advertisement for an investment manager of 45 or over to manage funds of £200 million in a Scottish institution, Alan Begg applied. Having passed the preliminary interviews, he was introduced to Sir Stanley, who offered him the job, but because of his relative youth, 35 not 45, knocked 25 per cent off the starting salary. Although Stanley was very careful with the company's money, he was more open and honest with policyholders than during his father's regime. For instance, under a clause in motor policies, a widow was entitled to £1,000 compensation, if her husband was killed while driving, a fact pointed out to executors' solicitors who had not noticed it.

Whereas his father had been full of drive, creating and expanding the business, Stanley was the conservative maintaining his inheritance. As managing director until 1963 and chairman from 1951 he gave little scope to his general managers Alfred Pearson and his successor Colin Little. Directors too had a limited rôle, as Lord Ogilvy, the future Earl of Airlie and chairman, found when he joined the board in 1962:

Stanley Norie-Miller asked if he could see me so I invited him to my home. When he asked me to become a director I was honoured and delighted. General Accident was a local company and my father had been a director. When I joined, directors were not expected to make a major contribution at board meetings. We were given no papers beforehand and when we arrived there was one sheet of paper on the table giving the bare bones of the updated situation. He was close to two directors, Scott-Dempster and Hicks Beach, lawyers who had both joined the board in the late 1940s and with whom he did discuss matters.

Annual reports retained their brief format and the annual general meeting was routinely conducted in 20 minutes, an interruption to the proceedings from the floor being unusual. The most memorable departure from routine occurred when Francis's widow, Florence, embarrassed her stepson by standing up and berating him for the miserable pension he was paying her.

When Stanley took over from his father not much changed within the paternal, frugal company as Philip Rhodes found when he joined the recently opened Lincoln branch in 1953:

It was seen as a fairly staid industry in which nearly everybody started as a junior clerk and ostensibly had a job for life. Promotion was slow because it was thought you needed considerable knowledge and experience to assume responsibility and leadership. There was the promise of becoming a trainee inspector by 25 and a resident inspector by your mid-30s. Meanwhile you did the mundane jobs like handling the monthly renewals, for which you could get a 2s 6d tea and supper allowance for more than two hours after hours; filing; collecting the National Insurance stamps; and for me cycling four miles, the first mile uphill, to buy meat for the branch manager's dog and delivering it to his home. The branch manager was soberly dressed, as we had to be, and aloof. I was commended for being 'tidy of mind and neat in numbering the outside of filing boxes'. Style, especially in dealing with people, counted because the business revolved around the service you gave.

The emphasis was on the branch as a unit rather than the performance of individuals. Branches could boast of having the lowest expense ratio. In

As car ownership grew post-war, motor insurance continued to be a popular subject for advertising.

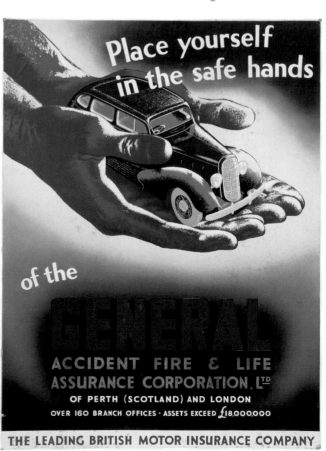

Place yourself in the safe hands

of the

GENERAL

ACCIDENT FIRE & LIFE ASSURANCE CORPORATION, L^{TD}
OF PERTH (SCOTLAND) AND LONDON
OVER 160 BRANCH OFFICES · ASSETS EXCEED £18,000,000

THE LEADING BRITISH MOTOR INSURANCE COMPANY

Mechanisation in the 1950s still meant labour-intensive operations. Here, in a prefabricated building, a group is preparing metal address plates. Computers, installed from the early 1960s, would get better offices.

1955 profit commission was abolished on the grounds that it was a group, not an individual, effort. Inspectors, whose figures were noted, continued to receive their production bonuses. They had to rely on the chance of being noticed within the hierarchy, the chief clerk assessing staff mentally if not formally. He could put in a good word when Leslie Nye, the agency manager from head office, visited. Ahead of the occasion staff muttered 'The Day is drawing Nye', knowing that the office would have to be cleaned and tidied to the point of cobwebs being removed ready for a military-style inspection. He was a stickler for presentation. In Dublin, for example, he went along with the branch manager's ruling that two-piece suits were only allowed if kept buttoned. Nye kept his own pithy notes in brown ink, for instance summing up one man as 'adenoidal and duodenal'.

Bill Hartley, who pointed out to Nye in his interview given to all ex-service staff that he had been getting tax-free army pay three times more than the General Accident salary subject to tax, was offered the position of motor and

accident superintendent in the Swansea branch at 11 a.m. and was ready to leave third class in a train at 2 p.m., with the cheapest-of-three removals to follow. He actually left three weeks later. When new salary scales came out, motor and accident superintendents were both Grade 3. As Bill was doing both jobs he argued that he deserved a salary increase, a view supported by his branch manager. Perth thought otherwise. A few weeks later, when he was writing a motor policy, he suggested a more efficient identification system for policies, which was adopted by head office. Within a matter of weeks he was invited to Perth for an interview with Sir Stanley, who spent most of the time admiring photos of Bill's son and discussing his development before offering him the number two job in the public liability department.

The largest branch was in London and there was an advantage in being there because Perth staff came down for insurance industry and other meetings that often led to chance encounters in the office, informal meetings at which quick decisions were made and people got to know one another. Personnel and salary systems, manually maintained like everything else at the time, were in operation but the reality of advancement was whether you were known or noticed.

A few graduates were beginning to be brought in annually as trainees. Tom Roberts, who on leaving Oxford decided against joining the Colonial Office administering a shrinking number of territories, joined Newcastle branch in 1953:

At first it was assimilation rather than training, reading policy binders and forms just as the branch manager, Sandy Doig, had done when he joined. I persuaded him to let me do a tour of departments to learn firsthand. So more by accident than design I got a thorough grounding over two years before going out on the road and getting oil on my hands. As an inspector I got to know the interface of the company, the agents and the public, which was indispensable.

Nelson Robertson, a future chief executive, joined the same branch as a graduate trainee five years later:

I also spent two years going round the departments learning something about the business before going to Sunderland sub-office as an assistant inspector. Going round the motor dealers I did benefit from the bonus system, a new business incentive, but although there was some monitoring from Perth of graduates' progress I was not really conscious of any career path or fast track personal development. There were graduates who were not prepared to make their way through the system and fell by the wayside.

They could well feel themselves a tiny minority without worthwhile prospects, sandwiched in an alien environment between old-style managers clinging to their authority and the mass of employees condemned to performing routine tasks. In an age of full employment and insurance not being the best paying of occupations graduates saw around them low quality staff doing low quality jobs. Manual systems were labour intensive and, not just in hindsight, inefficient. There was much retyping and keeping of records required only occasionally, often duplicating information that was held elsewhere. Head office, wanting to have its own set, would employ somebody to keep copies rather than spend money on calling a branch to settle a point. Share registration was in ledgers, with double entries and cross references of buyer/seller details from transfer forms. Rights and scrip issues in quick succession in 1957, 1959, 1961 and 1962 created a large volume of work, especially when rights were split between beneficiaries. With the company raising more capital for growth and institutions coming in as investors, the volume of share transfers increased tenfold. An index card was kept for each shareholder and separate ledgers for mandated dividends, one for each bank, and those to be paid directly on 1 June and 1 December.

In 1960 the company celebrated its 75th anniversary with a dinner-dance at Perth City Hall and an outing to the local theatre. Branches followed suit in local hotels, where they listened in unison at precisely 9 p.m. to a recorded exhortation by Sir Stanley. With the new decade the atmosphere began to change. The lighter mood of Swinging London penetrated the provinces, where people began to feel freer, less staid, more mobile. Jim Mahon, a solicitor experienced in claims, was invited to London and offered a job by Emil Savundra, who ran the cut-price insurer Fire, Auto and Marine. If he had taken it he would at least have doubled his salary and added perks such as a car. Not taking to his prospective employer, later publicly exposed by David Frost on television, Jim turned down the offer. Having had initial doubts about the quality of General Accident when he joined, he preferred the security of the company, which was starting to move, however slowly, with the times. Other employees resisted Savundra's blandishments.

When labour was comparatively cheap there had been little investment in mechanisation. Pencils, pen and ink were regarded as adequate. When biros came in they were issued individually, a new one only being taken from a locked drawer on proof that the existing biro could no longer write. As salary scales were raised, bringing them more into line with national levels, to offset

A commemorative cigarette box was engraved for a luncheon.

GENERAL ACCIDENT
FIRE AND LIFE ASSURANCE CORPORATION LIMITED
LUNCHEON
to mark
the 75th ANNIVERSARY
OF THE INCORPORATION OF THE COMPANY
GENERAL BUILDINGS, PERTH.
16TH DECEMBER, 1960

Margaret Cooper, who presented a bouquet to Sir Stanley's wife Grace at the company's 75th anniversary celebration said she was terrified, having been with the company only a fortnight. She was still there 39 years later.

higher pay, cost reductions were sought. Business efficiency had begun to improve in the 1950s with modest investment in labour-saving devices such as punched card machines (operators performing 20,000 key depressions an hour without repetitive strain injury), addressing and franking machines, hand-cranked desk calculators instead of pencil and paper, and better dictation equipment. In 1958 telex, first mooted in 1955, was installed in London and Perth. The first electric typewriter was provided on trial loan by Olivetti, then trying to break into the head office market.

These machines improved individual productivity but of all the changes in technology that would make the biggest difference to the company the most important was forming a data processing department and embarking on the use of computers. Manufacturers of what were still thought of as 'electronic brains' endowed with powers to revolutionise office life were selling grand concepts. In 1960 General Accident ordered an IBM 1401 with punched card input and magnetic tapes for storage of data. Needing staff to run it, the company recruited a chief programmer from an IBM user, Cheshire County Council, and carried out aptitude tests internally for support staff. Tony Luck in Aldwych accounts department was one of the six:

We went on a basic IBM course. In Perth I concentrated on one of the three areas, accounting and financial systems. The other two were motor and non-motor. It soon became apparent that the total demands were beyond the capacity of the

General Buildings were decorated to mark the Queen's visit to Perth in 1960. The event happened to coincide with the company's 75th anniversary year. Employees had a grandstand view of the visit.

machine so we had to double the size of the processor, add more tape drives and a line printer. Conversion of data from 74 branches, one at a time, was a big task. We were producing information that the company had not had before but, having been sold the idea of unlimited management information in a paperless office, management was expecting too much. Expectations were unreal.

Consultants, Urwick Diebold, were brought in – a sharp break with tradition. Until then the company had been very self-contained. Diebold was the US guru and the consultants brought a touch of realism: how could we get better value for our money and how could we get better systems?

Nelson Robertson, recommended by his branch manager and showing aptitude, was also one of the original six:

Macdonald, by then deputy chief general manager, saw the potential of a computer in handling tasks like payroll and renewals and creating a database. Unfortunately a Commercial Union author had published a paper in the journal of the Chartered Insurance Institute that was more theory than practice and we were expected to match the blue sky, which CU themselves did not reach. Our attitude was down to earth: what can we realistically do within the timescale which will be a base for future development? For my part it meant a lot of work on the systems side, business analysis, stressful in a nice way. You had to think it through for yourself because there was not much in the way of precedent.

Computer use was set to grow and with it the habit of people having to think for themselves. They could not wait for senior management to hand down approved tablets of thought because, beyond the broad objective, they had little grasp of the technicalities. The General Life, which to be closer to its main sources of business had moved back from Perth to London in 1956, soon followed its parent in installing a similar computer. Among other applications it may have been used for keeping monthly valuations on a consignment of whisky it held in the early 1960s as a security for a mortgage. During the 1960s General Accident made rapid progress in using IBM machines of increasing power.

Throughout the 20 years after the end of WW2 General Accident was progressing, adapting to the change from a sellers' to a buyers' market, business growing in line with social trends. More people were owning their homes, which had to be insured as a condition of mortgage, and equipping them with domestic appliances that raised the contents value. In a decade the number of private cars and vans more than doubled from the 2,307,000 registered in 1950, when petrol came off ration. Rationing after the Suez crisis, from 17 December 1956 to 14 May 1957, was too brief to stop the upward trend. Prices of small cars were falling in relation to earning power. Company cars, bought in fleets, were also becoming more common. In 1959, the year in which the £500 Mini was launched, weekend sightseers flocking to inspect the M1, the country's first motorway, were mass evidence of the increasing popularity of motoring. With the implementation of the 1963 Beeching report, closure of many railway branch lines boosted the road haulage industry.

As the major motor insurer, with rates undercutting the tariff offices and a higher commission to agents, the company benefited. Even in remote areas there were few garages that did not have a General Accident agency. Matching that network, the company had its own staff of motor engineers who examined and processed damage claims and prided itself on 'service that excels'. Exhibiting at the annual Motor Show helped to keep the company's name in front of the public and ensure a rising motor premium income. Although the royal warrant had been lost, the company continued to insure cars of the royal household and in 1948 issued a motor policy in the names of HRH The

By the early 1960s traffic by General Buildings in Aldwych had grown to a jam.

its nearest airport, Turnhouse. There was a growing opinion too that the airport facilities would have to be improved to make it worthy of the Scottish capital. Redevelopment was beyond the resources of its owner, the Corporation of Edinburgh, which in 1967 opened negotiations with the Board of Trade for a possible takeover.

In what were dubbed the Swinging Sixties the world around General Accident was changing faster than the company. To catch up, General Accident would have to take a great leap forward.

The most significant
General Accident
acquisition to date,
80 years after Francis Norie-Miller joined
the company, it marked the end of family
domination.

IN the 1950s the UK passed from the post-war Age of Austerity to the Age of Affluence, summed up by the Prime Minister, Harold Macmillan, in a 1957 speech on the financial situation as 'You've never had it so good.' That was true for consumers buying durable goods with rising wages and salaries but not for companies. By international standards British companies were not as productive as their competitors. Internal cost reduction programmes were by themselves not enough. A more effective way of becoming efficient and realising higher growth rates was to achieve the larger economies of scale, cutting out duplication of resources, through mergers and takeovers. In 1959, for example, the Alliance Assurance Company and Sun Insurance Office merged; so did the Northern Assurance Company and the Employers Liability Assurance Corporation, which did not make them invulnerable; Royal Exchange took over Atlas Assurance; Commercial Union the North British & Mercantile; and Norwich Union the Scottish Union. In 1961 Royal Insurance acquired the London & Lancashire with its subsidiaries, including Law, Union & Rock. The process was set to continue, for instance with Sun Alliance beating the Phoenix in the takeover of London Assurance in 1965, resulting in the emergence of a smaller number of composite offices. Each move relatively diminished General Accident.

Competition was sharpened by the emergence of brokers, large and small. Large ones could play off one company against another to secure the best terms for their clients. If they could not secure a better rate they argued for wider wording to broaden the cover. In the long run high street brokers, some of whom were quick to place their business with cut-price motor insurers, spelled the end of garages as the main source of General Accident's motor business.

There was a challenge too in life business, a growth area now that consumers could save more consistently and substantially. As well as existing life companies new ones were being formed to tap the expanding market for disposable income, the best known being Abbey Life, founded by Mark Weinberg from South Africa, and Investors Overseas Services, the brainchild of the American playboy-financier Bernie ('Do you sincerely want to be rich?') Cornfeld. They recognised a market and produced what the customer wanted. New savings products were being launched such as unit trusts linked to life assurance and there was a growing appeal of endowment mortgages promising a profit when the house was paid off.

Although General Accident had been in the life business since 1906 and in 1923 had acquired The English Insurance Company and in 1925 The General Life Assurance Company, it had never had a strong reputation in that field. The English, based in Croydon, had a profitable connection with Noble Lowndes on pensions but it was not a major force. The General Life was a conservative office, a follower by no means a leader, against the accident business a poor relation with a chequered history within General Accident. The few group pension schemes it had were small. Its priority was to reduce expenses, partly by moving out of Central London. Developing the company would have been slow and uncertain while competitors were pressing on. One suggestion was that General Accident should buy one of the Scottish life companies, thus strengthening its local roots. Jealous of its reputation, the company proceeded cannily.

Also bent on remaining independent was The Yorkshire. Following more mergers in the industry during the 1960s, even though it had taken over the Scottish Insurance Corporation it knew it did not have sufficient resources for further acquisitions that would change its status significantly. In fact it was eating into its reserves and its investment policy was conservative, with an emphasis on gilts rather than equities for a predictable return. Stock market rumours tipped it for takeover. Phoenix Assurance made an approach. Regarding itself as under attack, The Yorkshire response was to stall and talk to other companies, among them Guardian Assurance, considered to be a serious contender, Legal & General, Royal Exchange and General Accident. Phoenix thought it was in a strong position, indeed had a proprietary right to an association because Continental of the US, which had already bought the not so profitable American business of The Yorkshire, had a sizeable holding in Phoenix. Culturally, the two British companies were similar. Like The Yorkshire, founded in 1824, Phoenix was a tariff office, having been started in 1782 as a fire office by sugar refiners needing to cover the risks of their inflammable product. In contrast, General Accident was a non-tariff company below the salt. Preferring to describe itself as 'independent' and undeterred, it made a positive approach to The Yorkshire.

Robert Gudgeon, general manager of The Yorkshire, arranged a secret meeting at offices in Winchester House, London, where preliminary information was exchanged. The two companies were in many ways complementary and a merger made commercial logic. Both were provincial, having grown up in railway towns surrounded by agricultural areas that were a source of livestock business, with a base too in London. There, in the City, the General Accident account was only about a quarter the size of The Yorkshire account.

The Yorkshire, founded in 1824, conducted its business through agents, at first mainly in the North of Britain. Here is the agent's office in Market Street, Lancaster in 1860.

Whereas a greater part of the General Accident business was overseas, about half The Yorkshire business came from the UK and Ireland. General Accident had strong American interests; The Yorkshire none, but a sound foot in Brazil. It was also established in Australia, Canada with a company under its own name and the Canadian Pioneer, South Africa, Rhodesia, Denmark and, not very profitably, France, which might become important should the UK be allowed to join the European Economic Community.

The UK life portfolio, primarily from broker connections, accounted for a high proportion of The Yorkshire income, relatively small for General Accident. Redressing the balance, General Accident was strong in motor insurance, most of which came through agents. While general business was volatile, evident in the early 1960s, life business offered General Accident a stream of quality earnings. Their technology was compatible; both companies used IBM computers, though General Life was more advanced in adopting magnetic tape while The Yorkshire was still using punched cards. Culturally too, on the definition of 'a Yorkshireman as a Scot who has lost his sense of generosity', they could be said to have an affinity, though The Yorkshire staff were naturally apprehensive about their career prospects while General Accident people saw opportunities in an enlarged company. Later some on the General Accident side regarded The Yorkshire folk as greater globe-trotters round a smaller empire while being all too ready to offer advice on how to run the General Accident business. There was one conflict of interest in that both companies

Livestock was one of the main Yorkshire lines. This was a stand at an agricultural show in 1931.

had Schroder Wagg as financial advisers. The Yorkshire opted to move to Kleinwort Benson.

There were also important differences between the two companies. General Accident was centralised; there was no question that it was run from Perth but its chief general manager, Macdonald, was not a prisoner of the long-standing bureaucracy. Indeed, he was slowly changing it. An investment man who had been brought into insurance, he had a broader view, clearly seeing a business opportunity. On the other hand The Yorkshire was decentralised to the point of weakness, having two head offices and two general managers, one in London and one in York, with functions split between them. It had lost its chief actuary, Shaljean, who saw beyond mortality tables to management issues but realised he would not get the top job enabling him to put his ideas into practice. In the opinion of some colleagues he was the one man who, had he stayed, might have changed the course of events.

On 5 September 1967, the day before it had agreed to let Phoenix know its reaction, after the Stock Exchange closed The Yorkshire informed Phoenix that it would not enter into a voluntary association with it. On 6 September, The Yorkshire and General Accident issued a joint press statement:

The Yorkshire produced much of its print in-house. As befits an insurance company, the electrically driven guillotine was well guarded.

> *Following an initial approach by General Accident in March and an examination of the benefits to be obtained from a joint operation of their businesses they have decided to recommend to their respective stockholders and shareholders that The Yorkshire should become a member of the General Accident group of companies.*

Valuing each Yorkshire share at £3 3s 2d General Accident offered in cash and loan stock a total of £27.6 million. Phoenix countered with a bid of £3 14s in cash and shares, which General Accident just outbid, causing Phoenix to raise its offer to £4 1s 5d. Keen to pursue the opportunity but going through what one member described as 'a pretty fraught time', the General Accident board was prepared to raise its offer without securing its chairman's agreement. Wiser counsel prevailed. Keeping a low profile, the General Accident chief general manager and Lord Airlie, a director of Schroder, the merchant bank advising General Accident, took separate flights, one from Glasgow and the other from London, to Philadelphia where the chairman was on an extended visit.

Staff at work in the
Yorkshire head office at
St Helen's in York.

Lord Airlie well knew that the board had charged them with an important and delicate task:

> The purpose of our joint visit to Philadelphia was to use our best endeavours to persuade Sir Stanley that this acquisition was in the best interest of the General Accident shareholders. We were already aware that he was not in favour of this proposal and, if we failed to persuade him of the advantages, that we would be left with no alternative but to inform hin that this was a board decision and he was no longer in a position to veto it.
>
> At around 8.30 a.m. Macdonald and I entered Sir Stanley's suite in the Barclay Hotel, where we found him having breakfast. He looked up with feigned surprise and asked what we were doing there. He knew of course perfectly well but this was an encouraging start to our discussion! In the event we failed to persuade Sir Stanley of the advantages of this acquisition and he particularly objected to the price, which he thought was far too high. It then fell to me to tell him that the board had decided to go ahead despite his reservations, which he accepted with good grace. We then departed for luncheon, at the end of which I asked whether I could have a cigar. 'Certainly not,' he replied. 'We can't possibly afford that.' We had just spent several million pounds. The whole incident was a turning point. We all realised that it was no longer a family company but one subject to external pressures.

The Yorkshire had a strong local presence in Australia. For example, in the Hunter Valley town of Singleton, New South Wales, Chapman's Newsagency represented the company continuously for 50 years from 1918.

General Accident went to £4 9s 9d, which edged up to £4 10s against the Phoenix's eventual £4 12s 7d. At the climax on 2 November The Yorkshire chairman, Sir Richard Graham, summed up the respective cases for his shareholders, stressing that the differences in the offers in capital values, which fluctuate with share prices, were small enough to be ignored and that what mattered were the long-term values of their investments. Among other things he pointed out:

> Because of the solid strength and profitability of General Accident and the splendid record of growth and income which its shares have shown, the long-term advantages lie unquestionably with an association of General Accident and Yorkshire. The future dividend cover for General Accident shares is markedly better than the cover for the Phoenix dividend.

Life Assurance is highly competitive. Administrative efficiency is, therefore, important and as an example, a well-known insurance publication, Stone & Cox, shows the 1966 expense ratios, calculated on renewal premiums, as follows:-

Yorkshire	*6.13%*
General Life	*8.26%*
Phoenix	*10.13%*

It is clear, therefore, that a link with General Accident is to be preferred.

The performance of General Accident in the past five years is much the better of the two. These figures bear repeating: after crediting investment income and after payment of dividends, General Accident showed a surplus in that period of £5,160,000, whereas Phoenix showed a deficiency of £2,321,000.

Phoenix business in the USA has in the past been a serious source of loss. Under the new arrangements announced in conjunction with their bid, its success or otherwise in the future will depend upon the control by Continental of the common underwriting pool. It is valid to point out that over the past years Continental has made heavy losses on underwriting in the USA and last year (1966) they made an underwriting loss of $6,000,000, whereas General Accident made an underwriting profit of $4,400,000 in the USA.

Although the Phoenix bid was higher, offering a greater benefit immediately, General Accident won with over 50 per cent of The Yorkshire equity in a £41 million bid. A small number of The Yorkshire shareholders held out and were eventually bought out in a scheme of arrangement.

To Desmond Bean on the financial side of The Yorkshire it was not primarily a money matter: 'It was a people decision. Macdonald was the dominant figure.' The Yorkshire board thought that, although General Accident was the underbidder, their company would be better off in his hands. He was a good businessman, entrepreneurial, personable. The takeover was a personal triumph, but he was not one to gloat. To Lord Airlie the event had other aspects:

The deal established a firmer link between General Accident and Schroder, which for the duration of the transaction became involved almost daily. I felt I was getting to know General Accident in greater depth as well as bridging the cultures of the City of London and Perth. It was also the first occasion when the board made its presence felt as it hadn't done before. It showed its mettle. Hitherto, the board had been dominated by Sir Stanley, who sat in a chair with a cushion higher than anybody else and looked down slightly on the directors with a piercing eye, which tended to inhibit debate. Discussion was general rather than specific and he took the minutes.

The most significant General Accident acquisition to date, 80 years after Francis Norie-Miller joined the company, it marked the end of family domination. In place of the autocrat to which the board and staff had deferred there would develop a collective management with the board intervening at crucial moments. Until now change had been piecemeal, what little Sir Stanley could be induced to accept. That it would accelerate, as he was without heir, there had been no doubt. It had to wait until he reached 80, the age for retirement from the board under the articles of association as amended in 1947. A decent interval of a few months elapsed before Sir Stanley formally resigned as chairman and director on 10 April 1968, almost four months before his 80th birthday, handing over to the deputy chairman, Lord Polwarth, and like his father before him taking the title of governor. It was a satisfaction to Polwarth to whom in the words of another director 'Sir Stanley had given stick for going on and on with the bid'.

Publicly, at the last annual general meeting over which he would preside as chairman, Stanley acknowledged the reality of the situation:

> ...what has been a memorable year in which the acquisition of The Yorkshire takes pride of place as the most outstanding achievement in the history of the General Accident...The year has placed a very heavy load of work and responsibility on Mr Macdonald, our Chief General Manager, his colleagues on the Executive, and our Managers and Staffs throughout the world...I deeply regret that with the passing of the years I shall no longer be a member of the team. I look back with pride and satisfaction at the achievements of that team during my 49 years as a participant, and am more grateful than I can express for the friendships and loyalty which I have received from my colleagues throughout our worldwide organisation. I am indeed honoured that the Directors should have appointed me Governor in succession to my father, who laid the solid foundations upon which the Corporation has flourished exceedingly.

The Yorkshire identified itself with the twin towers of York Minster.

The change was not before time nor was it sudden. Simple certainties with which the family had grown up and prospered were increasingly no more. The company was operating in a post-imperial, post-paternal era, in a more complex, shifting business environment. Wisdom could no longer reside in a single head.

Inevitably the company culture would change with the passing of paternalism and the integration of The Yorkshire staff, the first outside group to penetrate the Perth fastness and looked upon as incomers. Integration at home and overseas took about a year. Macdonald had given a pledge that nobody in the acquired company would be worse off and he took trouble to fit people into the right jobs, which some General Accident staff regarded as favouritism. On The Yorkshire side it was seen as maintaining the confidence of the staff who decided to stay with General Accident and who, while prepared to accept the not particularly generous relocation expenses and move say from York to Perth, could have felt very much the junior partners. To them it was not so much captive Greece leading conquering Rome as a civilising influence from which everybody benefited. For instance the starting and finishing bells to which General Accident headquarters staff had been regimented disappeared. Desmond Bean, who moved from London to Perth to become responsible for overseas accounting to the chief accountant, Buchan Marshall, was told by the assistant company secretary Bill Hartley that 'Mr Macdonald does not like private correspondence'. Desmond pointed out that the two private letters he had received were from former colleagues wishing him well in his new assignment. In time the practice of all correspondence being addressed to the company and being seen by the general manager also disappeared, a change seen by Nigel Lister in another General Accident subsidiary, Road Transport & General:

The Yorkshire was more decentralised, more innovative. It had more senior level people, managers not processing, technician types. These people brought a different philosophy, style and culture to the business. They were managers who could change things.

For its part, General Accident became more outward-looking, taking a greater interest in industry affairs and what went on in London. A priority there was to convince brokers through a series of seminars, especially in the City, that the combined companies were able to handle the capacity that the market had to offer. Going to London was an unsettling experience for one Perth executive, who felt guilty at the extravagance of a hotel room with a bath being booked for him. Apologising when presenting his expenses, he was told that he was entitled as he would have had a bath at home. In continuing thrift the London office was moved from the older General Accident building in Aldwych to Becket House in Cheapside, rented by The Yorkshire since 1959 on a 42-year lease from the Mercers' Company at a fixed rent of £1 per square foot. It had the advantage of being near the heart of the City and the headquarters of the British Insurance Association, of which Macdonald became chairman in 1973–5, the first man from a non-tariff background to do so. He encouraged senior staff to be more outward-looking, taking a more positive rôle on industry committees. Charles Heath became the first non-tariff chairman of the Accident Offices Association and in just over 20 years the company provided three presidents of the Chartered Insurance Institute: David Blaikie (1975–6), Tom Roberts (1981–2) and Philip Rhodes (1996–7).

Jason Frangoulis was active in European discussions on competition and regulations. In his view The Yorkshire gave General Accident a new perspective on the world:

> When I joined General Accident in 1954 it was fairly Anglo-Saxon in its mentality. Europe wasn't important. The Yorkshire was influential in getting General Accident to widen its horizons, particularly with interests in Europe. Macdonald was able to build on this in a short space of time.

In Canada the addition of The Yorkshire raised premium income by more than 50 per cent to $30 million a year.

The fact that, against the opposition of a tariff company, a non-tariff company had taken over a tariff company was another indication that the days of the tariff were numbered. Historically it was a relic of Empire, developed when trade followed the flag but communications were slower. Its justification was that, in the interests of order across far-flung territories, staff on the spot needed it as a stable base on which to conduct business. With the granting of colonial independence, the 1960s were the decade of the end of Empire and in the UK consumer pressure on prices had made itself felt. Resale price maintenance had been abolished in 1964 and there were increasing political pressures on price-fixing among producers as not being in the public interest.

The tariff associations were largely rating bodies, setting minimum rates below which members could not charge. General Accident, which could usually undercut and had not been considered one of the élite, was now having a greater influence in the formation of industry policy. Tariffs for various classes of insurance would cease gradually. The motor tariff was undermined by a few specialist insurers that mushroomed in the 1960s, taking business with very competitive premiums. Although there were spectacular failures, notably of Fire, Auto and Marine in 1966, tariff companies were forced to reduce their rates to the point where the motor tariff ended in 1969. The Yorkshire adhered to the fire tariff in the transition period after it had been taken over and appeared on the same schedule, arranged by the Fire Offices Committee, as

The Yorkshire logo, incorporating York Minster, continued after the merger with General Accident, when the combined life company was known as Yorkshire-General.

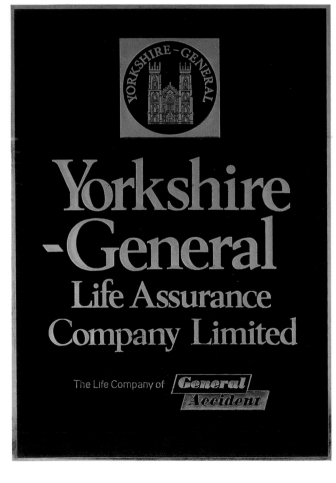

its parent. Typically the fire risk on a schedule was shared 65/35 in favour of the tariff companies, the non-tariff companies being asked to provide cover at a lower rate but with a higher commission.

As for The Yorkshire, it immediately created more work in General Accident's share registration department, adding up to 10,000 shareholders to the existing 35,000. It also brought a policy shift for investment secretary Alan Begg, who had taken over the responsibility in 1963:

General Accident invested in bonds, debentures and equities. The only property we invested in was our own offices, which we preferred to own rather than lease, so we had a premises but not a property department. As a life company, to which the income stream was important, The Yorkshire had a substantial property portfolio, owned shares in property companies and had some good connections. After the takeover only two of The Yorkshire investment staff transferred, neither of whom was a property man so we had to build a department from scratch. Our initial investments were in offices in good locations, for which there was an on-going demand, and then shops in similar settings.

For the first few years The Yorkshire, which had been regarded as a strategic acquisition, was not a brilliant business buy. General Accident shares underperformed peer companies for a period thereafter, indicating that the market and investors believed the company had overpaid, not unusual for something that one really wants. General Accident held on to nearly all of what it had bought, which included a specialised engineering inspection company, Scottish Boiler & General Insurance, founded in 1881. It disposed of a small reinsurance company it did not want to a Swiss-led European consortium. Livestock business increased, the combined company exhibiting at the Great Yorkshire and Royal Highland agricultural shows and doing well in the bloodstock line.

In Ireland, where there had been an excess of claims on the imprecise risk of infertility, livestock underwriting ceased. After a mass of small claims with relatively high administration costs and arguments with travel agents, travel insurance also finished. General Accident had debated whether to withdraw from Ireland altogether. It stayed because of the connection principally with the Irish Permanent Building Society, a growing source of new business, and through the merger with The Yorkshire, which had been allied with the Commercial Insurance Company of Ireland since 1922. Dublin, which until 1951 had had all its policies written in Perth on evidence the branch supplied, gained. It ceased to be part of the UK branch network, getting overseas status and becoming the head office for Ireland.

The other main post-merger argument was that, being largely a non-life company, General Accident had to understand what it had bought. A unit trust, GandA, was launched in 1969 but the company was not a major player in this growing form of investment. In the same year it merged The General Life with The Yorkshire, giving the combined company in York the compromise title of Yorkshire General Life Assurance Company, inserting a hyphen between the first two names in 1970 when the court process of merging the two life funds was complete. Soon afterwards the company launched a whole life endowment bonus that was too generous in its longer terms and, had it been allowed to stay on the market, would have seriously eroded life fund profits. It was quickly withdrawn. Learning what life in a new era was about would take a while, in the event a decade.

The middle years of the
century were the period
of the company's greatest
geographical extent.

AS the arsenal for democracy the US prospered in WW2 and its economy achieved more than under the New Deal of the 1930s. Defence industries grew up on a large scale in the continental US, untouched by enemy action. Making ships, planes, tanks and ammunition brought full employment with growth in average annual earnings outstripping price increases. California, for instance, became the veritable Golden State.

John H. Grady, assistant US manager since 1935, who succeeded Fred Richardson as General Accident's US attorney in 1938, was thus able to maintain within wartime limitations the momentum of a profitable branch. In 1943 it introduced a staff pension plan. There were adverse wartime effects such as a drop in investment income 1941–2 and in premium income 1943–4, when the war effort was at its peak, but the parent company was pleased with the US situation. At the annual general meeting in 1945, the chairman, Fred Richardson, said:

We have been able to bring into the Accounts an item of Profit on Exchange amounting to £197,298, mostly derived from United States remittances…We welcome the conclusion of a Treaty of Double Taxation with the United States. We have very large funds in the United States, and as is customary these have been translated into sterling at the pre-war rate of exchange. Therefore as long as the prevailing rate continues to favour the dollar there will be an element of potential profit on exchange.

When sterling was devalued from $4.03 to $2.80 in September 1949, the gain was over 30 per cent.

General Accident was well placed to benefit from the post-war boom. Workers had become consumers and there was a pent-up demand, increased by

Cartoons were used in 1940s advertisements by General Accident and its sister company The Potomac.

the rising birth rate, for houses and consumer goods, including automobiles, production of which was resumed. In New York State, where the company had its biggest slice of business, it enjoyed almost a six per cent advantage in auto rates over its competitors and did well. American aid for the reconstruction of Europe and Japan involved considerable expenditure in the home economy. Defence was still a national priority in the Cold War, even more important when the Korean War broke out in 1950, and weapons industries were sited in California and the Sun Belt, attracting further investment. Well established in the densely populated North East, on the Eastern seaboard, in California and Texas, and working through a network of loyal main street agents who knew their local communities and what to expect from the company, General Accident picked up more business in these states. Illinois and Iowa were states of slow growth.

At $121,832,257.32, net premiums for the three years 1948–50 were 48.37 per cent over the premium total for the preceding three years 1945–7. With more than half of its business in automobile, the company was primarily an automobile and property damage underwriter. In 1950 it issued its first policy covering fire insurance on an automobile. Workmen's compensation and liability accounted for more than a quarter of the business, accident and health about five per cent and a similar volume for burglary and theft. About one sixth of gross premiums came in re-insurance, mainly from The Potomac, over half being for automobile physical damage and one third for fire and extended cover.

As insurance was not a matter of inter-state commerce, rates were regulated by individual states. Each state had its rating bureau and rates recommended by the major trade association were filed with the state regulator. These still allowed companies flexibility in the actual rates they charged. Where possible General Accident deviated from bureau rates, which alone were not enough for success. The successful formula was combining competitive rates with conservative underwriting. As Tom Brett, later branch manager of Harrisburg, the Pennsylvania state capital, put it: 'Take the top 50 per cent of what you think's good and you'll make money.'

In 1949 General Accident had been in the US for 50 years. Welcoming John Grady to the annual general meeting in Perth, the chairman, R.G. Simpson, reviewed the accomplishments:

The trio most concerned with the USA: (left to right) Stanley Norie-Miller, who enjoyed visiting Philadelphia; Fred Richardson, who had made the US branch profitable; his successor, John Grady, US attorney 1938–51.

The original Deposits and subsequent remittances from the United Kingdom amounted to $5,300,000. Since then remittances received from USA down to the end of our financial year [31 December 1948] amounted to $21,500.000. Our annual premium income is approximately $40,000,000. We have an Investment Portfolio of $60,000,000 and at the end of last year a Surplus of over $23,000,000. These are impressive figures both from the immediate point of view of our Corporation and of our National Finances.

In 1950, to keep pace with expansion, General Accident bought the eight-storey Independence Building at the corner of Fifth and Walnut Streets for $817,720. Retiring in 1951, John Grady could look back on a good record, a worthy succession to Fred Richardson. For his last few months Grady had joint general managers understudying him: another Bostonian, Ed Moynahan, and William Bernhard, who like Grady had been manager of the premier branch, New York. Bernhard had been with General Accident for 34 years while Moynahan had joined The Potomac as recently as 1947, rapidly working his way up to executive vice-president. When in 1949 Moynahan became assistant manager for General Accident he linked the administration of the two companies at executive level. It was a smart move that gave him a lead over his rival because soon afterwards property and casualty business, which hitherto had to

Ed Moynahan, after Fred Richardson the longest serving US attorney. Taking over in 1951, he formally retired in 1972 but his presence was felt for another five years.

be handled by separate companies, could be written as a multiple line within one organisation.

Moynahan became the general attorney, a title he regarded as giving him more power than the average chief executive because he had no board, at least locally, to contend with. Given the character of the man, his appointment was an inherent contradiction, a Boston Irish Catholic running what was regarded from Philadelphia as the offshoot of a Scottish Presbyterian company. His policy was control, playing the American or Scottish card as suited. A health-conscious former football player and salesman, he kept himself in trim for business, got impatient with people late for appointments, dressed down subordinates in front of others, and lectured staff on the necessity of keeping down costs. Performance reports were on his desk quarterly. Correspondence to and from Perth went through him. If a telex was more than 20–30 words he thought it would give the Scots the impression the US was spending money. He decided how much information he would give head office and when, perhaps saving a report until Sir Stanley came over on what became more a social than a business visit or until he and his wife made a month's sea trip to Europe, during which he would visit London and Perth. In turn his own branches, which dubbed his executive 'the twelve apostles', held back information from him if they could.

Taking the line that the company was a guest in the US yet had to survive, he kept a low public profile but went for growth. Organically, the operation grew with the introduction of new policies such as in 1953 the homeowners' comprehensive package with a no claim bonus of a free sixth year's cover. This cover had been offered by the company in the UK since 1908. From 1960 a multi-peril policy provided under one contract broad coverage at a lower cost than for individual policies. To compete with direct writers of auto insurance, who offered rates and payment plans attracting the growing blue collar class, General Accident formed in 1955 a new company, Pennsylvania General. For growth in property insurance Camden Fire just across the Delaware River in New Jersey was bought in 1963. Philadelphia was ahead of Perth in computing, installing in 1956 a Univac 650 for handling the general accounts. It was also ahead of Perth in forming in 1953 a Quarter Century Club for employees with that length of service.

What Moynahan could not control was the level of claims. In his first year as general attorney there was a General Accident underwriting loss of over a million dollars, the first loss since 1925. Nor was it an isolated incident. General Accident was to report underwriting losses for the years 1956–9, during which having failed to secure rate increases it economised by consolidating many claims sub-offices; 1963–5 when there was a substantial deterioration in the

automobile account and hurricanes like Betsy did not help; 1969, the year in which a claim was paid on Teddy Kennedy's car going off a narrow bridge on Chappaquiddick Island, Massachusetts, causing Mary Jo Kopechne to drown; and 1974–7. The Potomac incurred losses in 1941, 1944–6, 1951, 1956–60, 1962–5, 1969, 1974–7; Pennsylvania General in 1955–9, 1963–5, 1969, 1975–7; and Camden Fire 1963–4, 1969, 1974–7. In short, there were some bad periods, with an amalgam of causes.

A patent one was financial. When John F. Kennedy said in his 1961 inaugural address:

Let every nation know, whether it wishes us well or ill, that we shall pay any price, bear any burden, meet any hardship, support any friend, oppose any foe, in order to assure the survival and the success of liberty.

he was announcing a formula for galloping inflation. Fulfilling the rôle of world policeman while remaining an affluent society at home was beyond the capability of even the American economy. Cost of the Vietnam War (1965–73), with its major commitment of resources, was of the order of $150 billion. In 1971 the balance of trade went into deficit for the first time since the nineteenth century. The dollar was devalued in August by being allowed to float against other currencies, the end of fixed exchange rates reducing in terms of sterling the amounts remitted to the UK.

In December 1973 the fourfold increase in the price of imported oil raised inflation within months to over 12 per cent. Gasoline shortage did lead to the introduction of lower speed limits, which in turn reduced the frequency and severity of accidents but it was a comparatively minor credit. Rates inevitably lagged behind increasing costs of, for instance, auto repairs and hospital treatment, and in economic hardship not only the bankrupt and the unemployed tried to win something from insurance companies. Getting rate increases meant presenting facts and figures to insurance department hearings state by state. For instance, in New York State, General Accident was the first to get rates raised for uninsured motorists coverage, under which an insured driver could extend his cover so that he could claim in the event of being hit by an uninsured driver. Such drivers' liability was covered by compulsory pool insurance, of which General Accident had to accept its share.

An outstanding example of the effects of inflation was the case of Thomas Roby, a jockey on whom a binder, a cover note, was written on a Friday afternoon in 1942. The next day he fell off his horse and was taken into the Mary Immaculate Hospital, Jamaica, New York, where the daily room rate was about $7, the amount of his initial premium. In a foetal position with his thighs hyperflexed against his abdomen, fed through tubes, completely incontinent and wearing a diaper, unable to communicate with anybody, Roby spent his time watching horse races on TV and needing the attention of three shifts of nurses. By 1958, when compensation and hospital costs had totalled $260,153.49 and because of the increased cost of nursing and medical care were running at some $25,000 a year, a report stated 'Unfortunately the prognosis is bad for restoration of functions, relatively good for preservation of life'. By the time Roby died, in the late 1960s, his room rate had risen to $33,000 a year. Fortunately for General Accident, it had reinsured the risk, which did entail special book-keeping. Following the Roby case no General Accident office in the US was permitted to write a policy involving horses.

The social map had been changing. Automobiles produced in ever increasing numbers led to more frequent and severe accidents. They also encouraged the development of affluent suburbs. Deserted city centres became rundown, places where an insurance inspector could be taken for a plain clothes cop. Insurance companies could avoid writing business there but not all areas with an above-average risk could be eliminated. Smart operators bought abandoned industrial premises, insured them, had them put to the torch and claimed high replacement costs. Insurers could never be sure when an urban riot with arson and looting might be sparked off, as for example after the shooting of the black civil rights leader Martin Luther King in 1968. General Accident itself was an ethnically integrated company, on one occasion experiencing difficulty in holding its annual outing at a country club.

Consumerism was a challenge to insurance companies. Activists challenged the basic concept of occupational underwriting, arguing that treating everybody in a group as the same risk discriminated against individuals within the group who had a good track record. Since the technology existed for distinguishing good risks from bad, insurance companies had no excuse for penalising people for their occupations. Aided by lawyers, benefiting either from a single fee or a continuing percentage, consumers were more ready to assert their rights, especially in matters of accident and personal injury, which might be mental as well as physical. Going to law became something of a national sport. Where their fees depended upon the level of the award lawyers had a vested interest in achieving higher compensation, to be paid promptly. In Pennsylvania, where the lawyer could get 20 per cent of the benefit for the claimant's lifetime, he did not want a client in failing health.

'If but for', in whatever circumstances, was often a catch-all phrase in determining the entitlement to and level of compensation. For instance, a New Jersey widow brought a dependant's benefit claim against the Ford Motor Company because her husband, who lifted boxes all day, had a heart attack. She

won her case and New York and Pennsylvania soon followed the lead of New Jersey in recognising other heart cases. Levels of compensation varied by state and the trend over time was upwards, total disability originally being paid for, say, a limit of 500 weeks becoming a lifetime benefit. Insurance companies, cast in the rôle of corporations with bottomless pockets bearing down on hapless individuals, had to weigh up whether it was worth going to court on a point of principle or cheaper to settle. Either way it was going to cost them. State by state extension of No Fault legislation reduced auto premium rates and mandated returns of premium on unexpired risks.

Underwriting losses had two effects on General Accident. Moynahan, who had majored in banking and money and taught his four children investment, concentrated his attention on that side of the account. Investment income could more than compensate for underwriting losses, even a run of losses. Although there were two men in the investment department under him, Moynahan made the decisions. As Charlie Niles, who joined General Accident as an assistant actuary in 1960, put it:

Moynahan fell in love with the theory of compound interest. In percentage terms he held more money in stocks than any other insurance company. At one point, when he was sitting on a paper loss of something like $100 million, he held on to the stocks until they recovered. Under him General Accident became an investment company rather than an insurance company. He did well on investments.

The portfolio, blue chip stocks held for the long term, was held on computer.

Pressure of social trends and underwriting losses meant that insurance companies in their own interest had to become more professional. From the early 1960s life became a little less social and a bit more practical. Whereas offices had been used to settling simple 'fender bender' claims over the phone, with rising compensation being sought, they now had to sense where something was wrong. While keeping to its slogan of 'Service that excels' General Accident could not afford to be Generous Accident. Had the claimant really been disabled by the whiplash injury? Did the suspicious back injury merit investigation, perhaps using undercover surveillance? Paul Bass, who specialised in workmen's compensation, wrote a booklet illustrated by a man with dollar signs in his eyes saying 'Oh that compensating back, oh that compensating buck!' Was everything stolen in the burglary brand new, the best that money could buy or genuinely a gift from somebody now deceased and without a receipt? Doctors' offices were not above 'confusing cases' and 'making arithmetical errors'.

Professional liability insurance was becoming less profitable and General

Facing page
When this South American advertisement, in colour, was sent to head office for approval it was immediately quashed. In this surviving black and white version it is not clear what the promotion was in aid of.

Accident withdrew from sectors as bad experience became evident. When auditors failed to detect corruption or impending bankruptcy, causing customers to lose money, it was time to cease covering accountants. Similarly, building faults were the responsibility of architects. The National Rifle Association had too many injuries and deaths from the improper use of firearms, the Professional Golfing Association incidents of errant balls blinding people. In addition long-tail claims on asbestos and some pharmaceutical products, for example an anti-abortion prescription for pregnant women that was later linked to genital cancers, were beginning to emerge, gathering in number to become class actions.

In spite of all the problems, Moynahan with his investment returns was running a financially successful operation, but it did not have the status to match his achievement. Over the border in Canada General Accident had long existed in the form of companies whereas in the US it was a mere branch. Moynahan, who had gathered round him an advisory committee of senior internal staff and prominent outsiders whom he could use as a stalking horse, wanted to head a domestic company. It would be the first step in the creation of a holding company structure being adopted by other insurance groups. At the end of 1968 Moynahan told his advisory committee:

> *The stumbling block is in the United Kingdom where the governmental authorities are holding to the position that a transfer of assets from the Branch to a domestic company would be held as a sale from one to the other at the current market value with a resultant capital gains tax on the difference between cost and market values.*

Total tax for the General Accident branch and its subsidiaries would be $63,832,696, entirely a UK obligation. As a payment of such magnitude was out of the question the advisory committee instructed Moynahan to communicate with the chief general manager, Macdonald:

> *urging that every possible effort be made to persuade the UK authorities that the change to a holding company concept was being 'forced' on the General Accident in the United States and an exception should be made to the general rule. It should be emphasised to the UK authorities that the General Accident Group, historically successful in the United States, is now operating under a serious handicap and its most satisfactory rate of growth will be slowed down unless the General Accident, like its forward-thinking competitors, is organised to provide a full range of financial services to the public.*

In 1970, when it looked as if the stumbling block might be overcome, the General Accident Insurance Company (New York) was registered as the first step to

Stanley Norie-Miller liked the relaxed luxury of ocean liners for long-distance travel but in the 1950s aircraft were beginning to compete. From September 1950 to January 1951 he and his wife took a world tour, the most extensive overseas visit in the corporation's history. It took in the USA, Canada, Australia, New Zealand, Singapore, India and Egypt. Here they are at Vancouver, ready for flights via Honolulu and Fiji to Sydney.

domestication, but the company was never licensed for business and at the end of 1973 was liquidated. Domestication would have to wait for almost a decade.

Moynahan's original request came at an inopportune time for the parent company, which hitherto had benefited by keeping so much of its liquidity in dollars. It had gained from the 1967 14.3 per cent devaluation of sterling from $2.80 to $2.40. However, the parent company suffered a 'deterioration in experience during the latter part of 1968 and the early months of 1969' placing 'a considerable strain on liquid resources'. A rights issue was considered. An alternative was to borrow up to $20 million from the US branch in addition to receiving annual remittances of $5.5 million. Lord Airlie and the general manager had

Stanley (second from left) in happi-coat for a Japanese dinner in Honolulu.

branch opened in 1966 as a showpiece, to attract business from large brokers. It was a recognition that Toronto, the Canadian headquarters of General Accident from its inception, had overtaken Montreal in the 1960s as Canada's premier financial city. Montreal had lost its status through extremist actions of the Quebec separatist movement, most evident in the nationalist riots of 1964, with fears of worse to come. Confirmation of the change came with the opening of General Accident's Ontario branch in 1967, the year that General de Gaulle exclaimed from the balcony of Montreal city hall *'Vive le Quebec libre!'* It was also the year that The Yorkshire, which had its local head office in Montreal, was acquired by General Accident. Integration was centred on Toronto.

The combined resources of The Yorkshire and General Accident, writing about $12 and $18 million respectively, appealed to large brokers offering business with premiums exceeding $1 million. Sizeable commercial business was a growth area when, as in the US, there was increased pressure on personal lines from direct writers, regarded at first as a fad that would not last. Consumerism, state involvement and fraud all added pressures. Consumerism affected the company directly through its participation in a compulsory pool for auto insurance. State involvement narrowed opportunities, as in British Columbia, where under National Democratic Party rule motor business was taken in March 1974 from the private insurance market. Greater fraud was a challenge, for example causing an inspector in the London, Ontario, branch to get a police permit to carry a gun when confronting a threatening claimant who had buried a 'stolen' truck with a bulldozer.

There was more money to be made from the corporate risks division carefully assessing organisations such as Imperial Oil for its ground, not down-hole, operations and municipalities of the size of London and Windsor than in increasingly competitive personal business. Canadian subsidiaries in the US could also be catered for, at least some of the reinsurance being taken up by Philadelphia. To make up some of the income lost by motor business going to the government in British Columbia, the company took over the non-motor portfolios of Perth Mutual and Economical Mutual in that state. In the East it acquired the loss-making fire, auto and casualty business of Norwich Union, which concluded that the expense of maintaining branch operations hundreds of miles apart was no longer worthwhile. By the end of 1974, when a future general manager, Howie Moran, joined General Accident it had what he described as 'a nice commercial book of business'. He made the move because he was not progressing as claims manager

Serious motor accidents can be caused by simple mishaps like a driver sneezing. Here in Brisbane, capital of Queensland, the driver was attacked by a wasp. Brushing it away from under his hat, he temporarily lost control of the car, which veered to the left, jumped the kerb and crashed head on into a weeping fig-tree. Swerving to avoid a kangaroo is commonly claimed to be the cause of an accident in Australia.

of a mutual casualty company with a similar premium income of about $40 million. What he found in General Accident was that its administration had not been able to keep up with its growth.

Whereas Canada was run by Canadians, Australia was not regarded as a mature territory, having a succession of expatriate managers. Harry Johnson, who succeeded Doig in 1938, by which time the branch had become profitable, was able to capitalise on his predecessor's groundwork. Notwithstanding staff shortages during WW2, loss of motor income, bushfire losses and heavier taxation, he was able to make a profit, improve the administration and give greater help to the branches, particularly with instructional material. From the late 1940s business noticeably picked up. With assisted passages ('Australia for £10') the government encouraged the immigration of skilled workers to develop the economy, wool prices rose, Commercial Union was ready to accept reinsurance from a non-tariff company, and General Accident introduced a business traders' policy

The Adelaide, South Australia, office put out the flags for the Queen's visit in 1954.

Floods in the wake of Cyclone Wanda caused widespread damage in 1974. Some 20 inches of rain fell in 24 hours. Among buildings affected was the company's Brisbane office.

covering seven risks with a discount for the package. Claims under Johnson's regime were carefully scrutinised. For example, after the Adelaide earthquake of 1954 a distinction was made between old, dusty cracks and new ones, against which there could be a legitimate claim.

Johnson's successor in 1958 was Charles Belton, a dour Scot, who in the traditional way had come out by sea. By then local industries, including wool textiles, were beginning to feel the effects of Japanese competition. There was compensation in the early 1960s when the development of mineral resources in Western Australia stimulated other industries. During 1962 the presence of the Commonwealth Games in Perth, Western Australia, gave it international prominence to the extent that for more than six months much of the mail for Perth, Scotland, was being delivered there. It had to be put into a larger Post Office box. Head office authorised its same-name Australian branch office to open the mail, deal with it or advise.

The Yorkshire acquisition helped Belton's successor (1965–8), the extrovert Clifford Fisher, in that the company was established in New Caledonia, New Hebrides, Tahiti and Western Samoa, was in the livestock business and had two local life companies. It was hoped that co-ordinated operations would reduce costs and the underwriting loss. When Cliff Fisher went back to York as general

Cyclone Tracy hit Darwin, capital of Northern Territory, on Christmas Eve 1974. It was the worst natural disaster in Australia's history, destroying 90 per cent of homes and killing 65 people.

As the Brisbane floods subsided, boats were the easiest form of transport.

manager of the life company he was succeeded by R.M. Trotter, previously New South Wales manager of The Yorkshire, who for just under two years before he stepped down in 1972 had a General Accident man from head office monitoring his work on the spot.

Motor and employers' liability business was unprofitable and a substantial volume of low quality risks was discarded, including compulsory third party motor insurance in all states except Queensland. One of the problems was that there had been no management training to prepare for the company's growth. The deficiency became obvious at a time when the market was changing with the advent of major brokers adopting London and US practices of putting large business on the open market. This trend strengthened soon after Jim Adam, yet another expatriate, took over in 1973. Under the Trade Practices Act 1974 the tariff was ended along with the ties between insurance companies and banks/building societies. In the new competitive environment loyalties were loosened and clients shopped around for the best deal. It was also the year of Cyclone Tracy devastating Darwin and floods in Queensland, leaving large claims in their wake. Expatriate managers in Sydney writing business across six different states still needed the political sagacity and welcomed the occasional business introductions of their advisory board.

New Zealand also had an advisory board, its managers Dennis Howe

(1947–51), Kenneth Mackenzie (1951–67), Jim Adam (1967–9), all being General Accident men who had had previous overseas experience. When Colin Little left for the UK in 1947 total premium income from the whole country was just £100,000 after 22 years' presence in the territory. During WW2, with bulk purchase agreements from Britain for primary products and the drive for greater self-sufficiency in manufacturing at home, the economy grew.

The country was essentially a series of local communities and General Accident was able to make progress through its branch offices in the main centres serving a network of agents. Branch managers met annually in Wellington to share experience. Business was domestic, rural, and small concerns: stock and station agents providing services for the farming community, garages and workshops. Premium income grew strongly enough for the company to select a new site for its head office in Wellington and have the prestige of the building being opened in 1966 by the Prime Minister, Keith Holyoake. Integration of The Yorkshire, marginally the larger local company, and the acquisition of its livestock business, principally bloodstock, farmed deer, pedigree bulls and goats, further strengthened the company. It was felt that The Yorkshire had a higher calibre staff, General Accident suffering from the stigma of being non-tariff and attracting recruits mainly from the government-owned State Insurance, who, unused to making decisions for themselves, tended not to perform well. Merging the two different administrative systems, bringing in General Accident's computer experience, fairly apportioning staff in the six branches and exercising more central control made General Accident a stronger national force. Keith Taylor, the manager from 1969, had been The Yorkshire manager of the Hamilton branch.

It was timely because the market was changing. From April 1974 much of the workmen's compensation and employers' liability business was no longer available to the private insurance market. The number of dairy farms and small farmers had been falling since the mid-1950s and there had been a corresponding growth in large dairy factories and complete animal processing in centralised freezing plants taking the place of local abattoirs. Developments such as these involved new fire hazards in polystyrene freezing chambers and damage to food on a larger scale, putting larger profits at risk and entailing more re-insurance. It was the kind of commercial and industrial business appealing to the emerging brokers, jokingly described by one General Accident man as 'bananas' because there was not a straight one among them. Some did the company a favour by educating their clients in the necessity of relating their insurance coverage more closely to the changing nature of their business.

The company developed its own niches by devising package policies to appeal to specific trades such as booksellers, builders, chemists, jewellers, motel proprietors and plumbers. So strong were the links that staff were invited to address annual conferences of some groups. Owner drivers with high hire purchase commitments on their trucks and workers in wood were groups avoided. Undesirable motor risks were actors, immigrants speeding on open roads and nuns enjoying freedom from the convent. Shooting deer from helicopters in mountainous country and retrieving the carcass was an accident-prone pastime. Disasters could be caused by earthquakes, floods, forest fires and snow.

Another area developed was marine insurance, New Zealand's trade having broadened away from Britain to Australia, Japan and the US. Stuart Hindmarsh, who had been with a Lloyd's broker in London and had opened a local brokerage, simplified a complex area for branches by producing a guide with six basic rates. Used to covering goods in transit, the marine department also handled the insurance for the literal moving of timber houses, removed on trucks from one site to another. The local company was well set when the tariff came to an end in the early 1970s, able to expand its business in the markets that it knew, consulting Perth on some major underwriting matters, in particular reinsurance arrangements. One ex-Perth man described the relationship with head office as 'quiet control, never obvious but there'.

By 1958, when it had been in South Africa for 50 years, General Accident had, as well as its headquarters in Cape Town, offices in Bloemfontein, Durban, East London, Johannesburg, Oudtshoorn, Pretoria, Lichtenburg, Port Elizabeth and Windhoek. In 1965 the company was domesticated, changing its name to General Accident Insurance Company South Africa Limited. From Cape Town it also controlled Botswana, Lesotho, South West Africa, and Swaziland. In 1969 the head office was moved to Johannesburg, the financial capital. Through the 1970s new branches were opened in Roodepoort and Vryheid (1971), Ermelo and Springs (1972), Grahamstown and Krugersdorp (1974), Pietersburg and Worcester (1975), Nelspruit (1977), George and Stellenbosch (1979).

The middle years of the century were the period of the company's greatest geographical extent. With the spread of nationalism after WW2, what had been captive Empire markets became independent states, many demonstrating their new status by seeking fresh international trading partners and investors or pursuing protectionist policies, restricting opportunities for the mother country. India ceased to be an open market and by 1955 General Accident withdrew, having left Pakistan a year earlier. Operations in China ceased in 1949 with the Communist conquest. Africa was the continent where most agencies were ended. Those in Libya and Nigeria finished in 1958. By the mid-1960s Aden, Eritrea, Ethiopia, Malawi, Sudan, Tanzania, Uganda and Zambia had ended too. The new republic of the Congo, where United Nations forces were trying to restore order, was by 1962 too unstable for the conduct of business.

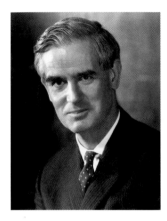

Lord Polwarth, chairman 1968–72, was also governor of the Bank of Scotland and a director of Imperial Chemical Industries. In 1972 he stepped down as chairman of General Accident and resigned his other directorships when he became Minister of State in the Scottish Office.

General Accident did gain territories with The Yorkshire acquisition, notably in Brazil, where in 1972 local interests were consolidated into one aptly named local company Corcovado Companhia de Seguros, Corcovado with its giant statue of Christ being the dominating peak of Rio de Janeiro. In the Middle East, Iran was to be a market until the fall of the Shah in 1979. When Papua New Guinea became independent in 1975 General Accident was registered to do business as a foreign company.

In Western Europe, underwriting experience in Belgium, France, Ireland and the Netherlands was generally unsatisfactory. Earlier in Germany the company had insured the local distributors of thalidomide, the Distillers' product that between 1959 and 1962 caused 2,000–3,000 West German babies to be born deformed. Insuring British armed forces in Germany, it had also become involved in accident cases of vehicles owned by soldiers, which had to be settled under German law. Under the Western Europe policy, military personnel could cover their vehicles. Over some 40 years many thousands of servicemen and women insured in this way through agencies such as NAAFI (Navy, Army and Air Force Institutes).

Ahead of Britain's probable membership of the European Economic Community the chairman, Lord Polwarth told the annual general meeting in 1972:

We are taking steps to ensure that our existing policyholders will be provided with General Accident service in the Common Market where this is not already available, but we shall be cautious in our approach to direct involvement in areas which at present are unprofitable and do not show prospects of success in the long term.

In the face of a fundamental economic shift it was a reiteration of basic General Accident policy.

Part of its success was
due to a more aggressive
presentation of itself.

AS governor from 1968 Sir Stanley came into the office less and less; Aonghais Macdonald, chief general manager and executive director, had more freedom, which he used over the next nine years. Tom Roberts, who had been agency manager for the South of England before returning to Perth in 1970 as an assistant general manager responsible for personnel and administration, saw:

A sea change. Macdonald changed the philosophy of the company from being the organisation with the lowest expense ratio. He wanted it to look outward, to grow by capitalising on its existing strengths. Macdonald took General Accident from being a successful and large but introverted, parochial company and put it on track to become a major international insurance group.

Aonghais Macdonald was, after Francis Norie-Miller, the second outsider to have a major influence on the company's fortunes.

Coming from a financial background, he was released from Norie-Miller constraints. Fresh from securing The Yorkshire with its life business and taking over from Commercial Union the motor and householder policies of the industrial life company Liverpool Victoria, he was in a strong position to effect changes. One immediately welcomed by the staff was the end of Saturday working and the benefit of a five-day week.

Yet, when in the country at large the patrician grouse moor image of Harold Macmillan had yielded to the youthful society of the Swinging Sixties, Macdonald was in many ways still a traditionalist. Ladies who had worked for 25 years now, like men, got a gold watch and both sexes received £50 after 40 years' service, men previously getting £25. There was some concession to modern times in that miniskirts were frowned upon but not prohibited. In 1969 he introduced a Quarter Century Club for the UK; to ensure that the family name was preserved in its adopted city, as Andrew Carnegie's was in a park in his native Dunfermline, the company gave to Perth in 1971 the Norie-Miller Walk by the Tay; a Norie-Miller chair of general practice was endowed at Glasgow University in memory of Sir Stanley, who died on 21 December 1973. Early in 1974 the company bought for over £1.3 million the 15,000-acre Ardnamurchan Estate in Argyll, intended to provide an income from farming, fishing and stalking deer. Income was minimal against the capital investment. More important in practice was Macdonald's exercise of the shooting rights.

The working regime was relaxed in 1974 when flexible working hours were introduced. Macdonald addressed colleagues by surname until the day he retired, when he relaxed into Christian names. His personal assistant thought it an accolade when addressed as 'My dear Rhodes'. Not so parsimonious as Sir Stanley, he no longer required an old biro to be produced before a new one was issued. He exercised careful control, prepared to spend money where he thought it would produce a return. No revolutionary, Macdonald proceeded step by step, gradually seeing less of the incoming mail, broadening the attitudes of those around him and, as *primus inter pares*, creating a collective management. A masterful man seen only by appointment, he gave managers responsibility, enabling them to grow. Alan Begg, who succeeded him as investment manager after 16 years, got on with the job without interference.

Integration of The Road Transport & General, Scottish General and The Yorkshire was accomplished paternally and, for the most part, smoothly. A few staff left because they did not like the idea but there was no question of redundancies or compulsory early retirements. People were found jobs, sometimes being given specialist or basic training at the staff college in Perth. To ensure everybody interested in career development had the opportunity to improve

Ardnamurchan, a country estate in the West of Scotland, was a 1974 investment that never fulfilled its original promise. It was sold in 1992.

skills a video unit was set up in 1972 and internally produced distance learning packages provided.

A rumour helped Macdonald reorganise his top management without wielding an axe. Word had got round that the government was going to change the rules on the commutation of part of one's pension for cash. So strong was the rumour that several senior managers, regarded as the old guard, offered to retire before the measure came in. It did not happen but they made way for Macdonald to appoint his own broader team. These were mainly seasoned staff including Alan Begg, David Blaikie, Jason Frangoulis, Bill Hartley, Charles Heath, Buchan Marshall, Tom Roberts, Nelson Robertson and Harry Waldron, and newcomers such as Eric Robertson, brought in from the management consultants Urwick Orr, in data processing. In place at the beginning of the 1970s, they were the men who in their various disciplines were to lead the company towards the early 1990s.

In a larger, more diversified company tight control from Perth was less and less possible. Jason Frangoulis saw it from an international standpoint:

There was more decentralisation of responsibility with reporting, whether the news was good or bad. Perth didn't have all the answers but it wanted to know what was going on. No longer could it rely on homegrown common sense to interpret situations. Under Macdonald we had 'scientific' management, with managers attending outside courses. In the past the attitude had been never to mind the theorists.

General Accident senior management 1975 in the boardroom: (back, left to right) Jason Frangoulis, Joe Hool, Graham Cadie, Harry Waldron, Eric Robertson, Nelson Robertson, Desmond Bean, Tom Roberts; (front) Cliff Fisher, Bill Hartley, David Blaikie, Aonghais Macdonald, Buchan Marshall, Charles Heath.

Macdonald also encouraged staff to enlarge their horizons by taking part in industry affairs, largely centred on London, which he saw as more a help than a hindrance to their work in Perth. They and the company would benefit from industry co-operation in many practical matters. His own commitment to the British Insurance Association amounted to three successive two-year stints as junior deputy, senior deputy and then chairman. Nor need travel be as tiring. Though they had been used to taking whisky nightcaps, managers had suffered night starvation on the sleeper train to London, where they often occupied almost a complete carriage. Now they could be fresher for work by flying from Edinburgh to London, if necessary returning the same evening. The expense was worth it. Moreover, flying would become more reliable after the British Airports Authority took over Turnhouse Airport in 1971 with the commitment to building a new terminal and a longer realigned runway that should reduce the frequency of delays and diversions. The new runway became operational in 1976, the year that British Airways introduced its domestic shuttles from Heathrow to Edinburgh, and the new terminal in the spring of 1977.

The emergence of professional managers who were allowed to get on with their business in a world that was changing as never before altered the rôle of the board, as Alan Begg saw:

In theory an investment committee of as many as 10 directors meeting monthly just before the board meeting laid down investment policy, which my department implemented. A fortnight later a sub-committee of the investment committee monitored performance. In practice it was different, because my predecessor, Macdonald, had decided what he was going to buy and then reported. Our quarterly valuation of some 400 securities was a bulky document for the investment committee to digest so I went over the salient points. Similarly, our year-end valuation covered about 37 funds. A few board members were deeply involved in investments but it was really left to the people who knew and were watching the market day by day.

Notwithstanding this the board was by no means a cipher. The directors, a body of common sense, were unlikely to be fobbed off with poor answers. Occasionally they objected to a management proposal, once shaving a motor rate increase.

In 1967 Macdonald asked Nelson Robertson to go to Glasgow and put on a new path Scottish General, faced as it was with redundancies when the companies were being integrated:

Macdonald had brought in an outsider to study motor insurance statistics and come up with a recommendation for developing the business. The recommendation was based on the twin concept of direct selling to customers via coupons in newspapers

When Ann Hathaway's cottage at Stratford-upon-Avon caught fire in 1967 General Accident met a claim for £20,000.

and direct billing as Pennsylvania General had in the USA. My job was to implement a cost-effective DC [Direct Communication] Plan, using computers for direct communication with policyholders. Simplifying the procedure was immediately regarded by agents and brokers as an attempt to sideline them. Fairly soon the emphasis of the DC Plan changed from direct selling to direct billing, General Accident giving intermediaries a reduced commission on the basis that they still had a rôle in giving advice and help. The whole idea was ahead of its time, and difficult for a company with a large portfolio of its business through intermediaries. The scheme was reasonably successful, attracting 100,000 customers.

It was from the management that innovations were coming, the process later being formalised with the creation of a four-man research and development department to examine new lines of business. Innovations of specific interest were a combined fire, theft and liability policy for farmers and a single rate policy for offices and surgeries.

Following the end of the motor tariff in 1969 that line was experiencing severe competition, especially from cut-price insurers. In 1970 the general manager in the UK, David Blaikie, raised General Accident's rates by 25 per cent, a move that prompted several phone calls:

Had I taken leave of my senses? It was a prudent move based on our own judgement. Inflation was one factor. We had also developed a greater art in estimating outstanding losses, those incurred but not reported, and making proper provision for them, something that the newer motor companies did not do. Many claims are settled after the end of the year, when the old premium rates are no longer adequate. With higher inflation, instead of reviewing rates annually we looked at them more frequently.

To justify an increase in rates it was necessary to put something extra in the policy. Harry Waldron in General Accident came up with the idea of Keep Motoring, a fortnight's free car hire after a claim. This was effected through Godfrey Davis while the policyholder's car was off the road. Recommended repairers, a 25 per cent starter discount scheme, and the payment of premiums by instalment through the company-owned Multiple Credit Services were also introduced. General Accident lost comparatively few policyholders, gained some when Vehicle & General crashed in February 1971 leaving motorists without cover, and maintained a healthy motor account until the difficult inflationary years of the mid-1970s.

One of the profitable uses of the IBM computer was to compile the statistics and research the patterns of motor claims. There were many factors, including the level of petrol sales, weather conditions, and types of injuries, which typically

A partnership with the car hire firm Godfrey Davis kept General Accident motor policyholders on the road.

amounted to one-third of damage claims. Policyholders taking advantage of the Recommended Repairer Scheme did help to contain costs while being assured of workmanship standards. From the April 1973 budget, on the introduction of Value Added Tax, an element in the tax structure of the Common Market, joined by the UK on 1 January, the company had to bear the extra cost of the goods and services supplied by the motor repair industry, which it could not recover because insurance was a zero-rated industry. A better understanding of the portfolio of risks enabled the company to tailor its offering at more closely related rates.

Part of its success was due to a more aggressive presentation of itself. Murdoch MacLeod, in the company's new advertising and public relations agency, which replaced Godbold's, a family-run agency that had its office in General Accident's Aldwych building, saw the switch in attitude:

It had been very provincial, small scale, low key. 'We didn't get where we are by spending large sums of money.' General Accident moved into the big time in advertising by appointing the London end of Leo Burnett, a large American consumer agency. The agency strategy was to change insurance from a commodity into a brand-conscious market, which meant investing millions. Ultimately the strategy didn't work but the company did get a lot of exposure for elements like 'Keep Motoring'.

A firm identity of General Accident was also established by the campaigns. Hitherto the company had been known vaguely as The General or by the clumsy acronym GAFLAC. The company's new image was not reflected everywhere though as Jim Mahon discovered:

Institutional interest in General Accident as a sound investment had been growing during the 1960s. With the quadrupling in the oil price in December 1973 the Kuwait Investment Office, having more oil revenues to recycle, was increasing its stake in General Accident to a level that could give us a problem with the US regulatory authorities. So I went to see the Kuwait investment manager and explained the situation. Being British, he was quite understanding, saying that as it was a poor Scottish company paying its staff lowly he would accede to my request.

The fourfold increase in the price of oil after the Arab-Israeli war of 1973 pushed the annual rate of inflation up from 10 to over 25 per cent. For General Accident the situation was made worse by specific events such as the explosion in 1974 at the chemical plant in Flixborough for which the company was the largest underwriter, incurring a net loss of over £1.5 million, its largest ever in the UK. Such events underlined the importance to industrial and commercial

Facing page
The most memorable advertisement in the Keep Motoring campaign was the squashed car.

organisations of risk management, examining safety measures and controlling losses. In a period of continuing high inflation it was especially important to make adequate provision against consequential losses.

A wider problem arose in household insurance, where the company had given a free sixth year to policyholders without claims. This had been funded by putting aside a reserve of one-sixth, now eroded by inflation. Administering the reserve became more expensive since brokers still received commission on a premium that was not collected. In 1976 the company announced that the bonus year would be phased out, every bonus policyholder having one last chance to earn a free year. That same year was remarkable for its long hot summer after a year of below average rainfall, leading to subsidence in some areas and claims totalling £4.6 million. Many policyholders also failed to update the value of their house contents in line with inflation and consequently became under-insured. Persuading them to raise valuations to realistic levels and accept increased premium payments was not easy when the cost of living was rising. So, unless policyholders asked for valuations to remain the same, at renewal the company applied automatic index-linking of sums insured. At first the media criticised this as a form of inertia selling. Then the media went on to complain that, because index-linking was geared to the retail price index and not the durable goods index, policyholders were paying still more than necessary.

Inflation combined with advances in medical research and improvements in treatment pushed up the cost of personal injury claims, further increased under the Administration of Justice Act 1969 by having to pay interest on court awards for damages. A young paraplegic who might have survived eight to ten years pre-war could now have a near normal life expectancy and hence higher expected earning capacity to be compensated. Not until 1983 did the wearing of seat belts in the front of a car become compulsory. Similarly, medical negligence, which The Yorkshire had covered through the Medical Defence Union, had a pattern of rising claims. In general, as the financial consequences of professional error became greater so liability claims grew, making General Accident more selective in the risks it was prepared to cover and sharper at estimating levels of claims case by case.

The company's new advertising agency used humour to bring home the point about insuring for contents.

Take every care
ashore or afloat

It pays to be protected by *General Accident*

Marine Insurance

Sailing was becoming more popular, enlarging the market for boat insurance.

Inflation also made it necessary to rationalise the business structure. Between the two world wars, when labour was cheap, business had been built up by an army of agents. An inspector would start off working from his home, appointing agents who brought in clients from their locality and reaching a turnover that justified the creation of a sub-office. Swansea, for example, had a network of them scattered over South Wales. Inevitably there had been duplication of records and administrative costs that could no longer be justified. With 10 per cent of UK agents being the source of 70 per cent of the business, it became necessary to draw a line below which business was not worthwhile and gradually, sometimes controversially, dispense with agents. A similar gradual process was followed with local boards of directors, once a source of new business contacts but now less important. In the City, an expensive centre in which to carry out routine processing, staff numbers were reduced from 290 to 160 over five years by establishing a personal lines branch at Bedford in late 1978 and handling non-personal lines in Perth.

Prudent management was still the order of the day because inflation was the biggest threat to Macdonald's underlying concern for financial strength. What he wanted to achieve was real organic growth to build up the company's reserves ready for the next acquisition that would make General Accident one of the giants in a much more competitive environment. All the main tariffs except industrial fire had been ended by 1972 and he was well aware of two significant trends that would continue to affect the industry. One was the number of foreign insurers setting up in the UK, American companies in particular regarding it as an Anglo-Saxon stepping stone to the Continent. After 1973 continental companies saw Britain as part of the Common Market. During the decade foreign companies were to more than double their share of the UK market to over 22 per cent. The other significant growth was in 'captives' set up by large industrial concerns that had adopted the disciplines of risk management. Underwriting and reinsuring risks themselves could be doubly beneficial, initially cheaper and often effected through tax havens.

Macdonald had two other challenges facing him, one internal, one external. Since the unsuccessful 1920 strike for recognition of the Guild of Insurance Officials trade unions had not been evident in General Accident. By the mid-1960s the atmosphere had changed. In an era of full employment and a less deferential society trade unions were a stronger force in national affairs, especially when the government was engaged in wage restraint. Their membership had grown, especially among white collar workers, including some General Accident branches, notably in the Midlands, and among computer staff, who felt their new skills merited suitable rewards. Collective bargaining was the way to secure them. In General Accident it was once again a question of representation, this time by which union. An internal or external one? If external, by which union?

General Accident had modified its attitude towards trade unions. The blacklist of the union-minded was probably destroyed after Francis Norie-Miller died and since 1966 the company had agreed to meet union officials to discuss individual cases. In The Yorkshire the union claimed to have a majority membership and had the right of representation, which on the takeover in

1967 became a minority not recognised by General Accident. It appeared inconsistent because General Accident recognised the union in the Irish Republic. When the National Board for Prices and Incomes published its report on General Accident staff salaries, which even after its recommendations left them below the general level in the industry, it recommended 'there should be a collective consultation with the staff in future on matters which affect them'. The outcome was a system of staff committees, which became Staff Association – General Accident (SAGA).

Enter, in the person of the astute and witty Clive Jenkins, the Association of Scientific, Technical and Managerial Staffs (ASTMS), which in 1970 had merged with the Union of Insurance Staffs, the renamed Guild. Jenkins' argument was that SAGA was not an independent trade union, rather a piece of – hated word – paternalism, on a par with staff communications. The staff magazine *Generalities* since its refoundation in 1949 (the brief pre-war publication ceased with wartime paper shortages) covered side issues on a par with 'hatches, matches and despatches'. Although *The General's Review* had ceased in 1969, the newspaper *Gen*, started in 1972 and edited by Alex ('Scoop') McIntosh, was regarded as a management mouthpiece, talking to but not listening to staff. Computer staff from women in data preparation to graduates in systems, radicals in a fairly stodgy industry, were pro-ASTMS. In a 1972 ballot to decide which union should be given representation rights ASTMS won a narrow victory over SAGA, 45 to 41 per cent. As neither had received over 50 per cent support the company refused to enter into sole bargaining rights, claimed by ASTMS. SAGA rejected ASTMS proposals for a merger. The Commission on Industrial Relations could only make recommendations on the desirability of a single staff organisation for collective bargaining.

The issue dragged on. SAGA became part of the Association of Professional, Executive, Clerical, and Computer Staff (APEX). The two unions, APEX and ASTMS, put the case to the Advisory, Conciliation and Arbitration Service (ACAS), which was unable to recommend sole negotiating rights to either union. General Accident, which in common with most of industry at a time when unions were regarded as too powerful had rejected proposals for their greater involvement in decision-making, an extension of union power into the boardroom, therefore proposed the formation of a joint negotiating council with equal representation for both unions. This was finally accepted at the end of 1977.

Unions had a contribution to make, especially on job evaluation, and co-operation was more fruitful than confrontation. It was a lesson learned in an industry that often paid lip service to the principle that it was a people business, that people were its greatest asset and should be treated as such. Nevertheless until the late 1970s women were forbidden to wear trousers in the office and young men could still be told to get a haircut. The company had spent more than ten years shedding some of its paternalism and being manoeuvred into modern personnel management, the most difficult part of its culture change, absorbing far too much top management time and energy.

In 1977 a self-financing productivity bonus scheme was introduced. If there was a profit in the UK then employees benefited. Following the 1978 Finance Act, an employee profit-sharing scheme was introduced, the profits being allocated in shares, giving the staff a feeling that they had a stake in the company. About two-thirds of employees retained their shares.

Macdonald's other major challenge was political. Following the collapse of badly managed insurance companies, especially those depending on motor business, through the Policyholders Protection Act the Conservative government gave the Department of Trade and Industry more powers in monitoring and supervising insurance companies, paying particular attention to minimum solvency standards. Policyholders were given protection against the inability of companies to meet their liabilities through a fund financed by a levy on all companies. Macdonald became a member of the five-man Policyholders' Protection Board, originally set up by the Labour government. Aggrieved as much as the public at the conduct of rogue companies, the industry was consulted, suggesting amendments to bills before they became acts. The General Accident chairman, Stuart Black, was unequivocal at the annual general meeting in 1975:

We are firmly opposed to any legislation which permits an option to rescue failing companies…As long as provisions are made to protect private policyholders put at risk by a failing company there is no commercial sense or social justice in keeping that company alive for its own sake at the expense of the policyholders of other companies. We must concentrate on protection of policyholders, not survival of companies.

One issue on which the industry was not consulted was the revived possibility of its nationalisation. In 1949 the national executive of the Labour Party had passed a resolution to that effect but it was a dead letter because the second term of the Labour government was short (1950–1). In October 1971 the annual conference of the Labour Party, against the recommendation of the executive, passed two resolutions: nationalisation of banks and insurance companies; nationalisation of all motor insurance. Conference policy made in opposition could be modified in government but the Damoclean threat hung over the industry.

When there was much discussion about Britain's industrial decline the finger was pointed at the major financial institutions as a cause. The basis of the

Stuart Black joined the board in 1950, bringing shipping and financial expertise. He was deputy chairman of Glasgow-based Donaldson Line and for 25 years a director of Scottish United Investors. From the 1960s he saw General Accident change from a family-dominated company to one under collective management. He was chairman from 1972 to 1979.

argument was that they had failed the nation by not investing enough in growth areas of the economy. Labour's *A Ten-Year Strategy for Britain* proposed that insurance companies and pension funds should be required to divert a minimum proportion of new funds to supporting manufacturing industry. Macdonald's view was that the willingness to invest existed, to wit General Accident's total investment in British industry and commerce reached £320 million in 1975, but the atmosphere, which it was the government's rôle to create, had to be right. To invest, industry needed confidence to look ahead, difficult in a period of high inflation when the profitability of British industry had been declining in real terms. It was the duty of insurers, investing for the protection of their policyholders, to seek the best return. In his eyes that was a commendably socialist view.

In 1976 the national executive of the Labour Party issued a pamphlet *Banking and Finance* recommending the nationalisation of the big four banks and seven largest insurance companies, including General Accident. The document was adopted as party policy at the annual conference in September but James Callaghan, who had experience as Chancellor of the Exchequer, knew it would not be a vote-winner at the next general election. He therefore sidestepped the issue by setting up a Committee to Review the Functioning of Financial Institutions, chaired by his predecessor as Prime Minister, Harold Wilson. General Accident and others made their case. For them the crucial paragraph in the committee's findings was:

David Munro's daughter Pat was the second generation of the family to work for General Accident. She had had good reports of the company from visiting her grandparents in Bournemouth, where they were chauffeur and housekeeper to Sir Francis's widow. Her father had been with the company for 46 years.

A year after David retired from Glasgow branch in 1979, Pat felt like a change from teaching maths at Perth Grammar School. Computing appealed and General Accident was the obvious place in which to work. There was also the attraction of a three per cent mortgage for staff. It made up for the initial drop on her teacher's salary.

Pat worked first on programming a mainframe computer in Perth and then on a system for producing international insurance documents, green cards, on an IBM 8100 of Scottish General in Glasgow. Her teaching experience led her into training.

Fancying another change of scene and wanting to see her sister in the US, she contacted the overseas department in Perth and arranged a transfer to Philadelphia, staying there from 1982 to 1984. She found the US organisation was ahead of the UK in computing but lagging in employee benefits such as subsidised mortgages, discounts on policies and sports facilities.

Returning to Perth, she became a full-time deaconess with the Church of Scotland.

Gordon Simpson, chairman 1979–87, made his opening statement to shareholders 'at the close of a year in which the Corporation's total world-wide premium and investment income exceeded £1 billion for the first time'.

Two chief general managers: David Blaikie (left) 1976–80 and Buchan Marshall 1981–89 by the River Tay, opposite the then headquarters of General Accident in General Buildings, Perth.

The insurance associations emphasise that their activities as investors should not be considered in isolation from their primary function of providing a service to policy-holders. Their rôle as investors is a result of the service they provide, not the object of their existence, and this fact is reflected in the prudential constraints imposed, externally and internally, on their investment policies. The basic objective, laid down by statute, is to ensure that at all times the funds will be able to meet liabilities to policy-holders and their 'reasonable expectations'. General (i.e. non-life) funds face liabilities which are more short-term and less predictable than those of life funds, and this is reflected in a greater emphasis on liquidity in the choice of assets. As a general principle, risk is lessened by matching the maturity of liabilities and assets, as well as spreading investments between different types of asset.

Labour lost the 1979 general election to Margaret Thatcher, under whom the doctrines were liberalisation and then privatisation of nationalised industries.

When Macdonald retired in January 1977 he had changed the face of a provincial, family company. Management consultants would have said there was much more to be done to bring the company thoroughly up to date with best modern practices, but in its own terms it had not seen so much done in a short time since the advent of Francis Norie-Miller in 1887. One part that had stagnated was the life company in York. After withdrawing the bond that if allowed to continue would have seriously eroded the profitability of the life fund, Yorkshire-General retreated into an ultra-conservative attitude dominated by actuarial caution while competitors were declaring better bonuses. Perth showed no interest in making more of its acquisition, some said through ignorance, others because of personality conflicts accentuated by distance.

Livestock insurance was understood in both places. In the early 1980s claims of over £210,000 were paid out on two horses: Shergar, the 1981 Derby winner, on which the company had two lines amounting to £144,000, was stolen; Troy, winner of both the 1979 British and Irish Derby and commanding a record stud fee, died of acute peritonitis. Undeterred, the livestock department covered the 1983 Derby winner Teenoso.

Change is usually followed by consolidation and that was the rôle of Macdonald's successors David Blaikie (1977–80), a long-time insurance man who, unable to afford to go to university, happened to join General Accident while on holiday in Perth in 1933 at the age of 17 and had risen through the ranks, and Buchan Marshall (1981–9), an accountant. More by chance than design the

Shergar winning the 1981 Derby.

company fell into a pattern of alternating financial and insurance men at the top. Although the board and top management were gradually becoming more of a team, with less of a them-and-us distinction between gentlemen and players, progress towards greater unity was not even. The relationship between the board and top management tended to be biased by the character of the incumbent chief general manager, whether he was by background an insurance or a financial man. In general, the more insurance-minded the chief general manager the closer he was to the board. Inevitably this affected the stance of the company.

To an observer it might have suggested a fundamental uncertainty of identity. Was General Accident an insurance company or a broader financial institution? That distinction would become greater as other organisations changed their profile, for example banks taking on insurance and building societies becoming banks. General Accident would have to determine whether it would remain as a traditional insurance company or to what extent it would become a broader financial institution, possibly in a partnership.

Meanwhile the company was jealous of its reputation, which Murdoch MacLeod, a public relations consultant, helped to project:

General Accident always wanted to be in control of what other people thought of them. They were loath to release information putting others in a position to make a

Senior management, including here three chief general managers and a chairman, could relax in the Ardnamurchan country estate. In the back row (left to right) Buchan Marshall, Gordon Simpson, George Bell, managing director of the subsidiary Grampian Properties, Aonghais Macdonald and David Blaikie. In front are two estate workers and Neil Morris, a director of Grampian Properties.

judgement on them. Like a number of other Scottish companies they had this canniness, reserve. They made haste slowly, doing things in their time, not yours. As the market changed that was no longer acceptable. They had to be more open, give information even when it was against their best interests. Come the early 80s, senior people were making presentations to institutions, not leaving it to a hired hand. My job was as an interpreter, to present the company consistently as it was. There was the General Accident way of doing things, with courtesy, formality and integrity. A Scot in London, I was the bridge to the media.

Another Scot who had experience of London was David Blaikie, who as chief general manager was not blinded by patriotism. After The Royal Bank of Scotland had handled a large rights issue with some errors, he had the next issue transferred to Lloyds Bank Registrars in Worthing, Sussex. Having performed well, Lloyds handled all future share registration, which up to now had been done internally. The action upset some Scots sentiments in Edinburgh and Perth. Having worked in London, he knew the importance of the market there, particularly the large lines of business that could be won through brokers. Income from the City office grew more than fivefold to £36 million in five years. At a time when physical communications had become easier Blaikie was able to bring London and Perth closer in understanding.

Things began to change as well for the better in York. When Cliff Fisher died just before retirement Charles Heath was appointed general manager of the life company. A General Accident man who had come up on the motor side of the business, he soon saw that Yorkshire-General had only one successful product, a whole life policy, and that it needed outside management to take it forward. He recruited Norman Graham, a broad thinker from the Royal, to begin the process. A year later Jack Philp, a General Accident man with a marketing flair joined him. Within a few days he wished he had not left Scotland:

The company in York was a moribund, sleepy outfit with no real drive, enthusiasm or leadership. There was no marketing to speak of. Norman had no knowledge of selling and I had little knowledge of actuarial practice. Together we were to have a nine-year partnership during which he came to understand the psychology of selling and I learned something about actuarial science.

Blaikie was also keen on simplifying insurance, getting plain English adopted in forms, starting with motor, so that the public could have a better understanding of what they were entering into. Previous wordings had stood the company in good stead in the courts and there were concerns that removing some of the legal phraseology, a process that took years, could open the floodgates to claims.

Instead the company won some awards for its approach. He was also keen on the social responsibility of the company, sports being sponsored, especially for young people. For the London area offices he opened a new sports ground at Ewell, Surrey, in 1978. Blaikie made a point of seeing all the complaints that came into head office and was much involved in discussions with Guardian Royal Exchange and the Royal on an overall response to the public. In 1981 the three companies founded the Insurance Ombudsman Bureau, to which General Accident committed £100,000. The ombudsman's function was to act as an independent arbitrator, resolving complaints after all of a company's procedures had been gone through. Subsequently, a majority of other UK insurers joined the Bureau.

These moves were aimed at closing another gap, some of the credibility divide with the public, which increasingly regarded insurance companies as bottomless purses that could compensate the ills and inequalities in society. 'The insurance will pay' was an argument that could be stretched to excuse lack of respect for property, manifested in higher incidence of burglary and arson, affecting even non-commercial premises such as schools. In 1976 the company's losses by theft exceeded those by fire in private houses. Rates for contents insurance, which had remained unchanged for over 50 years, were raised in early 1979.

A new factor in aviation insurance was terrorist hijacking of passenger aircraft in the Middle East. This is the scene at Dawson's Field, Jordan, where extremist guerrillas of the Palestine Liberation Organisation forced four aircraft to land on 6 September 1970. The aircraft were blown up.

An area of particular concern was Northern Ireland, where the branch manager had to make the underwriting decision whether or not to accept the risk of a public house or hotel, which could be a terrorist target. Responsibility for settling a claim depended upon whether the chief constable of the Royal Ulster Constabulary issued a certificate stating that the loss was a consequence of terrorist action. If so, the government would meet the claim. Initially General Accident indemnified policyholders awaiting settlement from terrorist actions because money was taking so long to come through from the Northern Ireland office. David Blaikie decided that enough was enough and that policyholders would have to wait upon the government. Other insurers followed suit.

Terrorists did bring bombs into the Belfast office in two holdalls. One was detonated in an explosion controlled by an army robot, the blast causing small damage and spreading petrol, which did not ignite the first floor landing; the other failed. Blaikie made a special payment to the staff in recognition of the tension under which they were having to work. Within the office itself there was no sectarian problem, the two denominations balanced in number as asked by the Fair Employment Agency and working as colleagues. Sadly, in 1971 one young woman on the staff, peacefully shopping near an army patrol, was shot dead from a passing car. As local chairman of the British Insurance Association and hence a spokesman for the industry, the branch manager always had to check underneath his car before daring to get in it. In the mid-1980s the company had enough confidence in its presence in Belfast to redevelop its site and profit from a higher rental income. At that time there was an arson problem in North Wales, when second homes of English people were being razed by nationalists.

Increases in the frequency and size of claims in, for instance, products liability were examples of the psychology of entitlement. Not just inflation but changes in social attitudes and advances in technology, the values involved in oil exploration, larger aircraft and tankers, were pushing up the numbers and sizes of claims. The impact of such market forces, bearing higher price tags, continually emphasised the necessity of marketing as distinct from selling. There were many reasons for building up reserves against a time when disaster might strike.

On the credit side, administrative savings made a difference to the chief accountant, Desmond Bean:

Scrapping of exchange controls in June 1979 saved us a lot of work. Before that we had to fill in a form for every remittance sent abroad. If we wanted to expand abroad we had to make sure that return on our investment would pay back quickly or else we had to pay an investment premium to the Bank of England for the overseas currency we had bought. Settling claims in overseas territories was also a bureaucratic process.

Scottish Boiler & General, a General Accident subsidiary, insured this crane, which toppled into the harbour at Peterhead, Aberdeenshire, in 1982.

The end of exchange controls made it possible to consider acquiring overseas companies previously regarded as too long-term in their payback. The cash was mounting. A mark of careful financial management during the inflationary 1970s was the threefold increase in premium income whereas pre-tax profits increased fourfold to £104 million in 1981, the first time of exceeding £100 million.

It was a figure that pleased Blaikie's successor as chief general manager, Buchan Marshall, later described in the *Financial Times* as 'a drily humorous, gravelly-voiced accountant from Clydeside', but then Buchan was not enamoured of the media. Nor was he just concerned with the bottom line; sponsorship was continued on a broader scale. In 1981 the company donated over £100,000 to over 100 different charities, universities and medical establishments. It sponsored a 20-centre UK tour by Scottish National Orchestra, to which it invited guests, and a digital recording of Mahler's 4th Symphony; a music study project for over 40,000 11–16 year old school children and a set of five full-colour *Instruments of the Orchestra* wall charts; first prize of £10,000 to the winner of the Enterprise Scotland scheme. Staff were seconded to the rehabilitation of Toxteth, one of the scenes of urban decay and riots. In 1982, despite underwriting losses, the Scottish National Orchestra tour of Canada and the USA was sponsored by the company, which also paid for an exhibition marking the 50th anniversary of the Royal Society for the Prevention of Accidents. Sport sponsorship came to the fore in 1984 with the 1,000 and 2,000 Guineas at Newmarket for seven years and the World Bowls Tournament in Aberdeen, the occasion for introducing an insurance policy for bowling clubs.

Buchan Marshall's concern was shaping the business. For the 1980s, in broadening its computer activities the company formed an Information Services Division, did its business systems planning with IBM and decentralised its computing, investing in a series of IBM 8100 machines for branch processing of files with telecommunications links to head office. At a time when competitors were centralising their computer operations distributed processing was a strategic decision, improving branch administration and lessening dependence on a single source. In early 1982, in pursuit of a nationwide pay claim, members of both unions, APEX and ASTMS, co-operated in industrial action. The first such action for 60 years, it affected the Perth computer in particular. A work-to-rule, an overtime ban, refusal to handle telephone enquiries, and a half-day strike disrupted business, especially the handling of claims. Unlike the 1921-2 dispute, this was settled quickly, in three weeks.

Some branches had grown. For instance, Sheffield had moved in 1980 into a 20,000 sq ft former British Steel building with drive-in inspection facilities for motorists with damaged cars. In Bradford 'The Black Elephant', a Victorian post office, was bought in 1981, cleaned and adapted at a cost of over £1 million before being occupied in 1984. In 1983 after a thorough investigation, while 63 branches were retained, almost half of some 150 sub-offices were closed as no longer being cost-effective. Even with industry co-operation in stabilising rates economies were necessary after two recessionary years of underwriting losses, mainly on property accounts, and more business was now being placed through High Street brokers. The General Accident reorganisation was still in the paternal tradition; nobody lost a job. Staff at Coleraine in Northern Ireland, for example, were taken daily by bus 50 miles away to Belfast.

Concentration in the field was mirrored in Perth, where a new £33 million head office in a 62-acre hill farm site on the outskirts of the city was opened in 1983, bringing together departments that had been accommodated in seven separate premises. It was the third head office in the city in almost a century. After the first small office, Francis Norie-Miller had wanted a prominent central site and building. In the 1970s the company opted for a modest, functional, almost self-effacing structure. Blending into a hillside in accordance with planning requirements, its five levels, finished in fawn ribbed concrete like the elephant house at London Zoo and non-reflective glass with greenery tumbling from rooftop gardens, looked when approached from below as though some large sprite had left open a low-rise chest of drawers after a careless search of

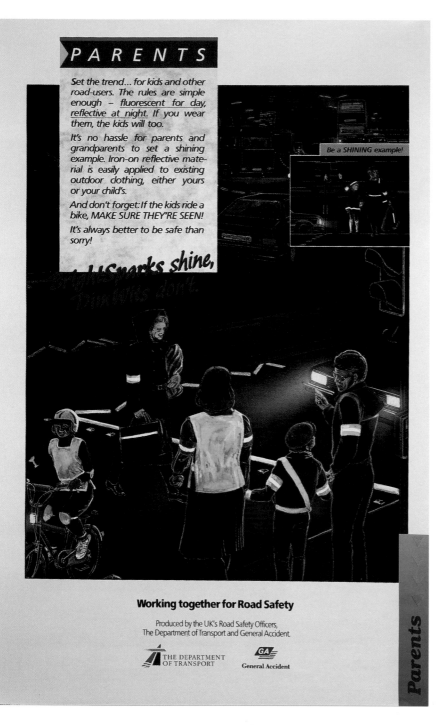

Promoting safety in conjunction with the government was one of the company's social responsibilities.

Some interesting facts

Site purchased in 1974.
Work started October 1979.
Completed June 1983.

The building covers an area equivalent to 4.5 football pitches.

It is largely a product of a 10-metre-square grid each one of which would be large enough to accommodate a modern-day bungalow.

309 cruciform columns (each weighing 3 tons) and 880 pre-cast panels (each of 1.5 tons) were used. They needed 3,000 tons of the chosen quartz aggregate.

The interior walls are lined with 2,500 veneered cladding panels.

17,900 cubic metres of concrete had to be mixed on site.

Also used were:
2,520 tons of reinforced steel
At least one million bricks and blocks
82 miles of cable
16 miles of pipe
480 tons of air-conditioning duct work.

Almost 190,000 square feet of top quality Wilton carpet – woven in Dundee – covers the floors.

The largest floor is Level 3, and measures 393 feet long and 328 feet wide.

The swimming pool in the Sports & Social Club is half Olympic length and is heated by waste heat from the computer suite chiller.

The main sports hall measures 6,372 square feet.

The company's new headquarters at Pitheavlis on the outskirts of Perth looked stark when first built. Cultivation of rooftop gardens has helped blend the building into the hillside.

their contents. It was not where most people would expect to find the head-quarters of a worldwide business, rather a prime example of the company doing its own thing after board debate and management planning extending over several years, a final decision being made in 1977. It was a Scottish project, James Parr & Partners of Dundee being appointed the architects, and Sir Robert McAlpine & Sons Ltd the contractors. Work started in 1980.

Not for General Accident the expensive and doubtful prestige of some city centre tower block. Most staff moved themselves in over a July weekend in 1983. Not long afterwards motor rates went up sharply, attracting some cynical press comment that motorists were paying for the new headquarters. Inside, all except the top management floor was open plan, which caused the company's tax expert to leave. Other employees experienced mysterious illnesses associated with moving to the new air-conditioned environment. For access to the town centre a morning, lunchtime and evening contract bus service was provided. On-site recreation facilities included a swimming pool, tennis courts, multi-sports hall and bowling green. Unfortunately the move coincided with a hard winter, when travel to and from country areas was difficult. If people had managed to get in but were doubtful about getting back after a heavy snowfall, they were given a half-day credit on their flexitime. Francis Norie-Miller's working regime had indeed relaxed. Abandoned too was a social occasion for Perth, the grand lunch at the Station Hotel for local dignitaries after the annual general meeting.

The old head office, complete with furniture, was sold for £1.5 million to Perth and Kinross Council. Features such as the marble entrance hall and staircase, the rosewood panelling in the chairman's office (now used by the Provost) and boardroom, and the boardroom table, which can comfortably seat 26 diners, have thus been preserved.

A change of place did not result in an immediate change of culture. On the whole graduates did not take to the regime. In the experience of a future general manager Nigel Lister, who in 1959 joined the Road Transport & General, a company with the same staid, hierarchical culture as its parent:

Graduates coming in on the Fast Track scheme did not endear themselves to existing staff, overtaking the experienced with long service. Both sides got disillusioned. Graduates, oversold with high expectations, found there was more to learn than they expected, a lot of experience to acquire. Often put on to project work involving several people, they didn't think it a proper job of the consultancy kind using high-level skills. So many of them left.

There were two minor pieces of reorganisation. To improve the productivity of

'The General' caricature helped to personalise the company.

engineering inspection services that element of Scottish Boiler was put into a new company jointly owned with Commercial Union, Plant Safety Ltd. Scottish Boiler continued to offer engineering insurance. As part of the company's concern for the way written-off cars were being bodged back on to the roads, stakes were bought in 1984 in two Kent-based companies, Autocrafts and Auto Economics. Autocrafts refurbished car parts and Auto Economics whole vehicles, enabling General Accident to control what happened to its wrecks, reselling only what was roadworthy.

During the early 1980s Yorkshire-General began to look up. Covermaster, term assurance with five- and ten-year opportunities to increase the sum assured without a medical, sold in some volume, as did mortgage protection policies and low-cost endowments through links established with building societies. After the conservation of life funds in the previous decade, Norman Graham as general manager and chief actuary was able to loosen the purse strings. The field force was organised in 16 separately managed life branches and their efforts backed by colour advertisements in the insurance press. New business began to climb. One major barrier was the company name, known to some brokers but not necessarily associated with the strengths of General Accident. From the start of 1985 it was changed to General Accident Life

The Queen visited Perth and the company during its centenary, 1985.

Assurance. The Croydon-based English Insurance became General Accident Linked Life Assurance in a refurbished office in York, specialising in group pensions and marking the corporation's re-entry into unit-linked products. Only a few Croydon staff chose to move to York.

In that year, 1985, which saw the end of the last major tariff, industrial fire, the company had been in business for 100 years. Her Majesty The Queen and the Duke of Edinburgh honoured the company by paying an official visit to head office on 2 July, although the actual centenary fell on 16 December. According to one member of the staff:

The anniversary, not long before Christmas, was just another day. Brokers got crystal goblets with the General Accident crest but there was very little for the staff. It was disappointing.

Funds were being saved for a spending spree.

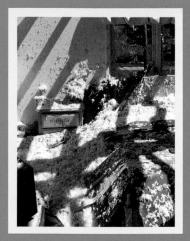

Hurricane Hugo was one of
a series of natural disasters
affecting the Caribbean
and the Eastern seaboard of the USA.

INTERNATIONAL CLAIMS

THE distance between UK-based corporations and their transatlantic subsidiaries is never constant. It varies not so much with the speed of physical communications and the state of telecommunications as the personalities of those heading the organisations. The possibilities of transatlantic communications improved rapidly throughout the period when Ed Moynahan was running General Accident's US branch: in 1958 the first jet services shortened London–New York journeys to just over six hours and more travellers crossed by air than sea; from 1956 undersea cables and 1962 satellites provided plenty of phone lines of better quality, over which data could also be sent; from 1970 direct dialling between the UK and US; from 1976 supersonic travel. Yet, when Perth was getting closer to London, Moynahan chose to keep Perth at a distance.

His successor, Jim Corcoran, sitting in the same office near where American independence was born, took a different view. If Moynahan was a Madison believing in strong central control then Corcoran was a Jefferson championing the devolution of power. For over 30 years the characteristic of insurance in the US had been decentralisation. Within six months of the Supreme Court ruling in 1944 in the case of *US v. South Eastern Underwriters Association* that insurers were subject to the Sherman Anti-Trust Act 1890, Congress passed the McCarran-Ferguson Act exempting insurers from federal anti-trust laws as long as the states regulated the industry. In the 1960s states appointed commissioners no longer content to follow the regulations of the New York Insurance Department, which had become in effect a national regulatory system. Meanwhile, in property and casualty, the centralising power of the industry rating bureaux had declined, individual companies taking advantage of 'deviations', as General Accident did in New York, the source of 30 per cent of its premium income. 'Deviations' inevitably led to open rating in the 1960s.

As in Perth, Philadelphia was slow to realise the implications of this trend for its own personnel. Though barely on speaking terms, in differing degrees Macdonald and Moynahan were both paternalists. Attitudes within General Accident top management on both sides of the Atlantic only really began to change in 1976–7 with the departure of the two men. On the day Jim Corcoran knew he was going to become the company's attorney for the US he said to his deputy, Charlie Niles: 'Charlie, we've got to turn this smartly not sharply.' His actions would be different but would not reflect adversely on his predecessors. He showed his gratitude and loyalty to the people who had built the branch to its present level by starting a retirement savings plan with the company adding to the employee contribution, improving medical coverage and uprating pensions at a time of inflation.

In Niles' view:

Jim brought General Accident US into the twentieth century. He knew changes had to be made and set about them. One of the first was the abolition of the salary committee, called by the troops a No-No committee. There were no job descriptions, grades or salary structures. He brought in proper salary scales and upgraded the office accommodation, starting with the troops, making sure they had decent restaurant facilities before the executive floor was refurbished. The place was no longer run by Jesus Christ and the Twelve Apostles. Outside he gave the company a presence it hadn't had. We got close to the National Agents Association, which didn't know we existed, and won awards as the top agency company.

Under the Growth Alliance Program special services were offered to the best agents. Money was spent on branches, making them individual profit centres more attractive for agents to visit. With head office as a support for field operations rather than a multi-headed command centre, branch managers were given more authority and responsibility for their results. They reported to one of three regional vice-presidents, their sole connection with head office. Costs were kept down by not over-employing and investing in automation, buying new computers instead of secondhand ones. Minicomputers were installed in all branches, the first agency terminal linked into the company, and the Policy Management System adopted. In 1983 General Accident joined in the purchase of AGENA, a company specialising in software packages for agents.

Throughout the organisation there was a new spirit, at least until there were some redundancies in the early 1980s. People's energies were released. Frank Coyne, who worked for Reliance Insurance in Philadelphia and joined General Accident as general counsel in 1985, saw the difference Corcoran made:

To an outsider General Accident had the reputation of being a good independent agent company with simple personal and small commercial products. Not an industry leader, it didn't attract a lot of high-powered people. The impression was of a military-style office with grey metal desks and linoleum floors. Within 30 seconds of meeting Jim Corcoran my view changed. In a big office he was an imposing figure, a thinker gazing out over the river. Sitting down, he was a soft-spoken doodler. When the

Jim Corcoran (left), US attorney 1977–91, brought Philadelphia and Perth closer together. He is seen here with Hollywood actor Raymond Burr — Perry Mason to TV viewers — who supported an anti-fraud campaign for the American insurance industry.

insurance industry lagged in terms of management discipline he was positioning the company to respond to change. He wanted to create greater shareholder value, as had happened in the auto, computer and pharmaceutical industries, while satisfying customers' demand for value for money.

These were large objectives during a difficult operating period. In only two years, 1978–9, between 1976 and 1991, when he retired, was there an underwriting profit. The marketing environment for insurance companies had deteriorated. Instances of fraud, particularly on auto repair and theft, had increased dramatically, operating at all levels within the industry, even being professionally managed by doctors and lawyers. Personal auto typically accounted for over half of General Accident's underwriting losses. So widespread was fraud that if it were a corporation it would rank towards the top of the Fortune 500 companies and be classed as a growth industry. Insurers responded by publicising the effects on honest policyholders – 'Fraud is not a victimless crime' – establishing investigative units and going as far as setting up sting operations with the authorities. Inner city juries favoured their own kind, the 'underdogs' left behind in the flight to the suburbs, when it came to awarding damages and there was the enormous problem of getting the residual market, better described as the involuntary business, under control. Having written smaller commercial policies, the company was not greatly affected in increasing reserves to pay for environmental clean-up under federal statute.

Fraud grew in the 1980s. The company stressed that it was not a victimless crime as honest policyholders had to pay higher premiums.

Facing page
Hurricane Hugo was one of a series of natural disasters affecting the Caribbean and the Eastern seaboard of the USA.

Pressure on industry-recommended rates grew in the late 1980s, forcing the trade association, the Insurance Service Office, to change tack. Loss costs were now developed in parallel with the companies arriving at their expense costs. By combining the two each company could determine its own rates. Paradoxically, as insurance became more necessary in society so states imposed more restrictions upon the companies, e.g. on their rights to cancel policies or withdraw from certain accident-prone markets. Massachusetts imposed compulsory participation in the state auto reinsurance facility but, because of its adverse experience, General Accident was able to withdraw from that state altogether in 1988. A prime example of continuing to serve customers where the company had a longstanding commitment was homeowners in the Charleston area, heavily hit in 1989 by the 135 m.p.h. winds and 17 ft walls of water raised

by Hurricane Hugo. Altogether that disaster, which began in Puerto Rico and the Virgin Islands, where 100,000 were made homeless and military police had to be called in to stop looting, resulted in a net loss of $38.4 million. At the same time new entrants such as banks were competing for bread and butter business through telemarketing, driving down rates.

Corcoran's policy, which he shared with Perth, making several transatlantic flights a year (he joined the main board in 1978), was to combine recovery with growth. Organic growth came from a greater range of products, concentrating on commercial rather than personal lines. Broader geographical coverage was achieved by making strategic acquisitions away from the north eastern states. His success was marked by two milestones: by 1986 written premiums topped $1 billion and in 1995 $2 billion.

The US branch was incorporated as a company in 1982 and this was achieved over a few months tax-efficiently by transferring the US assets of General Accident to the existing Potomac Insurance Company, changing its name to the General Accident Insurance Company of the US, and its registration from Washington DC to Pennsylvania. That gave the company under a chairman and chief executive, Jim Corcoran filling both rôles, a stronger American and international identity.

For diversification, in 1988 a 20 per cent shareholding was acquired in the United Fire and Casualty Company based in Iowa and three geographical acquisitions were made: in 1986, to gain a presence in the Pacific Northwest, the North Pacific Insurance Company and Oregon Auto Insurance Company from a steel company; in 1990, from the Royal, the Silvey Group in Oklahoma, which General Accident reckoned could be made profitable with a new strategy, including a sell-off of the life interests, and adjusting premium rates; and in 1991, to add to its presence in the Midwest, the Hawkeye-Security group of companies in Iowa. Redefining its position in New York State, General Accident formed in 1988 three new companies: General Accident Insurance Company of New York, General Assurance Company and PG Insurance Company of New York.

Also on the credit side was an outstanding investment performance. Moynahan, in the words of a colleague, 'was a seat of the pants investor, a lucky Irishman'. His record-keeping was inconsistent so that nobody knew exactly how well the portfolio had performed against standard indices. George Morris, who had a professional investment background, joined in 1975 but was not able to get his hands on the portfolio until Moynahan relinquished it in 1977:

General Accident took few risks in its underwriting, operating on the extremely low premium-to-surplus ratio of 1:1, way below the industry norm. Our investment policy was not conservative. The high risk portfolio of common stocks and long bonds, a flexible mix according to the state of the market, made a lot of money. Property we avoided, partly because we needed liquidity. Initially our performance in stocks was mediocre so I talked to the four best performers in the competition, who all had one person picking stocks. So I recruited a top man with an incentive bonus and three analysts, created a professional investment department. We outperformed the index.

When Jim Corcoran retired in 1991 the overall performance was quantified. If General Accident had done the average of the industry the surplus would have been $800 million less. A downside, however, was to emerge three years later when there was a downturn in the bond market.

In some ways Canadian business was like the American but on a smaller scale. It was concentrated in the East, with two-thirds of the total in Ontario and Quebec; independent brokers were the source; there were specific weather hazards, including tornadoes, as in Edmonton in 1987; in a big country each province had its own characteristics, government and regulations. Quebec, for instance, took over the bodily injury portion of auto insurance from March 1978. As in the US, society was litigious. There was a strong consumerist movement and policyholders were prepared to go to law, contributing to periods of underwriting losses in auto, the major area, and property accounts, as in 1979–81.

It was an unfortunate result on which the chief executive, Ed Burns, retired in 1981 after nearly 44 years' service. Nevertheless, he had persevered, focusing management attention on their business, insurance, and outsourcing functions such as data processing and print. A man who was an active leader in industry organisations, he took the line 'We're insurers, not in the information technology business.' Staff productivity was high and the expense ratio low. Market conditions with inadequate rates remained unfavourable for his successor, Len Latham, steering the company through over 200 competitors on a course to profitability.

The tornado that hit Barrie, Ontario, in 1985 wreaked havoc.

In spite of its unfavourable underwriting experience General Accident was not deterred from expansion in the fragmented Canadian market and in January 1986 acquired from Saul Steinberg's Reliance Insurance Company in Philadelphia the entire capital of Pilot Insurance Company, which wrote personal and small commercial lines in the province of Ontario. Brian Greenslade was the chief executive, operating from unpretentious offices in Toronto:

France, it was cancelled and branch and agency networks trimmed. A direct marketing operation for motor GA VOX, appropriately based in Le Mans, was opened in 1991 but the French were not yet attuned to that type of marketing.

In 1980 General Accident Reinsurance Company Limited was formed as a subsidiary but excess capacity developed in the market. In its traditional way General Accident proceeded cautiously, being conservative in its acceptance of risks. Offshore oil and gas operations featured prominently in casualty reports, especially as blow-outs increased. Around the world marine experience was not particularly good, aviation better and exposure to space risks was kept small because of inadequate rates. When airline rates began to fall the company closed its own aviation department, joining the British Aviation Insurance Company. This company subsequently merged its interests with Aviation and General to form in 1990 the British Aviation Insurance Group. The real international growth area in the late 1980s though was the Pacific Rim.

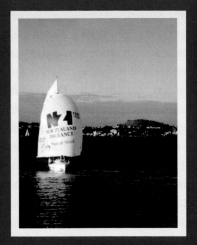

Viewed from the longer
term, NZI had given
General Accident a much
bigger presence in the world's fastest
economic growth area.

cover the insurance side and Ian Menzies (pronounced Mingis) the banking. They were accompanied by advisers from Schroder.

Robertson, an insurance man, had been brought up in General Accident's conservative ways. Menzies, who joined in 1985 as a general manager with overall responsibility for finance, came from the company's merchant bank, Schroder, where he had been a deal-maker. In General Accident his notable success was acquiring Pilot Insurance, a niche business in Ontario. NZI was a bigger and more diverse company, just over half its turnover coming from insurance and most of the rest from banking-related activities. There was too a pressure to seize what appeared to be a unique and long-awaited opportunity to expand in the Pacific Rim, the part of the world regarded as having the best growth prospects. General Accident was not the only interested party. There were at least six competitors.

Although General Accident had local companies in New Zealand and Australia, the situation was different from The Yorkshire merger a generation earlier. That association of complementary companies was negotiated directly between them over some months on home ground and settled in the stock market. The NZI acquisition was a deal among financiers. General Accident had to weigh up an unfamiliar overseas company nearly half of which was banking, a culture in which it had no background. It was in a position to take the risk though. In recent years City analysts had criticised the company for being

Strengthening of the Matahina Dam on the Rangitaiki River in North Island was insured by NZI. The NZ$260 million dam, damaged during the 1987 Bay of Plenty earthquake, needed partially rebuilding on its dry side. NZI insured the rebuilding over 18 months.

over-capitalised, a consequence of ultra-conservative Scottish thrift. At the end of 1987 its solvency margin, shareholders' funds as a proportion of non-life premiums, was 78.8 per cent, 60 points above the legal requirement.

Menzies and Robertson carried out what became their due diligence in New Zealand. What they were weighing up was the acquisition of a minority interest from another shareholder. To those on the spot and even more so in hindsight the examination of the banking side was too cursory. There were also rumours that within what was now a financial conglomerate the two NZI companies, banking and insurance, were running on separate tracks. Although most of the senior executives were from the insurance side of the business, neither side knew about nor did business with the other but had an entirely different external focus. Internally, there was a clash of cultures: risk assessment by the conservative insurers, regarded as stodgy; profligacy by the high-flying bankers, who saw themselves as thrusting entrepreneurs.

The two General Accident men went on to Australia, where NZI had larger interests. In conjunction with the Australian branch of Schroder they reviewed the banking book. Like their counterparts in New Zealand, General Accident senior management and non-executive directors in Australia had serious mis-givings about the proposed investment. Well aware of the need for the local company to grow to take it above a critical mass, they had been examining pos-sibilities of either acquisition or a reciprocal arrangement with another insur-ance company, as had been done in New Zealand. Neither move would have had the strategic impact of acquiring NZI. Senior people also had insights into some of the personalities involved with NZI and what had been happening internally. For instance, there was a strong inkling that all was not well with its bank. The gap in understanding between those from Perth pursuing a long-term strategy and those on the spot foreseeing immediate problems was enough to strain previous friendships within the company.

On its side NZI had to select its preferred purchaser. It rejected the Australian group Elders and unanimously favoured General Accident. Brierley Investments agreed only on condition that it could negotiate terms, including price, satisfactorily with General Accident. With the exception of price, all con-tractual terms were agreed. At a one-day meeting in Wellington attended by NZI representatives and their own advisers, the two General Accident men, following telephone consultation with their chief executive in Perth, agreed a price that management could recommend to the board. The price of Brierley Investments was struck after NZI had adjusted the issue price of the shares General Accident was subscribing for. For the year ending 31 March NZI had abnormal losses, writedowns and provisions totalling NZ$229 million (£93 million). In the total were provisions for bad debts of NZ$87 million written off by NZI Bank. These accounts, audited by NZI's auditors, KPMG, were available to General Accident before being released.

To go ahead or not? Advisers believed that the level of provisions for bad debts was adequate. Within General Accident opinion was divided. Those in favour of the acquisition assessed the maximum risk in buying the bank as no greater than the effects of a tornado in the US. Local management in Australia and New Zealand maintained their doubts. Ultimately the purchase was a corporate decision. On balance the General Accident board decided to go ahead. In the event General Accident paid £264 million for the 38 per cent of NZI held by Brierley Investments. Of the £264 million £116 million was in cash; the balance of £148 million was the proceeds of a placing of new shares, underwritten by Schroder, with institutions at 850p each. General Accident was to sell its own interests in Australasia and the Pacific Basin, worth about £100 million, to NZI in exchange for shares in NZI, and subscribe some £24 million for further NZI shares to bring its total holding to 51 per cent for an outlay of about £390 million.

Under New Zealand takeover rules it was not obliged to bid for the remaining 49 per cent. That came as a relief to the London stock market because a 100 per cent bid might have necessitated a rights issue. On the face of it the numbers looked favourable. General Accident had secured control of NZI at a very reasonable exit price/earnings ratio of about 10.5, paying a premium of only 20 per cent above the current stock market value. Through the mixture of shares and cash there was virtually no earnings dilution for General Accident and only a slight drop in its solvency ratio.

Nevertheless, the company's shares fell by 22p to 895p because analysts were sceptical about the wisdom of the deal, which was out of character with the company they knew. They were not inclined to believe that the otherwise canny company knew something that they did not. One analyst described the Australian non-life market as 'an historic graveyard of UK insurers', citing significant 1985–7 underwriting losses for British major composites there. Most criticism focused on the incompatibility of NZI's Bank with General Accident's philosophy, the *Financial Times* headlining its feature *The Abandonment of Caution*. General Accident was going to get 51 per cent of the profits but 100 per cent of the problems. Why too had the company chosen to expand Down Under when cross-border trade within the European Community was due to be liberalised in 1992?

As the main architect of the deal, Menzies stoutly defended the strategy:

Everyone is talking about Europe but who's doing anything about it? We're looking at that very seriously too. Last year the European Community, other than the

UK, accounted for about seven per cent of General Accident's premium income, £150 million out of £2,170 million, but nearly 15 per cent of the £96 million underwriting loss. By contrast, 'other overseas', mostly accounted for by Australasian, Brazilian and South African activities accounted for six per cent of premium income and only eight per cent of the underwriting loss. Down Under is not a good market, apparently, but it seems to be a darned sight better than continental Europe, notwithstanding the 1987 Bay of Plenty earthquake in New Zealand. Some say Australia is a bad market but they haven't looked at NZI's record. There are some very good parts of the Australian market and NZI has been in them.

He asserted that the Pacific Basin as a rapid growth area was firmly in General Accident's strategy and that the deal with Brierley was not opportunism. The company knew the insurance side of NZI was sound and believed that the problems in the bank could be sorted out within a year or so.

Optimism was unjustified. In January 1989 the New Zealand trading group Equiticorp International, to which NZI Bank had lent money, collapsed. It was just one public example of the downturn. NZI was by no means the only bank in the area to have experienced problems through lending. For instance, the state bank, Bank of New Zealand, was recapitalised by the government and split into good bank/bad bank. Westpac, an older, larger institution, also fell victim. Needing to restructure its capital, NZI decided on a rights issue but, as its clients fell like dominoes, responsibly cancelled it. For a few hours the stock exchange suspended its shares, which knocked confidence internationally. When the NZI results for 1988–9 were published, while the insurance side showed a profit of NZ$120 million (£45.4 million), loan loss provisions and write-offs for the bank reached NZ$336.48 million (£121.4 million). Assets had fallen in value and, in a depressed economic outlook, their sale would not be enough to make up the shortfall. To avoid recapitalising the company, which had an interest-bearing debt of NZ$800 million, General Accident accepted the invitation of the NZI directors and offered to acquire the minority stake.

Its offer valued NZI at around £228 million compared with £780 million when it acquired the 51 per cent stake a year earlier. Minority shareholders lost out. Ian Menzies acknowledged that the company had originally paid too much and asserted that it had to acquire the minority 'to take a severe grip of the banking side'. Analysts reckoned that as much as £200 million might have to be injected to clean up the banking operations. Press comment was unfavourable. 'Stuck in New Zealand's banking mire up to its waist' said one City journalist under the headline 'GA sucked into Kiwi mud'. Another observed that 'The General, the cartoon soldier used to advertise the insurance giant, is trying to avoid being demoted to Major Disaster'. The company's 'credibility has been badly dented'. Once descriptions like that got into newspaper libraries, they were destined to be tags for years to come.

General Accident became sole owner of NZI, what had once been New Zealand's only genuinely international company, a company then 95 per cent locally owned. Ironically, going for growth to avoid a takeover had resulted in just that. Now General Accident had to get to grips with sorting out its problems. Barrie Holder, 44-year old chief accountant of General Accident, was appointed an executive director of NZI and chairman of the bank. His strategy was to sell the parts of the package that the company either did not want or could not envisage becoming profitable. An early sale, in mid-1990, was of NZI Life in Australia to Zurich Insurance. Dealing with the major problem of the bank involved splitting it into good bank/bad bank in both Australia and New Zealand, salvaging the former and winding down the latter. He believed that within a year the company would see a 'totally different result' to current losses.

Deeper investigation revealed that the whole bank was bad, an unsaleable unit. Where General Accident can take credit is in taking an insurance approach of fully reserving for the liabilities at the time and in moving quickly to make recoveries from the loans, turning them into real assets wherever possible. In

The NZI logo is designed to make readers look twice.

April 1991 the company announced its intention to close NZI Bank and the licence was returned early in 1992. Winding it up took another six years. Assets from merchant banks to paintings had to be sold. A few items to which value could be added were retained, among them a horse-selling operation, a hotel and an office site.

True, a long-term aim had been achieved in that an international insurance business had been gained, strengthening General Accident's presence in the Pacific Rim, but at enormous cost in money and management resources. There were lessons to be learned. The most obvious was cultural. Insurance and banking in the way that they had been mixed had not worked. A quick reaction was that they were different disciplines never destined to succeed under one umbrella. Yet there were examples elsewhere of banks moving into insurance, of mutually owned building societies converting into quoted banks that branched out into insurance. What was at fault in the NZI situation was that the company's two main constituents, insurance with a pedigree of almost 130 years and banking of about 15 at most, were already an ill fit. What General Accident acquired was an inexperienced bank lending in a late 1980s entrepreneurial fever. Given a more thoroughly researched bank operating in a different climate, there was no reason for an association not to succeed. In short, the historical lesson was that General Accident was not necessarily to rule out in the future an association in banking *per se*.

There was a fundamental question, thrown into relief by the NZI episode. Since Sir Stanley Norie-Miller stepped down as chairman in 1968, ending the strong family connection, General Accident had taken its character from its chief general manager, who from 1988 would be called chief executive. Besides being men of a different stamp they came from different disciplines, alternating between accounting and insurance. The distinction was to become important when it came to a decision on direction. Was General Accident going to remain an insurance company or diversify into a broader financial institution? Abroad, notably in the USA, the source of a third of its business and where the impact on the business of social changes had been the greatest, it had come to rely on investments to make up for underwriting losses. In seeking to expand its insurance interests in Asia-Pacific it had acquired a bank, a business it did not understand. That had not worked, magnifying an uncertainty of identity into an identity crisis. In a financial world that was undergoing structural change General Accident had

Moving house in New Zealand can be a literal business and buildings in transit have to be insured. This 21m x 12m gymnasium, relocated from a boys' home in Hamilton to a school, was carried on four trucks with four trailers.

appeared to act out of character. Would it return to its roots or diversify more successfully? It could not stand still.

There was another fundamental problem, the rôle of Perth at the head of a company two-thirds of which was overseas. The relationship between Perth and its overseas organisations was largely a devolved one, a factor that had appealed to the management of NZI. Staff got on with the job in their territories; periodic management visits from head office monitored progress. What Perth did not want to happen was for a local office to get into difficulties so deep that the territory became no longer worthwhile. In that way the man on the spot had support without undue interference, but that was not making the most of the resources within the corporation.

General Accident had international operations but it was not a multinational organisation with meetings of top management from around the world. Local companies reported into Perth but there was no cross-fertilisation among them. Each company had to operate within its own market and set of regulations. In that sense the decentralised structure of the corporation was imposed. From its side, what the corporation lacked was a central cohesion at a time when physical communications and telecommunications had made possible real multinational companies that operated as global enterprises. The world had shrunk around Perth but it was not acting like a world headquarters, merely a head office.

Viewed from the longer term, NZI had given General Accident a much bigger presence in the world's fastest economic growth area. The company consoled itself that the disaster the press had tagged it with would be comparatively short-lived; the benefits would be longer-term. Two tangible ones came from within NZI. Its BONUS (Broker On-line User System) was an innovation in that it involved a General Accident underwriter being placed with a broker, the two working together to assess and cover risk on the basis of shared information. Developed in Australia, it could be applied profitably with international brokers across the world. It was an example of specific experience from which many General Accident companies could gain an advantage.

The acquisition of The Yorkshire had brought into General Accident a number of staff, who had helped to modify the paternalist culture and enlarge the outlook of the company. Similarly, NZI brought in a number of talented people whose experience and attitudes would help change what in many ways was still a traditional company. Russell Evans from New Zealand, for example, brought a fresh approach to planning and a strategic approach to information technology and human resources. He also had a sound knowledge of business in Asia. The outstanding man was a classless Australian, Bob Scott, a mover and shaker. Scott was the third outsider in the history of the company who would have a major impact on its direction and fortunes.

Through nearly a century of expansion abroad General Accident had struck a balance as an international company with about one-third of its business in the UK, one-third in the USA, and the remaining third in the rest of the world.

IN the second decade of the century General Accident worldwide had to come to the rescue of the troubled US branch; in the penultimate decade the US company bailed out its parent to the tune of $1 billion while maintaining a strong surplus and its A.M. Best insurance ratings. The sum was made up by remitting extraordinary dividends, loans and the purchase from its parent of the flourishing Pilot Insurance in Canada. Because of its low dividend rate to Perth for several years the US territory represented a high percentage of the worldwide net worth. In 1990 the US accounted for 61.4 per cent of the corporation's worldwide net worth while its premium volume was only 27.6 per cent of the world total. Comparable US figures for 1982 were more evenly balanced: 40.9 per cent of worldwide net worth and 36.1 per cent of worldwide premium volume.

The figures reflected the appreciation of the dollar against sterling, creating more value back in the UK. They also demonstrated the importance of continued successful investments, the income from that source more than making up for underwriting losses. These came mainly from personal lines, home and auto. In the 1980s private passenger auto performed worse than property; in the 1990s property losses were higher. Part of the better experience on auto was accounted for by the introduction of air bags. According to the Institute for Highway Safety, air bags reduced deaths among right front passengers in frontal crashes by 18 per cent and by 11 per cent in all types of crash. General Accident offered a premium discount off medical payments and the no fault portions of the policy of 20 per cent for cars with driver side airbags and 30 per cent for cars with both driver and passenger airbags.

To tackle underwriting losses a new strategy was adopted from 1991, when Walter Farnam, who had an actuarial background, became US chairman and chief executive. Frank Coyne, president and chief operating officer, outlines the change:

Walter Farnam.

Until 1990 General Accident was known as a class underwriter working from a rule-based manual. If we had continued down that track we would have been outrun by our competitors. So we began to diversify, identifying a known or emerging risk and evaluating it for profitability. We progressively became a risk underwriter with a broad product stream. That meant segmentation of the market and adding to the capabilities of the organisation by bringing in skilled commercial underwriters. For example we entered the competitive market of inland marine in mid-1993 and three years later our specialists had an average of 19 years experience in that area. We created a surety bond department in 1993, came up with a plan for the National Association of Wholesaler-Distributors in 1995, when we also went into BONUS services. Over five years we identified more than 15 segments in the commercial market and produced appropriate schemes. They offered our agents a much broader range of specific products and to us they were profit centres.

If there were any doubts about the new strategy they were dispelled by Hurricane Andrew in 1992, which caused damage estimated at over $15 billion, more than any other US natural disaster. The net cost to General Accident was $49.5 million. It was not an isolated catastrophe. There was a record number of tornadoes, several hail storms, storms in the North East where General Accident had a large exposure, and riots in Los Angeles.

Premiums grew steadily but were exceeded by claims. Improvement in the operating ratio in one year was no guarantee of continuity. Results depended upon such unpredictable things as weather, litigation and the degree of success in combating fraud. There was the consolation that, had it not been for the strategy of moving from class to risk underwriting, results could have been much worse. They also compared favourably with other property and casualty insurance groups in the US, where General Accident ranked in the top 30 of 2,700 companies.

It also had behind it an international strength. Since 1991, when chief executive Nelson Robertson called a global planning meeting in Perth and those attending had sat down in working groups with colleagues from other countries, there had been much more interchange of experience and information. People got to know one another as individuals, not just names. What was a federation of independent companies and branches had become a much more cohesive organisation. In 1995 the US organisation adopted the parent company's logo as its own. A practical example of 'globalisation' at work was the introduction of BONUS around the world. In 15 months it became operational in 17 US national and regional brokers. A similar concept was also applied to developing partnerships with independent agents, as Jack Doyle, senior vice president field administration, explains:

Agents are looking to accomplish the same things as BONUS: to increase revenues and decrease costs. If a significant volume of business exists in an agency, General Accident will place a business development underwriter in the agent's office as many

US advertisements used the themes of doing business via independent agents and client relationships with the company.

Sadly, Some Independen
Those Who Know GA Wil

ts Will Tell You The Sun Is Setting.
ou Quite The Opposite.

At General Accident Insurance, we believe the sun is rising on a whole new field of opportunity.

That's why we're renewing our ninety-year policy of unconditional commitment to Independent Agents, the same people with whom we've conducted business on an exclusive basis throughout our history.

Independent Agents are a vital part of GA, and we've been a vital part of thousands of independent agencies.

Family agencies have grown from small-town storefronts to coast-to-coast companies writing GA policies. Young agents have trained at our branch offices across the country.

And through the years, we've learned American consumers receive extraordinary added value from doing business with Independent Agents.

Independence means objectivity, so families and businesses get the right policies at the right price. And that's a traditional value that will never go out of style.

That's why GA, and the Independent Agents who know us, remain optimistic about the future of the Independent Agent system.

For protecting the family car, the hearth and home, and the businesses that fuel our economy, GA will keep putting its faith in the men and women proudly called Independent Agents.

Sure as the sun comes up tomorrow.

GA GENERAL
ACCIDENT
INSURANCE

436 Walnut Street
Philadelphia, Pennsylvania 19105
Telephone (215) 625-1000

days a week as required. Having a thorough knowledge of our portfolio, for example what can be done for the operators of short line railroads or in the towing and recovery industry, he can initiate plans and programs that help our agents to increase sales and market share. The emphasis is on developing relationships through face-to-face meetings, electronic communications and our regular publication Focus on Partnership.

Increasing automation and cutting out duplication of effort led to fewer jobs. During 1997 employee numbers in the US were reduced from some 5,600 to 5,000, with an annual cost saving of £27 million.

Like the US company General Accident in Canada faced adverse trends in auto and property insurance and activities of fraudsters. Its response to the challenges was similar: strengthening relationships with brokers and agents through partnership programmes; investing in technology for electronic communication with them; new lines; product innovation, especially for affinity groups and market segments; more investigation of possible frauds; growth by acquisition. In 1992 General Accident acquired the general insurance business of the Prudential Corporation of the UK in Canada for C$165 million (£63 million), a discount of C$40 million. Its quality portfolio provided a larger share of the Quebec market, a small increase in exposure in Ontario, where the auto market was difficult, and reinforced the standing in other provinces. As a result General Accident was now the biggest non-government controlled property and casualty insurer in Canada, with a market share of eight per cent.

When Len Latham retired in 1995 after 14 years as president and chief executive, he could look back on the growth of premium income from C$157 million to C$906 million. Losses had been sustained in three years: 1984, 1985 and over C$100 million in 1994. Latham's successor was Howie Moran, the fifth man to head the company in 90 years. Like his predecessor, he had to stay ahead of over 200 other insurers in the market and was also faced with competition from European companies setting up in Canada. There were several strands to his policy:

With about 60 per cent of our premium income coming from personal lines, for a more even balance we had to achieve substantial growth on the commercial side. That meant closer partnerships, for example with the reducing number of brokers, who were also facing competition from direct writers. Working with risk managers of large organisations would enable them to institute better loss control measures. Technology had to be used cost-effectively, for instance video teleconferencing saving the time and expense of travel for meetings or training. Internationally, within General Accident we were acquiring knowledge and sharing skills. We also had to leverage up our size, follow our customers so that General Accident could provide a worldwide service to large Canadian corporations.

Howie Moran.

Many of these strands came together with the C$600 million (£265 million) cash purchase in 1997 of Toronto-based Canadian General Insurance Group, the nation's eleventh largest property and casualty insurer. In the words of Canadian General's investment bank adviser, it was 'one of the fastest but deepest ever due diligence exercises we have seen'. A team of 25 experts – led by Perth but largely made up of staff from the operating businesses in Canada, USA and UK – made sure that General Accident Group was not taking on any hidden liabilities. Canadian General Insurance Group was a federation of businesses ripe for rationalisation. Before the deal was closed General Accident sold off parts of the business it did not want.

From the first day of due diligence, plans for combining the Canadian businesses were formulated. Integration of the two companies, a consolidation in a fragmented market, was expected to produce cost savings of C$75 million from 1999, mainly through reducing staff numbers, some 600 out of a workforce of 2,300, and the use of Canadian General's information technology systems. The combined companies were expected to have a 10 per cent share of the Canadian market.

Meanwhile John Denault, senior vice president specialising in marketing, adds a cautionary note on global marketing:

Learning what other General Accident companies are doing in market segments is very useful but we have to check the contents of packages against local situations because liability laws differ. For instance, where a hotel landlord serving drinks to customers is liable for their subsequent conduct, say as drivers or in cases of assault, we have to insist under the terms of a policy that liquor sales to individuals are relatively small against food sales. Packages for market segments cannot be standard around the world nor even in one country. Underwriting farm business for the huge acreages out on the Prairies is very different from covering rural Ontario.

Ice storms in Canada led to a rise in auto and property claims.

New Zealand continued to be a good market. Operating under the name New Zealand Insurance because NZI had been four times bigger and was better known than General Accident, the company was the largest commercial insurer and the second largest in the personal market. It aimed to be number one by providing 'Peace of Mind'. In what was an over-supplied market there were expected to be further opportunities for growth through rationalisation within the industry. As part of its strategy to withdraw from small life business around the world, the NZI life subsidiary was sold to the Prudential in 1997 for £70.6 million. When Hector Smith left as general manager of NZI in New Zealand to become managing director of the Australian company at the start of 1996 he could look back on a growth in written premiums and shareholders' funds, underwriting profits, and solvency margins around 50 per cent.

Australia continuing to be a problem, with disappointing underwriting performance, was a challenge. Various remedial actions were taken, including an alliance with a financial institution to sell home and contents insurance through telesales and direct mail. It would take some time though to turn round the company, also operating under the NZI name. In default of any immediate rationalisation of an overcrowded industry, the concentration was on profitable core business, drawing strength from General Accident worldwide.

Asia as represented by the 'tiger' economies of Brunei, Hong Kong, Malaysia, Singapore, Taiwan and Thailand was growing, becoming a larger portion of the Pacific area business. There were specific problems such as the theft of high value vehicles in Hong Kong and their rapid shipment to mainland China. In Japan, where the company had been a member of the British Insurance Group since the end of WW2, it had been unable to develop an acceptable market share and level of profitability and so withdrew from the group at the end of 1993. New Zealand Insurance was still represented there. South Korea and the reviving Vietnam were possible territories in which to open business.

In Europe the company had no more than footholds, not through lack of a genuine interest in the area, although in experience it was not a good market. As local acquisitions had been expensive the policy had been to get established, sometimes with the loose co-operation of the Italian insurer Generali, and then grow organically. Results were mixed, necessitating periodic local reorganisations, redundancies, the cancellation of unprofitable business and the imposition of higher rates and terms. In France in 1996 General Accident both opened a branch to sell unit-linked investments and withdrew from the construction insurance market. It also withdrew completely in 1997 from Denmark, Norway and Sweden, where the

In 1997 General Accident in Hong Kong flagged in its calendar that it was the only insurer in the territory to conform to the quality of the International Organisation for Standardisation.

operations had failed to reach a size necessary to produce consistent profits.

Ireland, for so long a territory of varying fortunes, enjoyed some good years in the economic boom of the mid-1990s. European Union money had been used to improve the infrastructure, notably of the road system, making the country a more attractive entry point for overseas investors in the single market. As a consequence well-educated young people did not have to emigrate to use their skills and were able to contribute to the home economy. In 1998, with an encouraging outlook for life and pensions business, GA Life opened an office in Dublin.

A significant move was made in 1996 with the acquisition in the deregulated German market of UAP Allgemeine, a company with a 1995 turnover of £116 million. It was amalgamated with the existing operation to form General Accident Versicherungs AG, making Germany GA's largest business in continental Europe. The new company was strong in the Saar region and had links with a national network of brokers. While BONUS units had been introduced in Belgium, France and Ireland, further benefits were expected from a closer integration of European operations, with the pooling of knowledge, expertise and best practice. Packaged products that had been successful in the UK, for instance, were being adapted for local markets.

While expanding through acquisitions in major territories General Accident retrenched in the interests of profitability elsewhere in the world. Following the severe hurricanes of the early 1990s and the likelihood that, with changing global weather patterns, a similar spate of natural disasters might be repeated, re-insurance costs rose steeply. Foreseeing unacceptable levels of loss, the company withdrew from the Caribbean region, selling operations in the Bahamas, Barbados, Dominican Republic, Jamaica and Puerto Rico, badly hit by Hurricane Marilyn in 1995. The business in Kenya was sold. In Brazil, after a period of hyper-inflation, the introduction of a new currency in 1994 benefited operations.

Where there was a promising prospect General Accident re-established itself. In South Africa levels of crime were the main cause for concern. Most of the Asian operations were consolidated under the General Accident brand name instead of perpetuating that of the subsidiary NZI. A representative office was opened in Beijing in 1994 and, in anticipation of obtaining a trading

Property investments, like this retail centre developed by Grosvenor Estate Holdings in Dublin, provide a steady income stream for policyholders.

licence to operate in China, two further offices were opened in 1996 in the developing cities of Shanghai and Guangzhou, and in 1997 in Chengdu. A joint venture was set up in Indonesia, General Accident taking a 60 per cent stake in the new company. In India The Yorkshire operations, mainly insuring small businesses and bloodstock, had been nationalised soon after the company was merged into General Accident in 1967. When the possibility of allowing participation by foreign companies was announced in the mid-1990s the company established a representative office in Mumbai (Bombay) and signed a memorandum of understanding with the Wadia Group, a leading manufacturing and trading company based in that city.

Through nearly a century of expansion abroad General Accident had struck a balance as an international company, with about one-third of its business in the UK, one-third in the USA, and the remaining third in the rest of the world. Its overseas strength was in the English-speaking world: in the USA, Canada, Australia and New Zealand. In the rest of the world when Britain was a great power and its Empire was intact, General Accident felt the imperative to be as widely represented as possible. After WW2, when Britain's status declined in relation to the superpowers and it relinquished its Empire, company representation was selective. Each territory was judged on its own merits as a market. Where governments nationalised the industry or restricted its scope by insisting on too high a proportion of local ownership and control or the risks and economic prospects were unfavourable there was no point in maintaining a presence. There was no overall commitment to a region that justified the continuance of a loss-leader in a particular territory. So, although Britain was a member of the European Union, it did not entail General Accident having a branch in every member country.

Towards the end of the nineteenth century, when General Accident was founded, steam had given man greater muscle and speeded travel through railways and ships. These were the means that transported Francis Norie-Miller around his expanding business empire. At the end of the twentieth century two technological advances had transformed the conduct of business by management teams. Oil was now the prime source of energy. Used in jet engines, it made the farthest places no more than a day apart and London/New York could be a supersonic day trip. More immediate, electronics handled information, storing, processing and sending it in microseconds. Technically the world had shrunk. It was a global marketplace, with features common across national frontiers. In insurance there was competition from direct writers, rising crime against personal property, a greater incidence of fraud, some of it on a large scale, and a bias in society towards the rights of the consumer. To deal effectively with common problems companies had to reorganise themselves. As the end of the century approached, Perth had to adopt a fresh perspective on the world.

The corporation had to take a hard strategic look at itself, be frank about its strengths and weaknesses, and decide where it wanted to be and how it was going to get there.

IN Perth, after the low-key celebration of the company's centenary, there was no immediate sense of embarking on a second century. Rather were the pressures coming from outside. In the interests of the consumer, who should be given the best financial advice, the Financial Services Act 1986 drew a distinction between tied agents offering the products of one company and independent financial advisers. Both should be properly trained as intermediaries for selling life and investment products and, for regulation of their conduct, the industry funded bodies set up under the Securities and Investments Board. It was a blow to many General Accident staff who had been encouraged by the company to sell policies to friends, neighbours and relatives.

Signboards of GA Property Services increased public awareness of the company as a whole.

General Accident's biggest life product was the endowment mortgage, about one quarter of which was sold through estate agents, few of whom were true intermediaries within the meaning of the new Act. If General Accident owned estate agents, it would gain a high street presence to sell endowment mortgages and be in a position to sell non-life products, such as cover for the property and its contents, at the time a house was bought. A separate company, GA Property Services, was therefore set up to operate as a tied agent and it set about acquiring existing chains of agents and single agencies. The preference was for those that were more professional, including chartered surveyors.

Other insurance companies, banks and building societies were seeking them as well and it was a sellers' market. In a two-year race to establish a national chain with a brand image, General Accident inevitably paid dearly, in hindsight sometimes twice as much as an agency was worth. Altogether 67 firms were bought, amounting to over 500 individual offices, with prospects of another 50–60 due to open. Areas in which the company emerged strongly were Scotland and in England the South East, where the highest value properties were, South West, West Midlands and North East. The latter became in 1992 the site of the head office, Newcastle-upon-Tyne.

Jim Boxall was appointed general manager of the division in 1990:

After the boom created by the Nigel Lawson budget of 1988, which sent house prices soaring while at the same time ending the possibility of two people claiming tax relief on the same mortgage, the market contracted sharply. Transactions more than halved in number and estate agencies were losing money. A few entrants cut their losses and got out. General Accident stayed in and trimmed its network to some 350 offices, selling off agencies with adjuncts specialising in things such as agricultural land and the sale of fine art. Concentration was in residential sales and lettings, with the accompanying survey staff. Commercial surveying along with investment work and property management was limited to a few major English cities. The major benefit from the agencies accrued not so much to GA Property Services as to GA Life, which received some 20 per cent of its new business in this way.

Also caught by the housing recession was mortgage indemnity, which caused heavy claims by the early 1990s, when interest rates rose, property prices fell and in the recession unemployment led to mortgagees falling behind with their payments and an unprecedented level of house repossessions. Fortunately, the company had a lower exposure than other insurers.

Under Britain's first woman Prime Minister, Margaret Thatcher, the Conservative government had increasingly moved from the estates to the estate agents. After the recession of the early 1980s she oversaw the release of energy in British business and the enterprise, profit-making culture of the latter part of the decade. Britain was now a post-industrial society, living on services, leisure and information technology, personified by yuppies, young, upwardly mobile urban professionals working in finance, the media and other services. Yuppies did not live in Perth, but in its way General Accident was part of the prevailing culture. Results for the three years 1986–8 were a record. An area in which it was fortunately not greatly involved was the sequence of major disasters that

In 1988 the prime minister, Margaret Thatcher, visited head office. She is seen here with Nelson Robertson.

occurred in the UK during the latter half of the 1980s. These included the cap-sizing of the *Herald of Free Enterprise,* the fire at King's Cross Underground station, the crushing of football spectators at Hillsborough, the Clapham Junction rail crash and the collision of the *Marchioness* on the Thames.

Nowhere was the success of the company more evident than in GA Life, the new name for what had been Yorkshire-General. Benefiting from a much clearer identity with General Accident, the company was progressing under the marketing drive of Jack Philp backed by the actuarial skills of Norman Graham. GA Life established its own branch network with on-line links to headquarters in York. Branch openings were occasions for publicising the new presence in local business communities. Field staff were selected through psychometric testing, trained, equipped with better products to sell, and moti-vated through commensurate awards and sales conferences, their activities being supported by advertisements in the insurance press. The new identity was more than just a name change. GA Life established connections with a number of building societies, among them Cheshire, Derby-

The purpose-built new office of GA Life in York enabled a number of scattered departments to come together under one roof, where new technology could be accommodated. Lord Airlie, GA chairman, opened the office on 29 September 1993.

shire, Leeds and Holbeck, and Newcastle, as tied agents. After years of bonuses less than competitors, a more progressive allocation to policyholders was justi-fied. Investment bonds, personal equity plans (PEPs) and unit trusts were developed and by the end of 1991 GA Life could claim that it was no longer a life department but a force in the life assurance business with its own invest-ment arm. In 1992 Bill Jack took over as general manager. Having a strong background in marketing and distribution, he concentrated on the develop-ment of the company's distribution channels. It went on to provide life admin-istration for building societies such as the UK's largest, the Halifax, and National & Provincial. Third party administration enabled GA Life to spread its processing costs over a larger volume of business. Expansion forced depart-ments to take scattered offices in York, which were brought together in a sec-ond major office in the city opened in 1993.

The one mishap it had in complying with the Financial Services Act occurred when, along with Commercial Union, it was fined £50,000 by the Life Assurance and Unit Trust Regulatory Organisation (LAUTRO) for a share-holding in the collapsed broking concern of Roger Levitt. This was a minor mishap compared to the scandal of pensions mis-selling, encouraging employ-ees to switch from occupational schemes into allegedly higher private pensions.

Here GA Life stood out as one of the best performers in the industry when companies such as Legal & General, the Prudential and Royal & Sun Alliance were being named and shamed in Parliament. GA Life did not appear in any name and shame list. In a national total exceeding two million between 1988 and 1994 the company, relatively small in that business and strong on compliance, had only some 1,900 questionable cases.

From the start of 1996 it moved more strongly into that market with the 1995 acquisition for £170 million of Provident Mutual, having previously shown interest in Scottish Equitable. Founded in 1840 as The Provident Clerks' Mutual Benefit Association and Benevolent Fund, its original policyholders were penurious, respectable City clerks like Bob Cratchit in the employ of Charles Dickens' character Ebenezer Scrooge. Until the late 1950s its main business was in the transport industry and since then it had moved into group and top hat pension schemes. In its first year as part of GA Life it brought in valuable investment expertise from the City and more than doubled the company's share of the UK pensions business. It was a weak brand that was soon integrated. Pensions and personal investment business accounted for 50 per cent of new business premium income in 1992; five years later it had risen to 80 per cent.

Provident Mutual logo.

Although small overseas life companies that failed to prove viable were sold, Silvey Life in the USA being a prime example, some new interests were developed in continental Europe, where France and Germany were the two largest insurance markets. In France from 1995 there was a branch operation and a subsidiary, GA Vie. In Germany from 1996 a similar set-up included the subsidiary Assecura, a Luxembourg company progressively acquired from 1990. Sweden had an agent, Yorkshire Forsakringar.

By 1988 it had become clear to General Accident that its market in personal lines was threatened by the growing appeal of insurers dealing directly with the public over the telephone. General Accident had to follow suit. One of its appeals, emphasised in the press, TV and below-the-line advertising, was that the company paid for the call on an 0800 121 number. For instance, the travel bond number 0800 121 007, echoing the fictional adventurer James Bond, was easily remembered. From the company's point of view it was also a low-cost operation. With only one or two locations, there was a concentration of running costs and economies of scale. The customer did not have to pay a percentage of his premium to an intermediary. The concept was a step beyond the way Scottish General operated, as the direct insurer for the insurance broker. Without the intervention of a broker, round the clock, motor and house insurance could be simply arranged through a short series of questions, the answers to which an operator entered on a computer screen.

Even though it knew it would face opposition from brokers, in mid-1988

General Accident set up in Hamilton, Scotland, GA Direct to handle initially motor insurance. This was less controversial than the introduction of the DC Plan in 1969 as the market had changed. Household insurance followed two years later. In the summer of 1990 a scheme was entered into with the Ford Motor Company, which provided free insurance on certain of its vehicles for a year. Like its predecessor Morris scheme in the 1920s it proved most unprofitable. Most of the enlarged operation moved in 1991 to Glasgow. Customer surveys revealed that Scottish voices exuded confidence and won the trust of customers.

John Parkinson, chief manager of GA Direct Division, explains how the original concept broadened:

With improvements in database, telesales and call centre capabilities, GA Direct Division evolved by late 1994 a structure to serve distinct customer groups. It also introduced travel and, uniquely, creditor insurance as direct offerings. Highly profitable, these innovations supported the increasingly competitive motor and home markets. Partnership Direct provided these facilities for clients of organisations such as the Post Office, the Halifax, Clydesdale Bank, and affinity groups such as Unity Financial Services for trade union members. General Accident Direct marketed the same products to its own customers, starting to call those on its existing database. Operating from intermediaries' offices, PLANet provided portfolio underwriting and marketing support via GA personnel and systems while Scottish General, still dealing mainly with motor, emphasised its low-cost delivery and electronic trading potential. Select Direct, a telebroking joint venture with the Aon Group, made GA an intermediary and provided commission income from callers who did not take up GA Direct policies.

Experience and software advances made it possible to learn more about customers and their buying patterns, showing up opportunities for cross selling and developing new business. Geodemographic data became more sophisticated, going beyond simple postcode identification of areas at particular risk from, say, burglary, flooding or subsidence. Mapping of claims experience was also easier, leading to accusations against insurance companies of 'red lining', refusing to cover certain areas. The reply was that whether or not to accept a particular risk is a commercial judgement.

Another centralised service established by the company was its own legal helpline, in 1989. Policyholders could call at any time for free advice on any legal matter, which did not have to be linked to or correspond with the policy. The advice, given by staff qualified in English and Scottish law, proved popular and some 300 calls a week were being answered. Analysis of the call reports revealed trends in policyholders' concerns. About a third of the calls were on consumer matters, another third on road traffic, and the rest on employment, family, landlord and tenant, neighbours, and miscellaneous financial affairs. An integral part of customer service was the provision of documents, all of which were produced in-house at a purpose-built print centre opened in Perth in 1993.

As elsewhere in the world General Accident was having to deal with an increase in fraud. Dave Crerar, who had plenty of branch experience in spotting and dealing with fraudsters and had visited Australia and the USA to confer with colleagues on the subject, set up in Dundee in 1993 a unit dedicated to combating the crime:

Fraud has always been with us. It was minor, on the level of the hot coal burning a hole in the hearthrug, the damaged article being passed from neighbour to neighbour. For many reasons there's been a marked decline in the standards of morality and a very noticeable escalation in the levels of fraud. There are people who live by their wits, taking advantage of the weak in the community and the powerful, the insurance companies, regarded like the Inland Revenue as fair game, a soft touch. A lot of fraud is an exaggeration of a legitimate situation, invention of or enhancing the value of missing items, the disabling back injury resulting from an accident. You can get some Oscar-winning performances staged to fool the medical profession. Being customer-conscious has also helped the dishonest to take advantage. Certain places and types of business have always been suspect. What was new in the mid to late 1980s was the scale of fraud and its spreading to all classes of society, including aristocrats and members of the professions.

In hindsight the Association of British Insurers (formerly the British Insurance Association) put the date when many otherwise law-abiding citizens decided to take advantage of a disaster as October 1987, when a hurricane hit southern England. Insurers quickly settled claims totalling £1.4 billion. Another storm, in January 1990, cost them nearly twice as much. Two years later the industry responded with a Crime-Check Campaign and in 1994 set up the Comprehensive Underwriting Exchange (CUE) for household insurance. Bob Scott of General Accident chaired Insurance Database Services overseeing the project. Motor was added in 1995, when a Crime and Fraud Prevention Bureau was also established to measure the scale of the problem.

Figures are best estimates. For General Accident, Dave Crerar believes that at any one time some £20 million worth of claims deserve investigation:

It's not just big cases. Repetition of frauds can mount up. So as well as the one-offs that don't smell right we're looking at patterns of crime, the luggage containing everything new that has a habit of getting lost, claims when the ink's scarcely dry on the policy, documents forged with modern technology. It's a battle of wits on an international scale. At times we're dealing with some remarkably astute people who have the brains to make a good honest living but they prefer to take a short cut. We have to stay ahead of their scams.

Two General Accident cases that made the media were the Dandonneau affair in France and the Lord Brocket case in England. In mid-1987 in the south of France a car crashed and burst into flames, killing the passenger, ostensibly a company director, Yves Dandonneau. On receiving a claim for over two million francs, the claim being tripled because it was an accident, General Accident's local life company, GA Vie, became suspicious as the policy was just over two months old. A company investigation revealed that Dandonneau had not been honest about his medical condition and that just before the accident he had sold his majority stake in a small company. Further investigation by the association for French life companies uncovered other suspicious circumstances and a string of policies with various insurers. Dandonneau, his face altered by plastic surgery, was traced. His victim, the passenger, was a drugged tramp.

Deeply in debt and with a failing marriage, Lord Brocket attempted to restore his fortunes by claiming that four classic Italian cars had been stolen from the electronically protected collection at his stately home in May 1991. Fighting his lawsuit because they believed but could not prove the £4.5 million claim was fraudulent, for three years General Accident and Lloyd's refused to settle. His scam was revealed by a blackmailer who had been involved in manufacturing evidence about an imminent sale of the 'stolen' cars. Brocket received a five-year jail sentence.

Severe road accidents emphasised the need for continuing road safety campaigns.

Rising fraud was not the prime management concern. With UK underwriting losses being recorded in the four years 1984–7, mainly through motor, the company launched in 1986, in a joint initiative with the Department of Transport, a road safety campaign. Over the next few years it was to spend some £12 million on promoting road safety. In 1985 the total casualty toll of deaths and injuries on Britain's roads amounted to 317,524 and in the first six months of 1986 the company paid out almost £100 million in motor claims. Other socially responsible sponsorships were the launch of Children's Traffic Club in 1989 and support for Neighbourhood Watch schemes. In 1988 UK underwriting was in profit, adding lustre to the record results for the corporation as a whole for the three years 1986–8. A setback came in 1989, when overall pre-tax profits were halved to £147 million. The downturn was attributed to losses in NZI Bank and a worldwide underwriting loss, mainly from Hurricane Hugo.

Worse was to come: losses for three successive years, 1990–2, the first in the corporation's history, reflecting the general performance of the market. Dividends were paid out of reserves, but there was no allocation from the

Incidents can occur at any time. This warehouse on the Quayside, Newcastle-upon-Tyne, caught fire on Christmas Eve 1989.

employee profit sharing scheme. The nadir was 1991, when an after-tax loss of £139.4 million was reported to the dismayed shareholders. In 1992, to pay maturing debt, £140 million preference shares were issued, the largest ever single preference issue by a UK financial institution. A further £110 million was raised in 1993. Like those of other composite insurers, losses resulted from a combination of the worldwide recession and underwriting results. For General Accident the situation was exacerbated by the drain of the NZI Bank. Just how much that venture cost the corporation, even threatened its survival, was a matter of much speculation. Estimates started at £250 million. That was almost the after-tax profit of £245.3 million in 1993, which almost made up for the previous three years' losses. From then on profits were on a rising curve.

Cyclical movements on this scale influenced management changes and drove management decisions. During the late 1980s, in tune with the times, the company culture was financial. Ian Menzies joined in 1985 as general manager with

GA's home city of Perth was badly flooded in 1993, causing an upsurge in claims from local policyholders. Out of local patriotism, many were insured with GA.

overall responsibility for finance and was appointed to the board. He was primarily responsible for three acquisitions: Pilot Insurance in Canada in 1986; UK estate agencies from 1988; and in 1988 the 51 per cent stake in NZI, followed in 1989 by the minority holding. Although he was the prime mover, each decision was ultimately down to the board. In financial terms each acquisition was less successful than its predecessor, contributing to a downturn in the corporation's fortunes. It was no exaggeration to say that a crisis was looming.

An outside observer watched the internal politics:

As chief executive Buchan Marshall had three lieutenants: Ian Menzies, a relative newcomer; Tom Roberts and Nelson Robertson, both seasoned insurance men. Buchan appointed both as joint deputy chief general managers. It was a signal to the stock market that one of them would succeed him and that Menzies' time at General Accident was coming to an end. He was not made a scapegoat. The realignment was a General Accident move in the old gentlemanly style, comforting to the market in that the company was returning to its previous culture.

Of the two deputies, Nelson Robertson was appointed chief executive from January 1990. It was a clear sign that the company had left behind its foray into the dealing world of the City of London and was back with its root Perth culture, insurance. Joining in 1958 as a graduate, Nelson had seen the old patriarchal regime under Sir Stanley and been part of the collective management under Macdonald and his successors. His experience was broad: working in a branch, computing, the first direct writing, life assurance, and monitoring overseas business, which did not include being tarred with the NZI brush. Having been responsible for business systems planning, he understood the rôle of technology and the fundamental importance of corporate planning, almost non-existent when he became chief executive. Without a corporate plan, the organisation lacked clear objectives and targets against which performance could be measured, dealing tactically rather than implementing a strategy.

The other outstanding weakness was the absence of international cohesion. Although two-thirds of the business was overseas the companies reported to Perth and seldom talked to one another, often spending unnecessary effort in dealing locally with what was a common problem. For instance, three General Accident companies, in Australia, UK and USA, independently evaluated and bought from one supplier the same piece of software to help with claims estimating and settlement. A more serious debit was that the corporation lacked synergy. It was not making the most of the resources it had.

Deploying his own resources, Nelson Robertson appointed Barrie Holder, who had left a small team behind in New Zealand to sort out the rest of NZI

Below a portrait of Sir
Stanley Norie-Miller,
Nelson Robertson, chief
executive 1990–5.

Bank, as a general manager responsible for finance. His elevation removed some responsibility from Ian Menzies, who continued to look after investments and estate agencies, adding responsibility for legal affairs. He left at the end of 1990. Three deputy general managers were appointed: Bob Scott and Bill Jack for the UK; Charles Barker Bennett for overseas. Jim Boxall took over the estate agency business. Following Bob Scott's appointment as general manager for the UK, a further reorganisation followed with Bill Jack being appointed general manager of the life company, taking over from Jack Philp and building on his success.

On his appointment Nelson Robertson realised that a fundamental review of the company's strategy was an urgent priority. The corporation had to take a hard strategic look at itself, be frank about its strengths and weaknesses, and decide where it wanted to be and how it was going to get there. Retrenchment was not the way forward. On the other hand, to keep options open, General Accident plc was launched as a holding company, permitting expansion into non-insurance activities across the European Community. To evolve positive policies, the new team sat down with members of the Boston Consulting Group to develop a corporate strategy. It had two principal strands: acting in concert worldwide, summed up in the word 'globalisation'; and responding to the market. Both involved explanation to employees, much of it through video, and training.

In January 1991 Nelson Robertson held a meeting in Perth of managers from around the world to introduce the corporate mission statement defining General Accident's goals for the next ten years. One of the fundamental points he stressed was returning to core competence, the business of insurance and the importance of underwriting. Investment had been successful in the US but that was not a reliable substitute for a well-run insurance operation, cyclical though that might be. His point and the pressure he applied were prophetic. In 1994 the US was over-invested in long bonds when interest rates rose. Depletion in capital value was largely rectified in 1995. The underlying reason for the success of the US company, as it had been in Fred Richardson's day, was its selection of risks, making money on the business it did not write. Focusing on smaller commercial lines, it was not exposed to larger long-term liabilities associated with lethal products such as asbestos and the reparation of environmental damage. Over the long term in the US the company performed slightly better than the insurance industry on underwriting but substantially better on the investment side.

Frank Coyne, executive vice-president from the US, summed up the mood of the 1991 meeting:

Car thefts were increasing.

At a very difficult time Nelson's style was an outward calm, a constructive approach to turning the organisation round. A great benefit of the meeting was that top people got to know one another much better, which made for more effective communications.

Changing what was still in many ways a federation of independent states was not going to happen quickly. 'Globalisation' had many aspects that all had to be dealt with before a revolution could be effected. For instance, an international electronic network had to be established for routine exchange of information. The possibilities of other technologies for bringing people together had to be explored. Having turned their attention from immediate problems, managers went back to their offices with their eyes on a new horizon and some ways of reaching it. Perth itself, the heart of the company, would be an example of what could be done.

While the strategic review was taking place results continued to deteriorate and it was reinforced to Nelson that this was not just a passing phase attributable to a run of bad weather in the UK and other external factors. More action was needed than simply raising rates and altering policy terms to keep pace with claims, although that did happen often as the recession went on. Underwriting results in the US and other major businesses were also causing concern, all reinforcing the need to focus on the core competence of insurance.

Of Nelson Robertson's recent appointees the one to make the most impact within the corporation was Bob Scott, who had been chief general manager of NZI in Australia. For Scott it was a return to Scottish roots but bringing with him an objective view born of broad insurance and managerial experience. His father, born in Edinburgh and qualified as an accountant in Dundee, joined the Vestey meat group and was promoted to Australia in 1938. When young Bob showed an interest in insurance through a holiday job with the Norwich Union Fire Insurance Society in Wellington, his father remarked 'There's a very good company in Scotland called General Accident'. An association was nearly 30 years away. In 1959 the 17-year old Bob joined the South British which, to keep him, offered two years in London and an opportunity to visit his grandparents. His grandmother's home was in Fife. In London he was a member of a team evaluating the company's loss-making business in the UK, which entailed fact-finding around the country. Back in New Zealand he turned his energies to promoting and implementing various reorganisations to improve results, and gained underwriting experience on the international side of the business. Having worked on the integration of NZI and South British, he went to Australia to turn that round. He had the qualifications for integrating NZI and General Accident in Australia.

Regarding General Accident as a sleeping giant and nicknamed Hurricane Bob not so much for handling the aftermath of a cyclone in Queensland as for his hands-on style – 'I want to know and be involved' – as general manager for

This motorway accident was close to home. When a transit van and trailer veered off the M90 near the company's head office in November 1992 the company secretary, Richard Whitaker, and the company nurse, then Margaret Wilson, were quickly on the scene followed by security staff. Although the van and trailer were badly damaged, the driver and passenger were unhurt.

support unit for the City of London. Service did not have to suffer. It could be improved, as it was in motor with the establishment of over 500 repair centres serving all comprehensive private car policyholders throughout the UK. GA BONUS was set up in 1992 as a separate unit, developing its own identity.

There was much 'fine tuning' and adjustment of rates on home and motor policies, one of the problems being that in the economic downturn more motorists were driving without insurance. Discounts were offered for fitting an approved anti-theft device to cars; cars were grouped in more rating bands and no claims bonus restructured; because of the unfavourable experience cover was declined for self-drive minibuses, one of which raised a claim for £1.5 million. In 1993, along with other companies, General Accident withdrew from the 'knock-for-knock' agreement. The deliberate policy was to reduce the volume of motor business, concentrating on the profitable parts of it. Cover was dropped for the family sport policy as well as point-to-point racing and hunter chasing. Stolen goods were replaced not in cash but in goods obtained at bulk discounts. Such arrangements were tactical details.

The company was interested to see how change was affecting the organisation. It commissioned consultants to conduct 'a culture mapping exercise and communications audit' by issuing a questionnaire to staff in Perth, the direct operation in Hamilton and the new model branches. Many staff had come to realise that, were it not for the changes, accompanied by the training programmes, they might well not have a job. They also found that in the new culture they had greater freedom

and flexibility to achieve results. All employees were organised in focus groups meeting quarterly to discuss issues, including the financial outcome. *Gen*, the staff newspaper, was succeeded by *Voice*, a colourful magazine.

Within branches life could be more satisfying. From 1993 Bob Thomson was in charge of personal lines business across branches:

In switching from a product-driven to a market-driven method of working we had two major projects in the branch network. Customer service was a culture change from making money. In underwriting we also considered customers' individual circumstances more closely. In home insurance, for example, where the property was. Was it exposed to floods, storms, subsidence, which with drier summers had become a major factor in losses on buildings? Natural hazards and the likelihood of crime affect contents ratings. We drew on specialist sources for more accurate data.

In 1992 the company appointed its first woman to the board, Louise Botting, presenter of *Money Box*, the BBC radio programme offering advice on personal finance.

Redundancies in the industry were not unique to General Accident. Other insurance companies, in which employees also felt they had job security for life, followed suit. In hindsight, General Accident was fortunate in taking action early. Coming from Australia, Bob Scott was untrammelled by personal local loyalties and was able to implement an objective business decision, cutting out layers of administration and driving down costs. The company emerged with a better balanced portfolio of non-life business with a more sophisticated monitoring of figures.

Taking shareholder questions seriously are (left to right): Nelson Robertson, chief executive, Barrie Holder, finance director, Bob Scott, general manager UK, and Walter Farnam, chairman and chief executive officer USA.

Taking over at the most difficult time for General Accident in more than a century, Nelson Robertson achieved a remarkable turnround. His six years as chief executive were evenly divided between the first three, losses making them the worst in the corporation's history, followed by the three best results ever. Sir Alick Rankin, appointed a joint deputy chairman in 1995, summed up the achievement:

Nelson was something of a white knight. Working with Lord Airlie, he pulled the company together, brought back self-confidence and put the company on track.

Under his leadership the company generally outperformed its peers. What Nelson had demonstrated was that the company's root strength in insurance, properly managed, could produce excellent financial results. It was not the old insurance of processing clerks, an army poorly equipped and led, firing off shots in all directions hopefully. The new breed of insurance man was competing in a market where traditional demarcations were being blurred in bancassurance and big retailers were adding insurance as another profitable line in their outlets. Traditional companies had to adapt, stake our their sectors of the market and go for them.

Bob Scott became chief executive in 1996.

When it came to Nelson Robertson's succession the pattern that had been followed, through happenstance, since Sir Stanley's day, a financial man alternating with an insurance man as chief executive, was a subject of speculation. To continue or not? In 1994 Nelson appointed two deputy chief executives: Barrie Holder, the financial director and a board member since 1990, who had effectively disentangled the affairs of NZI Bank and steered the acquisition of Provident Mutual; and Bob Scott, a director from 1992, who in the words of the *Financial Times* had 'been responsible for reorganising the group's sluggish UK business'. The board spent considerable time discussing the succession, which was announced at the dinner following the annual general meeting in April. Barrie Holder knew that he was going to have an important supporting rôle but, unfortunately, before he could take it up he died, of a heart attack on 30 November. That left a huge gap in the top management team to be filled when Bob Scott took over on 1 January 1996. After nearly 30 years the pattern had been broken, but there was an urgent need to strengthen the financial arm.

Bob Scott was not a deal-a-minute operator. His style was to do the homework with the team first and then act quickly.

AT home, one of Bob Scott's main relaxations was do-it-yourself. It was typical of the man: practical, hands-on, with the satisfaction of personal achievement. He applied the same operating principles in the office, understanding the business from the bottom up. His view of GA was unequivocally an insurance one: 'The company's underlying value is in its underwriting'. Throughout his career he had always reported to an insurance man, learning from his mentors and then doing it his way. Under Nelson Robertson, he had put an end to patriarchal, job-for-life attitudes. General Accident was no longer a large organisation under which staff could shelter. Every employee was now part of a discrete unit with its own focus, resources at its disposal, targets to meet and performance to be measured. Within a short span of time a new sense of personal responsibility had perforce been created. Some, especially in middle management, where the impact was hardest felt, saw it as an unfortunate shake-up, the end of a tradition, what had been for over a century a very personal company in which individuals counted. In its place was rule by numbers, the imperatives of each business to return a minimum of 15 per cent on allocated capital, a figure to which everything else had to bend.

The more objective view was that in a much more competitive environment Scott, like a spring gardener, had cut back to permit organic growth. Working in dedicated units, people had opportunities to grow the business. There was a new dynamic about it. People could see and appreciate the results of their own efforts. For the professionalism of its staff training and development the company received an Investors in People award. As chief executive, Scott's job was to take the company forward from its new higher base. Growth would be organic, venturing for example into self-invested pensions and selling pensions by telephone, and by acquisition. In the UK General Accident acquired in 1996 Sabre Insurance, which specialised in non-standard motor risks.

Secure in the knowledge that the UK was firmly on track, to see for himself he visited the General Accident world just as he had done the UK branches, coming up with ideas for development. Having worked in three places, Australia, New Zealand and Britain, his view was global, reflected in the continuing composition of his executive. There was not one man with a Perth background on it. Walter Farnam was chairman and chief executive of the US company. Russell Evans, responsible for overseas operations, came from NZI. In 1996 another outsider, Philip Twyman, replacing Barrie Holder, joined as an executive director with overall responsibility for finance and to provide board level input on life assurance. He had been with Australian Mutual Provident but was not a Scott crony. His appointment to the company was delayed by the board's admitted preference for a Scotsman. Philip and Bob had never met in Australia and his first job for him ended as a recommendation against buying a

US company Bob had been eyeing. Where the two men did see eye to eye was in the relative rôles of insurance and finance. In Philip's view:

General insurance has two basic components, underwriting and investment. Unless you can do either one better than your competitors then don't rely on it as part of your winning formula. Whereas in the long run one investment manager is about as good as the other, the skills that add value and make a difference to overall performance are in understanding and pricing risks correctly, settling claims efficiently, and maintaining good relationships with customers from major brokers to individuals. The important thing is to retain control of those processes and add something to them to earn a superior rate of return. That is particularly true the more complex products become.

Sharing knowledge through international meetings was now a normal, regular process. A practical benefit was the selective introduction of package policies in various territories. In the UK, Global and Corporate Risks was formed in 1997 out of two separate entities. Based in the City of London close to major international brokers, its rôle was to provide a worldwide one-stop service for large companies. Increasing its presence in that market was a significant development for General Accident, hitherto regarded as a leading insurer for small and medium-sized businesses.

Acting globally meant making much greater use of technology for transmitting and processing information. UK expenditure on information technology was running at over £60 million a year. Geographical information systems

As part of the company's return to China, in June 1998 Bob Scott attended the graduation ceremony for the first class of master's degree students at the South Western University of Finance and Economics in Sichuan Province.

refined postcode areas into smaller groups of addresses for more precise underwriting. E-mail brought day-to-day cohesion as a routine. Video conferencing saved senior executives the time and cost of travel, a two-hour UK-US connection costing less than £200. Initial sites for the system were Perth, London, Philadelphia and Toronto. If need be, all four sites could be linked into the same meeting. Communications links were not limited to the company. Electronic trading, started with independent financial advisers from late 1996, cut the cost of transacting life business, where customers also benefited from the use of document image technology.

The biggest advance was in computing. Near the end of 1996, to sharpen its competitive edge through a sustained application of information technology, General Accident outsourced the function to IBM. A joint GA/IBM team set about a two-year implementation project, Galaxy, based on the HUON integrated insurance package incorporating quotation, underwriting, claims, accounts, agency and ledger in one system. Bob Newton, UK general manager, emphasises the importance of the project:

Videoconferencing saves travel. Here Walter Farnam, chairman in the US, holds a transatlantic meeting with company secretary Richard Whitaker in Perth.

> *The HUON system, a proven package developed in Australia and implemented by IBM, is client-centred. A client's business connections with GA can be seen in one place, which improves both customer service and cross-selling. It is technology supporting our business strategy. Starting with home and motor products for Scottish General and GA Direct, phased implementation of the system across personal and commercial lines will give us a flexible, low-cost, sustainable platform to exploit the business cycle upturn expected from 1999. It will also be fully capable of dealing with the 21st century, when further product modules may well be added.*

There was an urgency about the project, the biggest ever undertaken by General Accident, because the world around the company was changing rapidly.

Outside its annual general meeting held in 1997 Scottish Friends of the Earth displayed a banner 'Insure our future: don't invest in climate disaster'. The protest on ethical investment was ultimately directed against Shell, an energy producer that was a source of greenhouse gases, leading to global warming and climate change. General Accident was in fact one of the few British insurance companies to have taken an active interest in the problem. Bob Scott was a member of the Business in the Environment committee and Dr Andrew Dlugolecki, the group assistant general manager responsible for underwriting, achieved international recognition for his continuing concern:

The insurance industry has traditionally worked on past statistics but, with the faster rate of change, past statistics are not relevant to the future. Man-made climate change will lead to major shifts in atmospheric and oceanic circulation patterns. These will directly affect the property insurance industry, which is vulnerable to variability in the frequency and severity of extreme weather events. Floods and subsidence are present UK examples. The cost of extreme events around the world could escalate dramatically because damage is not directly proportional to, say, a 10 per cent increase in wind speed. If the wind is gusting at 200 kilometres an hour the damage increase could be as much as 150 per cent.

Andrew Dlugolecki's concern is not limited to climate:

As we approach the millennium as well as catching up with the past it's more important that we anticipate the future. Insurance companies have written long-tail business involving unrecognized hazards such as asbestosis and pollution. When they were recognised they became sources of large claims. Repetitive strain injury is being compensated. There are debates on whether power lines cause leukaemia and repeated use of mobile phones cancer. We may encounter in the twenty-first century an epidemic of deafness from high-decibel music in conditions where the sense of hearing is temporarily dulled by drugs.

Other epidemics could affect the life and pension industries. At the same time genetic testing, an examination of the DNA pattern for any predisposition to a particular disease, made life expectancy more predictable. Those knowing they were at risk could benefit by taking out high levels of insurance at the expense of other policyholders. For the time being the accepted policy of the British insurance industry was basically not to ask people to take genetic tests when applying for life insurance.

Pensions were seen as a major growth area for insurance companies. As welfare burdens increased and state benefits provided a barely adequate basic, governments would encourage individuals to take out private pensions. It was another form of privatisation. Attitudes would take some time to change but, for the insurers, there was the prospect of providing low-cost pensions on a massive scale. There was also a growing market in portable pensions as employment patterns changed, with more people working part-time and on a series of short-term contracts instead of in lifetime jobs. A consequence for insurance companies of accumulating larger life and pension funds was the greater importance of asset management, looking after people's savings.

GA Life under Bill Jack had advanced rapidly in a short time. Before 1990, as measured by new annualised premium income, it was not one of the top 20 in its league in the UK. Within eight years strong growth and acquisitions took it as CGU Life into the first six, and with a good reputation. Unlike its peers, its involvement in pensions in mis-selling had been minimal. Moreover, its growth was profitable. GA Life was now providing about half of General Accident's UK profits. There was no reason why that proportion should not increase, especially if the company was able to ally itself with a comparably successful partner in the life business.

As the millennium approached the company began taking stock of itself, looking back and looking forward. It commissioned this history as an objective view. This is primarily a cultural history, setting the company in the context of its times and tracing the evolution of *A Premium Business*. For the first 80 years, almost all of them under the Norie-Miller family, father and son, the culture was patriarchal. That changed gradually under the succeeding collective management, lasting until the recession of the early 1990s, when the company was no longer able to provide the security of a job for life.

Until then the financial record had been one of steady progress. The losses in the first three years of the 1990s were a dip in fortune and not unique to General Accident in the insurance industry. Over more than a century the company had grown and prospered, a remarkable fact given that it was but one of many local insurance companies formed for a specific purpose. Starting in an

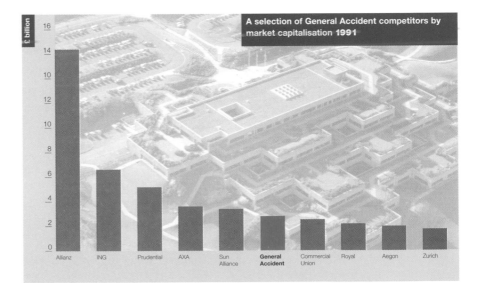

A selection of General Accident competitors by market capitalisation **1991**

agricultural community and a city that was by no means a major commercial or financial centre, its chances of survival were not great. They were on a par with an acorn becoming an oak.

That the company did survive from its second year is undoubtedly due to Francis Norie-Miller, a leader and innovator who largely guided its fortunes for 60 years. A man of independent mind, he was not a follower of fashion, believing General Accident should develop its own expertise and character from its own base. Research has revealed a more rounded character than the two-dimensional general proceeding from triumph to triumph. For all his human faults and physical weaknesses, his achievement is none the less. Without him, General Accident would long ago have been forgotten along with many quaintly named Victorian companies dedicated to local worthy ends, companies such as the Ancient Benefit Friendly Society of Cardiff, the St Columb District Mutual (fire) and the Torquay Mutual (plate glass), also formed in 1885. His achievement was not a lone effort. Behind him he had a growing number of lowly paid but dedicated employees who did the donkey work. Together they left his successors a solid international company on which to build.

While other Scottish general insurers were gradually acquired by larger companies, General Accident was the only one to maintain its independence. Stanley consolidated his father's achievement, growing the company organically. Under Stanley, Macdonald, the second significant outsider to make a major impact on the company, was responsible for the acquisition of The Yorkshire, which strengthened the company's life assurance business and overseas interests. Acquisition was followed by consolidation, organic growth and conservative financial management to accumulate funds for the next acquisitions. Nearly 20 years elapsed between the acquisition of The Yorkshire and three large purchases at the start of the corporation's second century in the latter 1980s: Pilot in Canada, estate agencies, and NZI.

Part of the cultural shift within the company was the change in the composition and rôle of the board, which from the beginning had been an assembly of 'the great and the good' so typical of traditional insurance companies and banks. The shift to a more professional board began in the 1960s with the appointment of Lord Airlie, a merchant banker, as a director in 1962 and during the chairmanship of Lord Polwarth (1968–72), who at the time headed the Scottish Council concerned with development and industry. He and his successors took an active part in the company's affairs, Stuart Black (1972–9) and Gordon Simpson (1979–87) both travelling extensively to examine the company's interests. Gordon Simpson, who was with Edinburgh stockbrokers Bell, Laurie, Macgregor & Co and in the mid-1970s was a deputy chairman of the Stock Exchange, looks back:

I was invited on to the board partly because Stanley Norie-Miller knew me slightly through my uncle, a former director, but largely I think because Harry Polwarth felt that someone with day-to-day investment experience was required. This was in 1967. During the 1970s and early 1980s the composition of the board changed and by the time I left in 1987 it was almost entirely financial, industrial and a smattering of retired civil servants or near civil servants.

The shift was reflected in a change of lunch arrangements:

When I joined we had a long exhausting lunch always finishing with vintage port which had to be finished. I often wonder if I would have passed the breathalyser test on motoring home from Perth. I made myself slightly unpopular with some members by forbidding port at lunch, much as I enjoy it myself.

In the cultural shift of the 1970s and early 1980s there was more significant change to be made:

Once when appalling results were reported from Canada for about the third year running our industrialist said: 'Why don't we just close it down now? I would in my company.'

The problem always was that anyone not steeped in insurance could not be fully aware of all the complexities of the detail and on such detail the board had to rely on management. Occasionally the trust was surely tried but fortunately it nearly always resolved itself.

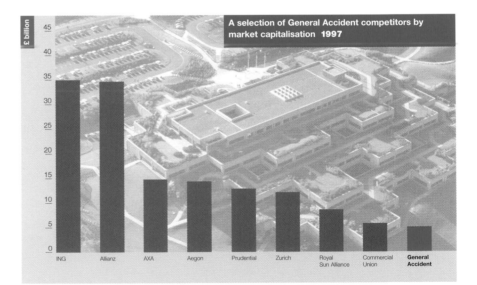

A selection of General Accident competitors by market capitalisation **1997**

The appointment of senior managers to the board brought directors and management closer together. What emerged was a cohesive, unitary board reviewing plans and strategy and acting as a shareholders' check on management. It also had major decisions to make about the company's future.

With the millennium less than two years away, General Accident was apparently in a strong position, a broadly based company with rising profits. In its total return to shareholders it was outperforming the insurance sector as a whole, as it had done more often than not since 1965. Sir Alick Rankin, now a deputy chairman, assessed the company's standing:

We were in a good position for the short term. General Accident had become more efficient, harder, sharper. Bob Scott had given the company an urgency, an incisiveness. Things could have been difficult for the longer term. The fundamental question was whether the company, ultra-Scottish in its location and philosophy, could remain independent and grow out of Scotland. Apart from where we would manage our assets and how we could enlarge our life base, there were cultural issues affecting the conduct of the business: whether we could recruit top people to Perth and develop there the competitive, pulsing, vibrant attitude of our competitors based in London.

The world around the company was changing fast. Faced with new challenges and major shifts in risks in a global economy, when exposure could be on a much greater scale, the insurance industry was regrouping. In the UK Royal and Sun Alliance merged in mid-1996. In early 1997 the Prudential acquired Scottish Amicable for £2 billion. The insurance interests of BAT, Eagle Star and Allied Dunbar, were merged in late 1997 with Zurich Insurance, creating a £23 billion group. Also in Switzerland, Winterthur merged with Crédit Suisse. Allianz in Germany outbid Generali of Italy for the French group AGF. As the process of liberalisation within the European Union gathered pace there was increasing potential in a pan-European operation. Compared with the giant Continental insurers and many banks, though, General Accident was a dwarf.

All sorts of combinations of the likely companies were speculated upon. General Accident was concerned to be better known and carry greater weight in the City. At the end of 1996 it ended its contract with Murdoch Macleod of Financial Public Relations, who for 20 years had faithfully presented Perth to journalists and analysts, moving the account to a larger consultancy, Lowe Bell Financial, which had recently been working with Macleod. At the annual general meeting in 1997 Lord Airlie, having reached the retiring age of 70, stepped down as chairman. In his 34 years as a director he had seen operating profits multiply a hundredfold, from £4.2 million in 1962 to £421 million in

1996. He had always been an encouraging chairman, meeting the staff in UK and overseas branches, steering the company through the difficulties of the 1990s while looking for growth opportunities. His particular interest had been re-entry into China. It was a good legacy to his successor, a deputy chairman, Sir Alick Rankin, the first GA chairman who was an industrialist.

Rankin and Scott were so much of a hands-on pair that some GA staff wondered how they would get on. The concern was unfounded. Having operated in both rôles, Rankin was fully aware of the respective responsibilities of chairman and chief executive. Moreover, where his predecessor as chairman, Lord Airlie, who was also the Lord Chamberlain, may have been uncomfortable in, say, a controversial merger, Rankin would have no such inhibitions. The new chairman, who would be seen in the office more often, had a reputation as a no-nonsense

operator who made and implemented big decisions. That had been his main appeal to the board. As chief executive of Scottish & Newcastle from 1985, through acquisitions and disposals, over ten years he transformed a provincial brewer into a brewing, pub and leisure empire. His greatest coup was buying in 1995 for £425 million the English brewer Courage from Elders IXL of Australia, which in 1988 tried to take over Scottish & Newcastle in a hostile bid. Chairman of Christian Salvesen and a director of the Bank of Scotland, Sears, and Securities Trust of Scotland, he was later described by *The Scotsman* as 'the pugnacious Scottish grandee'. By his own admission, his notoriously robust style was not to everybody's liking.

Lord Airlie, chairman 1987–97.

What Scott and Rankin shared was an outsider's perspective, an objectivity. Neither had qualms about facing the realities of the market without prejudice. They also had to resist government pressures to remain in Scotland, whether this made commercial sense or not. For 113 years Perth had been the world headquarters of General Accident but that was looking less possible. What had started as a local insurance company had grown to a global reach with, inevitably, an important investment side. On both counts Perth was not an ideal centre. The issue had come into focus after the acquisition of Provident Mutual from 1 January 1996. At a stroke this doubled managed life funds to £14 billion and brought in a second, London-based professional investment team. Who was going to manage what and where? Douglas Hay, general manager responsible for investments, outlines the background to the decision:

Fund management, regulated by the Investment Management Regulatory Organisation, has become a much more professional and competitive business. In GA we're concerned with two basic types. In life and pensions we invest for growth, aiming to beat the relevant index so that GA is well positioned in the league tables of performance, which in turn help to bring in more business. In general insurance we need ready access to funds to meet claims. Because the skilled investment staff were available in sufficient numbers in London and that was the area where most of the life and pensions business originated we transferred by the end of 1996 the majority of our UK investments to London, leaving the management of the general insurance funds in Perth. Overall control of the worldwide operation remained in Scotland.

This apparently sensible move, involving at most 45 UK employees, upset Scottish sentiment. Roseanna Cunningham, the Scottish Nationalist MP for Perth, commented that the move was 'a kick in the teeth for Perth'. Local newspapers and the Manufacturing Science and Finance Union (MSF) took issue with the company, ignoring the fact that over the last five years it had created over 1,000 jobs in Scotland. Transfer to Dundee of work done in London had resulted in 800 fewer jobs in the capital.

At the end of 1996 in its strategic review for the board management asked the question 'Is Perth appropriate?' The conclusion was that it was a great place to run a British business. In Perth there was quality labour at a lower cost showing a

Sir Alick Rankin, chairman 1997–8.

higher loyalty and with a lower turnover. The problem was that the company needed an infusion of new people and it was not easy to attract them to Perth. Running an international business from there was hard and there was not the convenience of being a few minutes' walk from leading investment institutions, as you could be in the City of London. In contrast, it made good business sense to run the main UK businesses from outside London: general insurance from Perth; life assurance and savings from York.

Scott and Rankin were unfazed by what, in the context of was happening in the wider world, was essentially a parochial protest over the siting of 45 staff with specific skills. At stake was the efficient management of over half of the corporation's investment funds. By 1997 these had risen to £29 billion, managed in three principal centres: the UK, USA and New Zealand. Even so the corporation had to look for yet greater resources and strength. Deputy chairman Lord Nickson put its situation into context:

British insurance companies have grown infinitely more slowly than our competitors on the continent of Europe and in one or two cases in the United States. The advent of technology, communications and the global market have meant that size, as well as quality, has become an essential factor in the ability to compete. General Accident has for a long while seen itself and has been seen as a global player but our scale of operations, heavyweight in the United Kingdom and significant in the United States, was midget in many other countries, particularly Continental Europe. We were number 22 in size in world terms. Our balance of life and general business, dramatically and successfully improving in the UK, was less than attractive anywhere else. The tendency for the largest brokers to concentrate meant that their buying power was becoming like that of the supermarket to the village shop.

GA had looked seriously at the possibility of merging with Guardian Royal Exchange, but GRE was not big enough, nor were its life interests. The GA board debated whether to intervene in the 1996 marriage of Royal and Sun Alliance. Not to was a knife-edge decision. An aggressive move on Sun Alliance was not in GA's style and the extent of City support for the Perth-based company was questionable. No other composite insurer was regarded as a worthwhile target. The Prudential acquisition of Scottish Amicable in early 1997 showed that life companies were commanding a much higher price than when GA acquired Provident Mutual less than two years before.

In mid-1997 GA came close to making a major acquisition in the US but refused to pay more than what it considered a fair price per share, a decision confirmed by the subsequent performance of the stock. While aggressively seeking strategic solutions the management was convincing the board that a deal was necessary. This episode demonstrated that management had a coherent strategy, analysed a situation and stood by its findings. Given authority by the board, it would not do a deal for the sake of it. Bob Scott was not a deal-a-minute operator. His style was to do his homework with the team first and then act quickly. Not having a major acquisition in the US to integrate meant that the company was free to reconsider options in the UK.

These were well-kept secrets but London stock market rumours of other alliances within the industry persisted. Ideally GA did not want to lose its Scottish headquarters or become a junior partner in an alliance but in Bob Scott's view immediate action was necessary:

By the year 2000 we would have been less able to compete with the new larger companies emerging in Europe and the USA. Size, reach, breadth and depth of skills, backed up by strong financial resources and a low cost operating base are now a sine qua non in order to compete.

The board concluded that in all major markets in which it operated it needed scale quickly. The ultimate alternative was loss of independence, possibly to an overseas company. In November 1997 GA was in a good bargaining position. Operating results were better than ever, profits and the share price were strong. The company had an opportunity that might not occur again for a near 50–50 deal with a larger partner.

Bob Scott and Sir Alick Rankin put the proposition to the board that an earlier tentative discussion with Commercial Union should be pursued. Talks began with Commercial Union, which had failed to agree terms with BAT on acquiring its insurance interests. Having different origins, General Accident and Commercial Union had developed into similar companies. It was a match if not a neat jigsaw. CU was founded in London in 1861 as Commercial Union Fire Insurance Company following the blaze in the wharves and warehouses of Great Tooley Street, the most serious blaze in the City since the Great Fire of 1666. CU quickly diversified into life and marine insurance, expanded within the British Empire, Latin America and China. Ten years after its foundation it was writing fire insurance in the USA. It did not embark on accident insurance until 1901. Like GA, CU also grew by acquisition. Soon after its merger with North British & Mercantile in 1959, the enlarged group decided to build a new headquarters at St Helen's in the City. Completed in 1969, it was destined to become the head office of an even larger group. Together the two companies represented 250 years of accumulated experience.

In the 1997–8 merger negotiations advisers to GA were investment banks Goldman Sachs and Schroder; to CU it was Morgan Stanley. Negotiations moved quickly and there was a remarkable level of agreement on crucial issues that cause major merger talks to fail. In particular, with Sir John Carter retiring

The last GA board meeting, June 1998. Standing, l. to r., Lord Lang of Monkton; Sir Anthony Cleaver; F Ranald Noel-Paton; Walter Farnham; Sir Peter Middleton; Lyndon Bolton; Philip Twyman; Richard Whitaker, (company secretary). Seated, l. to r., Louise Botting; Lord Nickson; Sir Alick Rankin; Bob Scott; The Earl of Mansfield.

as chief executive of CU, there was less of a problem in deciding that Bob Scott would be chief executive of a merged company. The size of the board and its composition by name was agreed. Strong egos were not obstructing a merger nor was there a fudge in the sense that everybody at the top had to be given a job. Further, there was agreement on who would fill senior management positions. The timing of the merger was opportune. Sterling commanded a high exchange rate, deterring overseas rivals from making a bid for either of the companies.

On 25 February 1998 the boards of Commercial Union (advertising slogan: 'We won't make a drama out of a crisis') and General Accident announced that they had agreed the terms to merge the two companies. As CGU, it would rank in the top 20 UK companies and be the UK's largest broadly-based insurance group, combining written premiums of £15.1 billion and a 1997 operating profit before tax of £962 million, with some £100 billion of assets under management worldwide. Based on the relative equity market capitalisations of the two companies, Commercial Union shareholders would hold 53.6 per cent and General Accident shareholders 46.4 per cent of the issued ordinary share capital. For tax reasons the merger would be arranged as an agreed bid by CU for GA.

Nevertheless, it was presented as a merger of equals having a common culture, with the 14 directors being drawn equally from the two companies. Bob Scott (1997 salary and benefits £515,000) would become group chief executive and Sir Alick Rankin (£123,000) deputy chairman. The other current GA directors on the new board would be Philip Twyman, Lyndon Bolton, Louise Botting, Sir Peter Middleton and Lord Lang of Monkton. Group headquarters would be in London while UK general insurance would have its head office in Perth, ensuring continuing employment and a large satisfaction to Scottish sentiment, and UK life business would be centred in York. In the USA, after a century in Philadelphia, the head office would be in Boston. The overall aim was to become a more efficient productive unit. Within two years, the expected time of the integration, costs would be reduced by 10 per cent, at least £225 million, from savings in staff, information technology and property. Of the 5,000 anticipated job losses, 3,000 would be in the UK, in the more expensive London area and where there was duplication of branches and functions.

Abroad there were areas of duplication. Local regulatory authorities would also have to be satisfied. For example, detailed filings would have to be submitted in eight US states where there were domiciled companies. In the US it would rank as the 15th largest general insurer. There were also places where strength could be added to mutual benefit. CU was notably stronger than GA in Europe, with substantial life operations in France and the Netherlands. In Ireland GA had its own network of offices while CU had a substantial minority interest in a local company, Hibernian. In products CU had a fairly even balance between general and life insurance, with a strong presence in the long-term care market, whereas GA's general business was about twice the size of its life side. It was also much stronger in direct telephone selling. Both companies had been pursuing a segmentation strategy in commercial insurance. CU had for 10 years or so been the standard against which to judge customer service and since the end of 1994 the two companies had vied for top place when it came to dealing with commercial customers. Following careful consideration, the decision was made to adopt CGU as the trading name for most of the business operations.

Since the surprising 1996 level of Scottish reaction against moving the bulk of GA's investment operation from Perth to London there had been a marked shift in sentiment. Losing Scotland's third largest quoted company was now the way of the world. It was recognised that London was a world financial centre, the place where international companies congregated, close to the Continent, where markets would be trading in a single European currency from 1999 and links were being established between stock exchanges. For many aspects of GA's business, communications and computers had abolished geography, but geography could not be completely history. To run a global company, top management had to be in the heart of Europe's financial centre, London.

Perth was not going to come off badly out of the merger. Among the older generation of General Accident employees there were regrets at the loss of name and with it identity. To the younger generation, some of whom would happily see their children follow them into the business, the move could mean some job losses in the short term. In the long term it was a means of preserving them against the many competitors.

Overall market reaction to the merger was favourable. It might be defensive but was none the worse for that. The partners were compatible in culture, geography, products, technology and, at the top, there were no clashing egos to upset the commercial logic. The chairman and chief executive of CU were both retiring and the new chairman of CGU, Pehr Gyllenhammar, former chairman of the Swedish vehicle manufacturer Volvo and before that chief executive of the insurer Skandia, was a dynamic man with an international reputation. As chief executive Bob Scott would take direct responsibility for the UK general insurance operation. Responsibility for key geographic and product areas was shared among three executive directors. From the GA side Philip Twyman would be in charge of the UK life business and worldwide asset management. One of his aims was to attract third party investment business.

Shareholders' and regulatory approvals were obtained earlier than expected. Ahead of schedule, on 2 June 1998, just over three months after the announcement, the merger was finalised. After 113 years it marked the end of General

Accident as an independent company with its head office in Perth. Its final board meeting was held there on 24 June.

Planning for integration with Commercial Union, organised through a committee of seven, of whom four were GA and three CU, started before the merger was finalised. Their theme was 'Being One'. In both companies employees' queries were answered weekly through an electronic postbox. There were many concerns. Who would get what jobs? Would there be new or different jobs? Differences in grading, salary and benefit structures had to be harmonised, as did other conditions of employment. For instance, retirement ages differed: 60 in CU; 62 in GA. The process of integration, involving 13,300 GA staff and 8,400 CU in the UK as well as people overseas, was expected to be substantially complete ready for the next century and the new millennium.

The new identity CGU would embody some of the century-plus character of General Accident. As Sir Alick Rankin, who as deputy chairman would be based in Perth, observed in his first and last chairman's statement to GA shareholders:

While it is sad to see the passing of an era, you can't lament positive and dynamic change and the excitement which is generated by a macro-alliance will quickly spread across the full range of our businesses, ensuring adrenalin in the corporate step.

Facing page
The CGU logo united the initials of the two companies, combining their strengths ready for the new millennium.

APPENDICES

MAJOR STEPS IN THE INTERNATIONAL GROWTH OF GENERAL ACCIDENT

UNITED STATES

1899 United States branch opened in Philadelphia (Muir & Haughton)

1900 Mutual Accident Association of Boston acquired

1911 Potomac Insurance Company of the District of Columbia acquired

1955 Pennsylvania General Insurance Company formed

1963 Camden Fire Insurance Association acquired

1982 US branch operations incorporated into a US company, General Accident Insurance Company of America – Head Office in Philadelphia

1986 North Pacific Insurance Company and Oregon Automobile Insurance Company acquired

1990 Silvey Group, Oklahoma acquired
1991 Hawkeye-Security Group, Iowa acquired

EUROPE

1899 Agency opened in Antwerp, Belgium

1902 Branch opened in Paris

1996 UAP Allgemeine acquired

AUST/NZ

1903 Australian agency opened in Melbourne

1925 Local agency opened in Auckland

1987 Australian branch operations incorporated into an Australian company, General Accident Insurance Company Australia Ltd

1989 NZI Corporation Ltd acquired

CANADA

SOUTH AFRICA

BRAZIL

1906 Incorporated as The General Accident
Insurance Company of Canada

1908 Canadian Casualty & Boiler Insurance
Company acquired

1908 Chief office opened in Cape Town

1965 Branch operations incorporated into
a South African company, General Accident
Insurance Company South Africa Ltd

1967 Companhia De Seguros Gerais
Corcovada, Rio de Janeiro (acquired with The
Yorkshire Insurance Company)

1986 Pilot Insurance Company acquired

1992 Canadian property & casualty business
acquired from Prudential (UK)

1997 Canadian General Insurance Company
acquired

PREMIUMS

General Business

1887–1923 £ MILLION

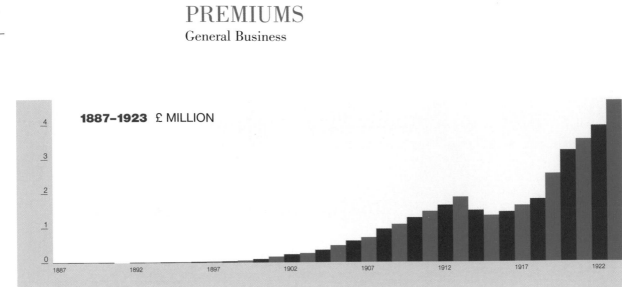

Source: Annual Report and Accounts

1924–1960 £ MILLION

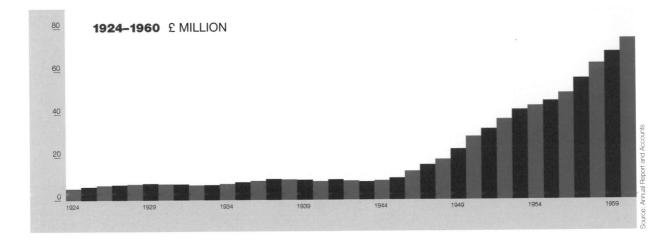

Source: Annual Report and Accounts

1961–1997 £ BILLION

Yorkshire Insurance Company
acquired 1967

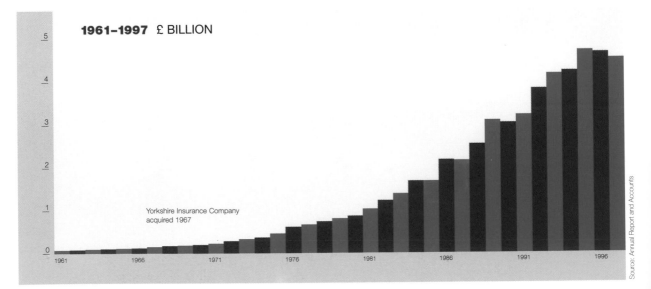

Source: Annual Report and Accounts

CLAIMS
General Business

1887–1923 £ MILLION

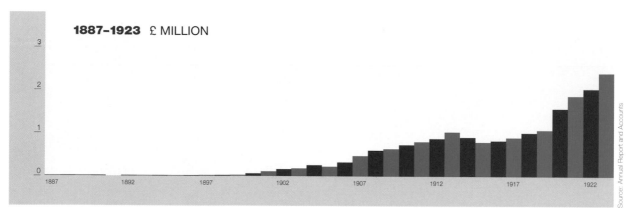

Source: Annual Report and Accounts

1924–1960 £ MILLION

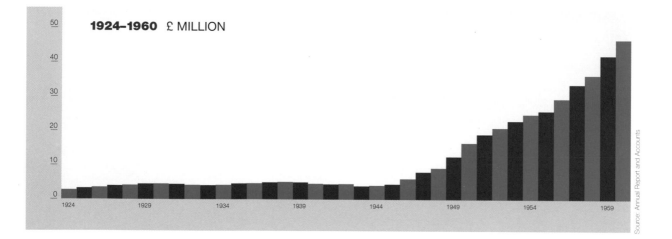

Source: Annual Report and Accounts

1961–1997 £ BILLION

Yorkshire Insurance Company
acquired 1967

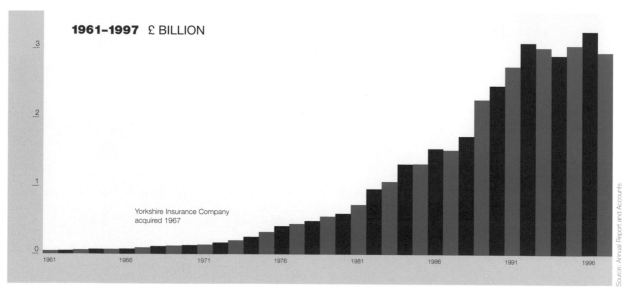

Source: Annual Report and Accounts

INVESTMENT INCOME
General Business

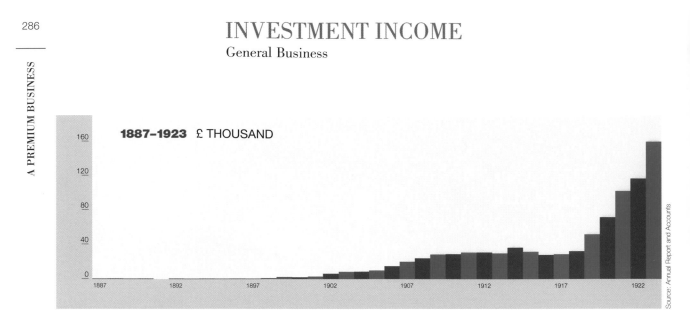

1887–1923 £ THOUSAND

Source: Annual Report and Accounts

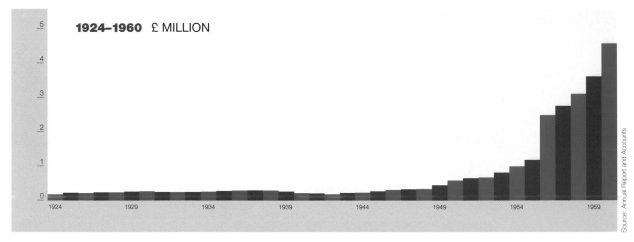

1924–1960 £ MILLION

Source: Annual Report and Accounts

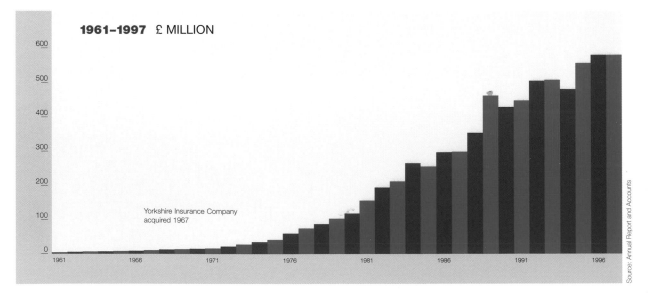

1961–1997 £ MILLION

Yorkshire Insurance Company
acquired 1967

Source: Annual Report and Accounts

£ billion

**Long Term Business Premiums
1965–97**

2.5

2

Provident Mutual Life Assurance
Association acquired 1996

1.5

1

.5

Yorkshire Insurance Company
acquired 1967

0

65   70   75   80   85   90   95 97

Source: Annual Report and Accounts

LONG TERM
LIFE PREMIUMS

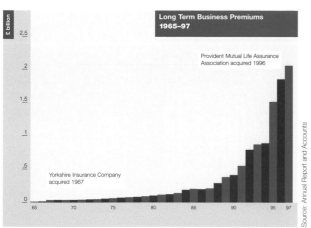

£ million

**Long Term Business Profits
1965–97**

150

Provident Mutual Life Assurance
Association acquired 1996

100

50

Yorkshire Insurance Company
acquired 1967

0

65   70   75   80   85   90   95 97

Source: Annual Report and Accounts

LONG TERM
LIFE PROFITS

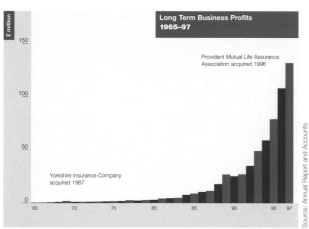

£ billion

**Market Capitalisation
1967–97**

5

4

3

2

1

0

67   72   77   82   87   92   97

Source: Datastream

MARKET
CAPITALISATION

PICTURE ACKNOWLEDGEMENTS

The author and publishers are grateful to the following for permission to reproduce photographs and illustrations:

p.2, photograph courtesy of St Andrews University Library; p.3, University of Reading Rural History Centre; p.4 (margin), copyright Auchindrain Museum, photograph courtesy of National Museums of Scotland; p.4 (top), courtesy of Perth Museum and Art Gallery, Perth & Kinross Council, Scotland; p.10/11, Science and Society Picture Library; p.16, photographed by Bradshaw & Sons; p.25 (1908), City of Salford Museums and Art Gallery; p.28, photograph R.L. Warham; p.30, p.34/35, p.56 (margin), p.172, Hulton Getty; p.38, KPMG. photograph by John Arnison; p.41, James L. Dillon & Co, photographer; p.54, Waihi Arts Centre and Museum, Assn, Waihi, NZ; p.75, copyright Campbell-Gray and British Empire Exhibition; p.78/79, p.248/249, © D.C. Thomson & Co. Ltd/*Dundee Courier*; p.82, print courtesy of the British Film Institute; p.87, Associated Press/Topham; p.108, *Kent & Sussex Courier*; p.119, p129, *The Perthshire Advertiser*; p.123, p126, p.256, p.269, pictures courtesy of Louis Flood Photographers; p.134, photograph A.R. Coats; p.137, Scottish Daily Record; p.169, D. Darwin Smith photographer; p. 170/171, p173, The Fairfax Photo Library, Australia; p.182, *Stratford Upon Avon Herald*; p.192 (bottom), FT Syndication; p.193, Gerry Cranham; p.199, copyright John Borowski Photography; p.202, Sean Bolan; p.211, *The News and Courier/The Evening Post*/C.F. Boone Publishing Co, USA; p.215, Andrew Taylor/*The Sydney Morning Herald*, Australia; p.227, Des Jack of Jack House Transit, New Zealand; p.237, Frank Fennell Photography; p.251, Dod Miller/Network Photographers; p. 257, Fergus Wilkie/FT Syndication.

Every effort has been made to obtain permission for the reproduction of the illustrations and photographs in this book; apologies are offered to anyone whom it has not been possible to trace or contact.

All other illustrations were obtained from General Accident's archives, with grateful thanks to all those people who have donated their pictures and memorabilia to it.

INDEX

To see the pattern of property insurance and avoid an undue concentration of risk, branches plotted the distribution on large-scale local maps. Mapping clerks either coloured in insured properties or stuck in pins. Map colours distinguished the materials of which buildings were constructed. Details such as roof construction and profile, types of walls, the presence of hoists. lifts and skylights as well as items such as boilers, chimneys and hydrants were identified by symbols.